The Imperial History Wars

Debating the British Empire

Dane Kennedy

Bloomsbury Academic
An imprint of Bloomsbury Publishing Plc

B L O O M S B U R Y
LONDON · OXFORD · NEW YORK · NEW DELHI · SYDNEY

Bloomsbury Academic
An imprint of Bloomsbury Publishing Plc

50 Bedford Square	1385 Broadway
London	New York
WC1B 3DP	NY 10018
UK	USA

www.bloomsbury.com

BLOOMSBURY and the Diana logo are trademarks of Bloomsbury Publishing Plc

First published 2018

© Dane Kennedy, 2018

Dane Kennedy has asserted his right under the Copyright, Designs and Patents Act, 1988, to be identified as Author of this work.

All rights reserved. No part of this publication may be reproduced or transmitted in any form or by any means, electronic or mechanical, including photocopying, recording, or any information storage or retrieval system, without prior permission in writing from the publishers.

No responsibility for loss caused to any individual or organization acting on or refraining from action as a result of the material in this publication can be accepted by Bloomsbury or the author.

British Library Cataloguing-in-Publication Data
A catalogue record for this book is available from the British Library.

ISBN: HB: 9781474278874
PB: 9781474278867
ePDF: 9781474278898
eBook: 9781474278881

Library of Congress Cataloging-in-Publication Data
Names: Kennedy, Dane Keith, author.
Title: The imperial history wars: debating the British Empire/Dane Kennedy.
Description: London; New York: Bloomsbury Academic, an imprint of Bloomsbury Publishing Plc, 2018. | Includes bibliographical references and index.
Identifiers: LCCN 2017014897| ISBN 9781474278874 (hb) | ISBN 9781474278867 (pb)
Subjects: LCSH: Great Britain–Colonies–History. | Great Britain–Colonies–Historiography. | Imperialism–History. | Imperialism–Historiography. | Postcolonialism–History. | Postcolonialism–Historiography. | History, Modern–Historiography.
Classification: LCC DA16 .K435 2018 | DDC 355.0209171/241–dc23 LC record available at https://lccn.loc.gov/2017014897

Cover image: From the Cape to Cairo/Keppler (Courtesy of the Library of Congress, LC-DIG-ppmsca-25696)

Typeset by Deanta Global Publishing Services, Chennai, India
Printed and bound in Great Britain

To find out more about our authors and books visit www.bloomsbury.com. Here you will find extracts, author interviews, details of forthcoming events and the option to sign up for our newsletters.

The Imperial History Wars

CONTENTS

Acknowledgments vi

Introduction 1

1 Imperial History and Postcolonial Theory 7

2 The Boundaries of Oxford's Empire 23

3 Imperial History and Postcolonial Studies Revisited 39

4 Exploration and Empire 57

5 The White Man's World 73

6 Debating the End of Empire: Exceptionalism and its Critics 87

7 On the American Empire from a British Imperial Perspective 101

8 The Means and Ends of Empire 123

9 The Imperial History Wars 131

Epilogue: Does British History Matter Anymore? Reflections on the Age of Brexit and Trump 149

Notes 155
Works Cited 177
Index 208

ACKNOWLEDGMENTS

Given the fact that this is a book that concerns the ideas and debates about the British imperial past that have circulated among historians and other scholars over the past few decades, the fullest measure of my intellectual debts is likely to be found in the list of authors that appears in the "Works Cited" at the end of this book. But that list fails to identify or acknowledge those friends and colleagues who either went out of their way to read and comment on one or another of the following chapters or provided some other forms of assistance and insight. I want to offer special thanks, then, to Ed Berkowitz, Phillip Buckner, Antoinette Burton, the late John Cell, Sandy Freitag, Dorothy Helly, Graham Huggan, Edward Ingram, Will Jackson, Philippa Levine, Trevor Lloyd, Wm. Roger Louis, John MacKenzie, Tom Metcalf, Tim Parsons, Doug Peers, Richard Price, Ben Rader, Mrinalini Sinha, Andrew Thompson, the late Marilyn Young, and Lynn Zastoupil. I am also extremely grateful for the ongoing support of my editor at Bloomsbury, Emma Goode, and for the spot-on advice offered by the anonymous reviewers of the manuscript. Finally, I want to acknowledge the assistance of Jonathan Adams, a George Washington University student who helped me edit and format this book.

The Introduction and Chapters 5 and 6 appear here for the first time. Chapter 1 originally appeared as "Imperial History and Post-Colonial Theory," in the *Journal of Imperial and Commonwealth History* 24, no. 3 (September 1996): 345–63; Chapter 2 as "The Boundaries of Oxford's Empire," in *International History Review* 23, no. 3 (September 2001): 604–22; Chapter 3 as "Postcolonialism and History," in *The Oxford Handbook of Postcolonial Studies*, ed. Graham Huggins (Oxford: Oxford University Press, 2013): 467–88; Chapter 4 as "British Exploration in the Nineteenth Century: A Historiographical Survey," in *History Compass* 5, no. 6 (2007): 1879–1900; Chapter 7 as "On the American Empire from a British Imperial Perspective," in *International History Review* 29, no. 1 (March 2007): 83–108; Chapter 8 as "The Means and Ends of Empire," in *Comparative Studies in Africa, Asia, and the Middle East* 34, no. 3 (2014): 604–10; and Chapter 9 as "The Imperial History Wars," in *The Journal of British Studies* 54, no. 1 (January 2015): 5–22. A portion of the epilogue originally appeared as "Does British History Matter Anymore? Reflections on Brexit," in *Perspectives in History* 54, no. 7 (October 2016): 26–7. I have made some changes to all of these texts, and Chapter 4 is a substantially revised version of the original essay. Chapters 1, 2, and 7 are reprinted by permission of Taylor and Francis. Chapter 3 is reprinted by permission of Oxford University Press; Chapter 4 by permission of Wiley; Chapter 8 by permission of Duke University Press; and Chapter 9 by permission of Cambridge University Press.

Introduction

The British imperial past seems to stir up a new public controversy almost every month. In August 2016, it was a tweet by Conservative member of Parliament Heather Wheeler, claiming that the "British Empire," miraculously resurrected from its grave, was ahead of the "Rest of World" in the Summer Olympics medal count. In May 2016, it was Canadian prime minister Justin Trudeau's official apology for the Komagata Maru incident, named after the Japanese ship loaded with Sikh immigrants that was prohibited entry to Canada a hundred years ago. In April 2016 it was now foreign secretary Boris Johnson's provocative assertion that US president Barack Obama's "part-Kenyan" heritage had imbued him with an "ancestral dislike" of the British Empire. In February 2016 it was the high-profile campaign by Oxford students to remove a statue of Cecil Rhodes from its perch in Oriel College. This had been preceded in May 2015 by an Oxford Union debate about whether Britain owed reparations to India for its colonial subjugation, which provoked a heated exchange in the British and Indian press. And in March 2015 students at the University of Cape Town had generated international attention and inspired their counterparts at Oxford by launching the "Rhodes Must Go" campaign, which led to the removal of Rhodes's statue from their campus after a prolonged struggle.

What are we to make of these and other controversies that connect the British imperial past to the present? Can they be dismissed as the last flickers of nostalgia or, alternatively, outrage against an empire that is fading from public memory? If so, why have so many people—not just Britons but Canadians, Indians, South Africans, and others—felt compelled to actively pontificate and agitate on these issues? Can they not indicate instead that the imperial past is not truly past, but endures as a point of departure for making sense of the present? While the British Empire no longer exists, its afterlife lingers on, and, indeed, its relevance to contemporary concerns seems resurgent.

One way to measure this resurgence is to conduct a Google Ngram metadata search of the words "empire" and "imperial." If we track their usage over the past fifty years, what we see is a parabolic pattern. Starting in the 1960s, with decolonization reaching its climax, "empire" and "imperial" appeared with far greater frequency than they would do over the next couple of decades. The trend lines began to turn upward again in the 1990s, and from 2004 there has been a noticeable spike in the use of "empire" and "imperial."

Academic interest in British imperial history has followed much the same pattern. My own career as a historian of the British imperial world began in the midst of the Ngram's terminological trough. The subject attracted little attention in the 1970s and 1980s. Those historians who did study the empire stayed close to familiar shores, trawling increasingly depleted fisheries for their evidence and analysis. By the 1990s, however, newcomers had arrived on the scene, sailing into deeper waters that offered richer returns. Fleets of vessels were soon plying these imperial seas, each seeking to assert its own dominance and drive out its rivals. They flew the flags of postcolonial studies, subaltern studies, the new imperial history, settler colonial studies, the British World, and other piratical projects. To strain this metaphor still further, they transformed a once tranquil, even stagnant, backwater into a stormy, turbulent sea. They created what can be called the imperial history wars.

This book seeks to make sense of these wars. It is the product of several decades' worth of reading and writing about the increasingly large and varied scholarship concerning the British imperial past. The ramifying nature of this scholarship, which has broadened the scope of historical inquiry from political, military, and economic concerns to social, cultural, and epistemological ones, bringing historians into dialogue with literary scholars, anthropologists, geographers, and specialists in other fields, has meant that any examination of the subject must necessarily be a running commentary, sensitive to shifting contexts and concerns. I offer no apologies, then, for including in this volume a number of previously published essays, each of them highlighting a particular point of rupture in the ongoing debate about the British imperial past. I also include several newly written essays, which take up topics that have generated a great deal of interest among imperial historians in recent years. Taken as a whole, this collection is intended to trace the transformation of British imperial history from its rather staid—some might say stagnant—state of affairs in the 1970s and early 1980s into the intellectually vibrant and politically charged subject it has become today. As John Darwin recently observed, "there has never been a better time to study the history of empire—or write about it."[1]

I have sought in these pages to adopt an independent, often skeptical stance toward the various schools of scholarship that have contributed to these debates about British imperial history. To be sure, I have preferences for particular methods, approaches, and interpretations, as will become evident in the chapters that follow, but my intent throughout has been to carry out historiographical reviews that offer informed and engaged assessments of the state of the field and establish the larger contexts within which that field has taken shape. Some of the chapters examine the challenges that postcolonial studies, the new imperial history, and other self-proclaimed intellectual projects have posed for the standard historiography, and especially for the historical consensus that became enshrined in the multivolume *Oxford History of the British Empire*. Other chapters review recent scholarship on subjects ranging from exploration to settler colonialism to decolonization, tracking shifts in the terms of debate and exposing points of conflict. Still others reflect on the comparative uses of British imperial history, especially as they relate to the United States' recent role in the world. My overriding aim throughout the book has been to bring to these topics a spirit of intellectual curiosity and critical engagement.

It is impossible, however, to make sense of the scholarly debates that have transformed the historiographical landscape—or seascape, if you will—of the British Empire in recent decades without also acknowledging and examining the ways in which these debates have resonated with and responded to current events and concerns. It is this aspect of the imperial history wars that relates most directly to those public controversies I noted in the opening paragraph of this Introduction. Historians' renewed interest in the British imperial past cannot be divorced from their heightened attentiveness to its contemporary echoes in world affairs. As the book's concluding group of chapters suggest, these echoes have reverberated with particular force in the hotly contested assessments of the US-led coalition's invasions of Afghanistan and Iraq, which continue to haunt the political scene both in America and in Britain. The past's echoes in the present can also be heard in the debates that raged around the referendums on Scottish independence and Brexit. Still, this resurgent interest in the British imperial past started well before any of these events occurred, and it requires, as I argue in Chapter 9, an examination of an earlier, more deeply rooted set of issues.

Historians are no more immune to presentist preoccupations than anyone else. The questions we ask about the past are invariably informed by the environments we inhabit and the challenges we confront. In *How Empire Shaped Us*, a collection of autobiographical essays I recently coedited with Antoinette Burton, various historians whose work has dealt in one way or another with British imperial history take up this issue in the contexts of their own lives and intellectual interests.[2] They reflect on the connections between their personal career trajectories and the broader social and political forces that shaped their academic interest in, and approaches to, the past.

Let me offer my own experience by way of example. I was drawn to British imperial history as an undergraduate at the University of California at Berkeley when the Vietnam War was at its height. For those of us who protested the war, it was a shameful act of imperialist aggression by the United States. Studying British imperial history helped me make sense of this traumatic conflict. I went on to pursue a doctorate in the field and selected as a dissertation topic the experiences of white settlers in Kenya and Southern Rhodesia. My choice came at a time when the renegade white regime of Rhodesia was entering the terminal stage of its struggle against African guerillas and international sanctions. Rhodesia became the black-majority-ruled country of Zimbabwe in 1980, the year before I received my doctorate. Thus, imperialism and colonialism seemed very much present and meaningful to me in the years I trained to become a historian of the British imperial world.

There was nothing particularly unconventional about that training, though it did occur at a healthy distance from the orthodoxy that pervaded the field's Oxbridge heartland. Only in the early 1990s did I become aware that the imperial past as I understood it was under assault—from anthropologists who were giving increasingly critical scrutiny to their own discipline's origins in empire, from feminist historians who were turning imperial history's masculinist orientation upside down, and, above all, from the literary-inflected school of postcolonial studies that Edward Said did so much to inspire. My efforts to make sense of postcolonial studies and the challenge it posed for imperial history resulted in the first chapter in this book. While sharply critical of certain aspects of this seemingly subversive scholarship, I also applauded its success in opening up cultural and epistemological avenues of inquiry that mainstream historians of the British Empire had all but ignored. Those historians' conception of the parameters of their subject found its fullest expression in the publication in 1998–9 of the five-volume *Oxford History of the British Empire*, the culmination of decades of scholarship and a counterblast to postcolonial critics. The appearance of this work gave me an opportunity to reflect on the "boundaries" of this historiographical consensus—by which I mean its methodological and theoretical limits—in the essay that appears here as Chapter 2. Recently I revisited the issues raised in the first chapter, reexamining the relationship between imperial history and postcolonial studies several decades after the latter school of thought had made its initial splash. What strikes me most forcefully in this reassessment is the degree to which recent work in imperial history has taken up themes, concepts, and methods introduced by postcolonial studies, while reshaping them in important ways. Indeed, I argue in Chapter 3 that much of the most innovative and influential work arising from the forces set in motion by postcolonial studies is currently coming from historians.

Chapters 4 through 6 address historiographical debates that have arisen in recent years about specific topics in British imperial history. The first of these chapters examines the resurgence of interest in the history of exploration. Largely ignored by imperial historians for decades, exploration has recently enjoyed a revival as a subject academics should study. Pioneering work by literary scholars, historical geographers, and historians of science have exposed the crucial contributions that exploration made in shaping British perceptions of other peoples and places, setting the terms of engagement across cultural divides between the British and indigenous interlocutors, and laying the foundations for modern scientific practices and the formation of an environmental consciousness. Chapter 5 takes up another important topic that until recently was relatively neglected in imperial history circles. Neither the *Oxford History of the British Empire* nor its postcolonial studies and new imperial history critics devoted much attention to the large settler colonies that arose in Australia, Canada, New Zealand, and South Africa, despite their immense economic, political, and social importance to the empire. Over the past decade, however, two distinct schools of scholarship have sought in very different ways to rectify that neglect. Both settler colonial studies and the British World contingent have given penetrating attention to settler societies, but the similarities end there: they adopt such starkly different approaches to the subject that they might as well be about completely different realms of experience. Why this is so can be explained largely in terms of the contemporary agendas that inform their lines of inquiry. A similar dynamic is at work in Chapter 6, which examines the contentious historiographical debate that has arisen about British decolonization over the past decade. What was once the exclusive province of political and diplomatic historians has now become fertile ground for social and cultural historians as well, and a process that had once been characterized as a relatively peaceful, consensual transfer of power has become reframed as a fiercely contested, often violent upheaval that has left lasting scars all around. These interpretive shifts are not simply the products of new methods or evidence, though both have certainly figured prominently in this historiographical debate. They also are the result of recent events that have reshaped the international order, placing the course and consequences of decolonization in a very different light.

The final group of essays—Chapters 7 through 9—and the epilogue address this relationship between the past and the present in a more explicit and systematic fashion. Written in the aftermath of the al-Qaeda attacks of 9/11 and the wars they set in motion, Chapter 7 surveys the upsurge in the array of works that characterized the United States as an empire and raised questions about the consequences of this imperial order for the post–Cold War world. Commentators of various political stripes sought to draw lessons for American policy in Afghanistan and Iraq from the British imperial experience. I address the uses and limits of such comparisons in this chapter. This theme is developed further in Chapter 8, which critiques one of the most systematic comparative studies of the American and British empires to appear to date, Julian Go's *Patterns of Empire*. The final chapter revisits and reframes many of the topics and themes that have appeared throughout the book, connecting the changing perspectives on British imperial history over the past few decades to a series of contemporaneous social, cultural, and political developments in Britain and the United States. It simultaneously stresses the enduring influence that the imperial past exerts on our current preoccupations and the double obligation it imposes on the historians: to maintain an awareness of our own subjectivity as products of our time while doing our best to uphold the disciplinary standards essential to the integrity of our profession.

The epilogue reflects on the implications of the two seismic elections of 2016—the British referendum to leave the European Union and the American election of Donald Trump as president—for the future of British history as a field of study. The Brexit campaign and the commentary that has appeared in its aftermath have demonstrated that memories of the British imperial past still exert a powerful influence over many Britons. An opinion survey conducted by YouGov in 2014 found that 59 percent of the British public thought the British Empire was something to be proud of (compared to 19 percent who were ashamed of it and 23 percent who did not have an opinion).[3] Is it any wonder then that the pro-Brexit forces made not-so-subtle appeals to imperial nostalgia? More surprising, perhaps, is the fact that many Republican politicians and right-wing intellectuals in the United States have embraced Winston Churchill as their inspiration and model for leadership. Why this is so and what it reveals about the lessons they draw from the British imperial past for the America they hope to remake is sobering. What will come of these initiatives is beyond my capacity to predict, but they point to the enduring presence of the empire as an object of longing in an age of discontent.

There is, of course, a danger in drawing such direct associations between the present and the past, both because the present is the product of a bewildering array of forces and because it becomes the past in the blink of an eye. My concluding comments on Brexit and Trump are likely to look dated soon enough. But they serve to remind us that we understand the present in the context of the past and vice versa. This is, in fact, the theme that runs through all of the chapters in this volume. And it is a theme that holds particular weight and relevance when it comes to the relationship between the British imperial past and the postcolonial present, both in Britain and elsewhere around the world. What is at stake in the historical debates that are the subjects of this book is not simply a matter of how to make sense of the past, but how to make sense of the present.

1

Imperial History and Postcolonial Theory[1]

Postcolonial theory—also known as postcolonial studies and colonial discourse analysis—burst onto the academic scene in the early 1990s. For most historians of the British imperial world, it was a strange and disorienting development. This new field of study took up many of the same issues that preoccupied imperial historians, but it drew on theoretical, methodological, and rhetorical strategies that made little sense to them. The following essay, which originally appeared in 1996 in the main journal for imperial historians, The Journal of Imperial and Commonwealth History, *was the product of my early efforts to understand and explain postcolonial scholarship. It reflects both the strong objections I had to some of its premises and practices and the high hopes I had for its ability to free imperial history from its narrow and stultifying framework.*

The historiography of British imperialism has long been colored by the political and methodological conservatism of its practitioners. Arising as it did from the imperial metropole in the late nineteenth century, it originally served as an ideological adjunct to the empire.[2] Its purpose was to contribute historical insights into past exercises in overseas power that could be used to inform and inspire contemporaries to shoulder their obligations as rulers of a worldwide imperial system. Decolonization robbed imperial history of most of its practical incentives. Yet it continued to cling to the methodology and mentalité of the "official mind," as Ronald Robinson and John Gallagher termed it in their enormously influential work.[3] The persistence of this paradigm is evident even in the most recent scholarship. Peruse any issue of

The Journal of Imperial and Commonwealth History, for example, and you will find a succession of articles that still tread the path pioneered by John Seeley more than a century ago. They remain wedded to the same official documentation, persist in addressing the same political, economic, and military manifestations of power, and continue to employ the same narrative conventions. They seldom stray from an adamant empiricism. On the rare occasions when they do flirt with theory, it generally derives from well-worn models. P. J. Cain and A. G. Hopkins's acclaimed two-volume study of *British Imperialism*, which is widely regarded as the most important and innovative contribution to the field since Robinson and Gallagher, resembles nothing so much in its theoretical stance than that old warhorse of imperial theory, J. A. Hobson, with a pinch of Schumpeter thrown in for flavor.[4] This return to the concerns of Edwardian radicalism is taken within the field for theoretical daring. It is hardly surprising, therefore, that imperial history has acquired a reputation for insularity and inattention to the methodological advances made both by historians in other fields and by scholars in related disciplines.

Perhaps because so many historians of British imperialism have been content to plough the same narrow plot over and over again, their professional domain has been invaded in recent years by a wide array of academic interlopers. Interest in imperialism and colonialism has intensified among specialists in anthropology, area studies, feminist studies, and, above all, literary studies. The latter have proven especially energetic and adept at claiming squatters' rights over imperial history's unclaimed provinces. Armed with the latest poststructuralist theories, the literary invaders have opened up and exploited some surprisingly rich and provocative intellectual terrain. It is their colonization of imperial studies and its implication for the field that this chapter proposes to address.

There can be no mistaking the success that literary scholars have had in making the topic of imperialism their own. Teaching positions in colonial and postcolonial literatures appear to be one of the booming fields in English departments these days. New works with titles like *The Rhetoric of Empire* seem to come off the presses every week. Thick anthologies of influential and representative essays have begun to appear for use as textbooks in college courses.[5] Leading theorists such as Edward W. Said, Homi K. Bhabha, and Gayatri Chakravorty Spivak have become superstars of the academic firmament. In America, *The Chronicle of Higher Education* has highlighted the phenomenon with a feature story, the popular academic journal *Linguafranca* has attacked it in a cover story, and *Time* magazine has devoted several pages to a flattering profile of Said, its principal founder.[6] In Britain, interest among the intellectual community has been equally intense.[7] Clearly this is a scholarly industry to be reckoned with.

The problem is that historians of British imperialism have for the most part failed to reckon with it.[8] This is a pity both for the historians, whose methodological horizons could be broadened by serious engagement with this literature, and for the literary scholars, whose theoretical excesses could be checked by the sober scrutiny of the historians. In proposing that historians enter into a dialogue with their literary trespassers, I do not mean to suggest that the two parties can be entirely reconciled with one another. Some of the differences that divide them are unbridgeable. Even so, a good deal can be gained, I believe, from historians conducting a critical reconnaissance of the territory that literary theory has claimed as its own. So let us explore.

* * *

The new and growing body of scholarship that concerns us here is generally known either as colonial discourse analysis or as postcolonial theory. Colonial discourse analysis refers to the examination and interpretation of particular colonial texts. Postcolonial theory refers to the political and ideological position of the critic who undertakes this analysis. In practice, the two terms have become virtually interchangeable, so much so that several recently published "readers" have put them in harness in their rather ponderous, mirror-imaged titles, *Post-Colonial Theory and Colonial Discourse* and *Colonial Discourse, Post-Colonial Theory*. Although objections have been raised to the teleological implications of the tag *post*-colonial,[9] its evocation of an anti-imperialist political stance and a poststructuralist theoretical one has ensured its usage. Indeed, the label "postcolonial theorist" seems to carry rather more cachet among the practitioners of the trade than "colonial discourse analyst," even though the latter designation is often the more accurate one. Perhaps the term "analyst" has unwelcome associations with financial and/or military functionaries; certainly the term "theorist" has an inflated prestige in lit-crit circles these days. For the sake of convenience and consistency, I will refer to this literature as postcolonial theory, but I caution that much of it is less engaged in developing a body of theory than in making gestures of obeisance to it.

It is generally acknowledged that Edward Said's seminal study, *Orientalism* (1978), is the foundational text for postcolonial theory.[10] Its transfiguration of the term "orientalism" from an arcane field of academic study to a synonym for Western imperialism and racism has been accepted and applied across a wide spectrum of scholarship, as has its central thesis and theoretical concerns. Said starts from the poststructuralist premise that knowledge is a discursive field derived from language and he draws from Foucault the insight that its significance lies embedded within systems of power. His study of Orientalism, by which he means Western representations of those parts of the world the West identifies as the Orient, seeks to show that this body of knowledge tells us little about the so-called Orient, which may or may not exist outside the Western imagination, but much about the West's efforts to impose itself on the peoples and cultures who came under its hegemonic sway. Orientalism, then, pushes past the conventional conception of imperial power as a material phenomenon, presenting it instead as an epistemological system. Moreover, because the West's power is linked to the cultural representations it constructs and imposes on the minds of colonizer and colonized alike, it is able to survive the political decolonization that occurred after the Second World War. Indeed, it exists even within the purportedly objective scholarship of Western academia. The full implication of this analysis is that the dismantlement of Western modes of domination requires the deconstruction of Western structures of knowledge. Hence the claim that this is a postcolonial theory.[11]

These central propositions have been endorsed, elaborated upon, and modified in varying respects by subsequent practitioners of postcolonial theory. Although Said has his critics within the fraternity, his influence has persisted to a remarkable degree over the years since *Orientalism* first appeared. Many of the weaknesses as well as some of the strengths of his enterprise have become magnified in the works that have followed its lead.

Perhaps the most obvious characteristic of postcolonial scholarship is its theoretical promiscuity. Said draws mainly on Foucault for inspiration, but other influences on his work include Antonio Gramsci and Erich Auerbach. This odd ménage creates certain tensions and contradictions in his argument. Aijaz Ahmad has observed that Said vacillates between a Foucauldian position that places the origin of Orientalism in the Enlightenment project of the eighteenth century and a Auerbachian stance that traces it all the way back to classical Greece.[12] Dennis Porter has pointed out that Said's use of Foucault is at odds with his use of Gramsci—the former presents a totalizing conception of power that absorbs knowledge itself, while the latter conceives of hegemony as historically contingent and subject to subversion.[13] Various critics have drawn attention to the ambivalence, if not outright obfuscation, in Said's position regarding the fundamental question raised by his study: is it possible to attain a true knowledge of the Other? For Said to charge that the West's representations of the Orient are distorted seems to suggest that he regards an undistorted representation as attainable, but this conflicts with his poststructuralist insistence that the Orient is nothing more than a discursive phantasm. "Orientalist inauthenticity is not answered by any authenticity," notes James Clifford.[14] Such are the conundrums that arise from the effort to appropriate such incompatible theoretical perspectives.

Said's progeny have taken the turn to theory in ever more tortuous directions. As Stefan Collini has remarked with regard to cultural studies in general, it suffers from "a disabling deference to the idea of 'theory'."[15] In addition to the obligatory bows to Foucault and Gramsci, postcolonial theorists have drawn upon Althusser, Bakhtin, Barthes, Benjamin, Bourdieu, Derrida, de Man, Fanon, Heidegger, Lacan, Lyotard, and other mainly postmodernist theorists. Conspicuously absent from the postcolonial canon is Marx, whose work is considered irredeemably Eurocentric.[16] This seems rather ironic in light of the fact that, except for Fanon, none of the names cited above ever exhibited the slightest intellectual curiosity in the issue of

European colonialism or the concerns of non-European peoples.[17] Yet the fascination with such theorists, especially if they are French, continues to run high among the postcolonial coterie. The latest initiates into the canon appear to be Foucault's contemporaries, Gilles Deleuze and Felix Guattari, whose Wilhelm Reich-inspired work *Anti-Oedipus* is advanced by Robert Young as an important new source of post-Saidian inspiration.[18]

The infiltration of these varied theoretical influences into postcolonial studies makes for a literature that is often dense and sometimes impenetrable. Arguably the most fashionable figure in the field at the present time is Homi Bhabha, whose ruminations on the cultural effects of colonialism draw inspiration from poststructuralist psychoanalysis and semiotics.[19] Traces of Lacan, Derrida, and the like are all too visible in the style and substance of his essays, which pose a formidable challenge for those who seek to decipher them. One of Bhabha's most sympathetic commentators has suggested that his baffling prose is a deliberate strategy to disorient the reader so as to prevent "closure" and thereby subvert the "authoritative mode" of Western discourse, a claim also offered in defense of Gayatri Chakravorty Spivak, whose work is often equally difficult to penetrate.[20] One has to admire the over-the-top audacity of this assertion, but the fact remains that the principal reason readers have trouble with Bhabha, Spivak, and certain other postcolonial theorists is they make such indiscriminate use of words, expressions, concepts, and doctrines from so many different, sometimes incompatible, sources. The literary scholar Elaine Showalter rightly complains that the "difficult languages of high theory ... have become a new orthodoxy as muffling as scholastic Latin, expressive straitjackets which confine all thought to a prescribed vocabulary."[21] Postcolonial theorists' vocabulary has become clotted with highly specialized, often obscure terms like heteroglossy, alterity, aporia, synecdoche, aleatory, elide, and metonymy. Even familiar words such as gaze, gesture, site, space, efface, erase, and interrogate have taken on highly specialized, almost metaphysical meanings in their writings. Metaphor has metastasized into metaphoricity, narrative into narrativity, origin into originary, fact into facticity. One critic of this plethora of arcana has put tongue-in-cheek in recommending a Devil's Dictionary of Cultural Studies to make its terminology accessible to the uninitiated.[22]

It is easy, of course, to mock almost any academic genre for its jargon, but what makes postcolonial theorists especially vulnerable to criticism are the claims they make for the relationship between language and liberation. Language, as they see it, is the key to emancipation from colonial modes of thought. This is the objective the Kenyan novelist and essayist Ngugi wa Thiong'o has referred to as "decolonizing the mind."[23] His strategy for doing so has been to write in his native Gikuyu language (although this does not extend to the programmatic tracts in which he presents his rationale for doing so). The strategy adopted by the postcolonial theorists is to subject the language of the colonizers to critical scrutiny, deconstructing representative texts, and exposing the discursive designs that underlie their surface narratives. This is seen as an act of transgression, a politicized initiative that undermines the hegemonic influence of Western knowledge and brings about the "cultural decentering of the [European] centered world system."[24] Bhabha, for example, presents his work as an effort to turn "the pathos of cultural confusion into a strategy of political subversion."[25] Its intent is to escape from the totalizing claims of the West. For the sake of argument, let us accept the postcolonial theorists' assertion. Let us agree that the non-Western world remains in thrall to the discursive system of the West, to the system that Said identifies as Orientalism. How do the postcolonial theorists propose to liberate these hostages? By writing in a manner that is utterly inaccessible to most of them? By writing as the acolytes of Western theorists? By writing to mainly Western audiences from mainly Western academies about mainly Western literature? By writing?[26] These questions may seem unnecessarily harsh, but they force to the fore the premise that stands at the heart of postcolonial theory's sense of itself—the notion that the sort of recondite textual analysis it practices offers a weapon to break free from the cultural and indeed political oppression of the West. One need not be a Marxian materialist—though this stance has supported a healthy skepticism regarding postcolonial theory—to consider this proposition as dubious, if not delusional.[27]

The issue that concerns us here, however, is not what this literature can or cannot do to decolonize the minds of contemporary non-Western peoples, but what it can or cannot do to deepen our understanding of the history of colonialism. What complicates this issue is that postcolonial theorists hold contending views about the value of historical analysis. For postmodernist purists like Homi Bhabha, history is nothing more than a text, a grand narrative that operates according to the same rules of rhetoric and logic as other genres of Western writing. As such, its significance is limited to the part it plays in the discursive field that the postcolonial critic seeks to dismantle, rather than the contribution it makes to our knowledge about the nature of colonialism. Bhabha keeps out the stuff of history by plucking random works of literature and other texts from their contextual soil and sealing them in the hermetic chambers of a psychoanalytic essentialism. Suspicion of history as an accomplice to the West's discursive drive to dominate the Other is a disturbing motif within a significant element of postcolonial theory. Edward Said's position is an ambiguous one, professing on the one hand the importance of a historicized understanding of Orientalism while suggesting on the other hand that the discipline of history is itself implicated in the Orientalist enterprise. John MacKenzie complains that Said's efforts to achieve a historicism untainted by Orientalist assumptions are essentially ahistorical, a charge that I think overstates the case and cuts off the opportunity for interdisciplinary dialogue.[28] The same accusation can be made, however, against some of Said's confederates. Gayatri Spivak praises the members of the subaltern studies group for engaging in what she regards as the deconstruction of a "hegemonic historiography" and urges them to break from the premises of historical analysis altogether.[29] The influential cultural critic Ashis Nandy denounces historical consciousness as a "cultural and political liability" for non-western peoples.[30] In *The Intimate Enemy*, his best-known work, he proclaims that his aim is to present "an alternative mythography which denies and defies the values of history."[31] This view of history as a mythography concocted by the West to further its hegemonic ambitions is one that Robert Young argues to be at the core of the postcolonial critique. He traces the intellectual genealogy of this effort to expose, decenter, and deconstruct what are seen as the totalizing claims of "white mythologies," or history as it has been practiced in the West.[32] For historians who have come under the influence of postcolonial purists, this attack on history has occasioned considerable hand-wringing. Some of the younger members of the subaltern studies school of Indian historiography in particular have begun to agonize about whether it is possible to write history when "Europe works as a silent referent to historical knowledge itself."[33] This is a real and serious epistemological problem, and I do not wish to demean the struggle to reconstruct history from a non-Eurocentric perspective. But this is not the agenda of the postcolonial purists, whose efforts instead are directed against a historical mode of understanding altogether.

What happens when history is set aside? Some recent examples of postcolonial scholarship suggest that it leads to a willful neglect of causation, context, and chronology. The authors of *The Empire Writes Back: Theory and Practice in Post-Colonial Literatures* blithely pour the literatures of Africa, Australia, the Caribbean, the United States, and other regions of the world into the same postcolonial pot, ignoring their profoundly different historical experiences except insofar as their "complexities and varied cultural provenance" are taken as signs of the decentering pluralism that identify them as postcolonial literatures.[34] Laura E. Donaldson acknowledges the need to address "concrete historical circumstances" in the introduction to her *Decolonizing Feminisms: Race, Gender, and Empire Building*, but this appreciation is quickly forgotten as she flits from *Jane Eyre* to *Uncle Tom's Cabin* to *The King and I* (the novel, the play, and the film) as well as a bewildering array of other texts in an analysis that conflates colonialism with racism, sexism, and oppression in general.[35] One of the most egregious examples of this aversion to history is David Spurr's *The Rhetoric of Empire*.[36] Subtitled "colonial discourse in journalism, travel writing, and imperial administration," this astonishing book insists that the same discursive forms recurred over more than a century in the diverse genres of writing that Western travelers, officials, and others produced about the profoundly varied peoples across the globe with whom they came in contact. In this "global system of representation,"[37] it seems to make no difference whether the rhetoric is British, French, or American, whether the author is Lord Lugard, Andre Gide, or Joan Didion, whether the text is a colonial report, a scholarly treatise, or an article in National Geographic, or whether the place is nineteenth-century South Africa, early twentieth-century Mexico, or the contemporary Middle East. All are indiscriminately advanced as evidence of the depth of the West's discursive drive for power and domination. It might be supposed that reductionism could not be carried much further, but Spurr shows otherwise. Following in the footsteps of Derrida, he tracks his quarry all the way back to writing itself: "The writer is the original and ultimate colonizer, conquering the space of consciousness with the exclusionary and divisive structures of representations."[38] Rarely does a theory chase its own tail with such single-minded intensity. We will not trouble Spurr with such obvious questions as whether he too is complicit as a writer in this colonization of consciousness or whether the imperial implications of writing are also applicable to the literatures of non-Western societies. We will merely observe that his analysis is entangled in what postcolonial theorists might call a "double bind": it seeks to convict historically specific parties of historically specific crimes while exonerating itself of any accountability to historical specificity.

* * *

Fortunately, other literary scholars have shown far more sensitivity to the historical record in their work. While operating under the general rubric of postcolonial theory, these scholars have rejected the antihistorical orientation of the theoretical purists. They recognize the distinction that exists between history as a text and history as a tool, between its presence as a discursive product and its use as an analytical practice. By placing their arguments in a historical context and testing them against the historical evidence, they have enriched our understanding of the imperial experience in ways that historians have been slow to appreciate.

Mary Louise Pratt, like David Spurr, concerns herself with the rhetoric of European travel writing in her book *Imperial Eyes*, and like Spurr, she ranges freely across centuries and continents.[39] Unlike Spurr, however, she does not conflate one century or continent with another. She takes some care to place the texts she has selected within the contexts of their particular time and space and she readily acknowledges the appearance of discordant discourses along the way. While her main aim is to trace the taxonomic impulses of an emergent European hegemony from the eighteenth century to the present, the story she tells is far from the univocal, unilinear one presented by Spurr. For many historians her enterprise still may seem unduly speculative and her arguments insufficiently grounded in the empirical record, but her efforts to establish the historical textures of her texts make her study of European travel literature much more nuanced and sophisticated than some of its counterparts.

Various other works of postcolonial scholarship have engaged in a profitable if often provisional association with history. Gauri Viswanathan's flawed but intriguing study of the British effort to introduce the study of

English literature into the curriculum of Indian schools draws much of its force from the author's immersion in the early-nineteenth-century debate between Orientalists and Anglicists about how to make Indians more amenable to British rule.[40] The self-proclaimed "historicist" reading of British explorers' accounts of East and Central Africa that Tim Youngs proffers is successful in showing that these representations of Africa were shaped in significant ways by class-specific preoccupations with identity that had their impetus in Britain itself.[41] Jenny Sharpe overcomes the simplistic assumptions that often accompany discussions of gender and race in the colonial realm by placing her study of rape as a trope in Western fiction about the Raj within the context of the shifting patterns of power from the pre-Mutiny to the postindependence eras.[42] Patrick Brantlinger's sweeping survey of British literature and imperialism in the nineteenth century succeeds as well as it does partly because it understands that the British Empire was a widely varied phenomenon that inspired different responses in different places and at different times.[43] Each of these works evidences a significant degree of sensitivity to the historical record, and although historians in the relevant fields can doubtless demonstrate that distortions and simplifications persist, the fact remains that these examples of engagement with imperial history by scholars influenced by postcolonial theory demand our attention.

This increased fraternization with history has inspired its practitioners to question some of the cruder premises that postcolonial theory brought to the study of imperialism. One of the most dismaying of these is the tendency to essentialize the West, a discursive practice no less distorting than the West's tendency to essentialize the Orient.[44] In Said's *Orientalism* and much of the scholarship it has inspired, the West is seen as an undifferentiated, omnipotent entity, imposing its totalizing designs on the rest of the world without check or interruption. Ironically, this emphasis on the power of the West countenances the neglect of that power as it was actually exercised in the colonial context, ignoring its plural and particularized expressions.[45] Further, it fails to appreciate the uncertainties, inconsistencies, modifications, and contradictions that afflicted Western efforts to impose its will on other peoples. Marxist-inspired critics in particular have taken postcolonial theory to task for ignoring what Sumit Sarkar calls "the microphysics of colonial power."[46]

With the appearance of more historically attuned studies like those cited above, we have evidence that postcolonial scholarship is capable of more subtle and persuasive treatments of the West and its widely varied imperial agents, interests, and aims. Javed Majeed's *Ungoverned Imaginings*, for example, shows that Sir William Jones, Thomas Moore, James Mill, and other major British interpreters of India in the late eighteenth and early nineteenth centuries constructed profoundly different versions of the Orient to serve profoundly different purposes, purposes that were often directed as much toward Britain as they were toward India.[47] Monolithic conceptions of the West and its intentions have also proven increasingly unsatisfactory for many feminist scholars, whose analyses of the role of white women in colonial societies have exposed an obvious fissure in the facade of a homogeneous ruling elite. While some feminists have sought simply to acquit Western women of complicity in Western imperialism, others have understood that the construction of colonial power was a far more complex and contradictory process than the theoretical purists suppose.[48] Jenny Sharpe observes: "The notion of a discourse that is traversed by an omnifunctional, free-floating power breaks down any distinction between relations of domination and subordination"[49]—by which she has in mind in particular the distinction that confronted white women as members of both a dominant race and the subordinate gender. These sorts of distinctions are essential for making sense of the ambiguous, ambivalent positions of memsahibs, poor whites, and various other subordinate or marginalized groups within white colonial society.

If postcolonial theory is to move toward a more nuanced, historicized understanding of the colonial experience, it also has to overcome its tendency to abstract the colonized Other as an undifferentiated, unknowable category. Given their ideological loyalties, this may seem a rather surprising position for the proponents of postcolonial theory to take, but it derives directly from their answer to a crucial question: can the deconstruction of the West's misrepresentations of the Other open the door to a true representation? Most theoretical purists say no, arguing that any effort to retrieve the experiences and attitudes of the colonized is doomed to fail because it is inescapably enmeshed in the positivist premises of Western knowledge. Homi Bhabha argues that the best that can be done is to monitor the traces of the colonized inscribed in the margins of the colonizer's discourse, an enterprise enigmatic enough in its interpretation of silences, ambivalences, and contradictions to escape almost any kind of external assessment.[50] Gayatri Spivak insists that the voice of the colonized subject, and especially the colonized female subject, can never be recovered—it has been drowned out by the oppressive collusion of colonial and patriarchal discourses.[51] The implication of this stance is made clear by Gyan Prakash, who declares that the "shift to the analysis of discourses" means the abandonment of a "positivist retrieval" of the experience of the colonized and the search instead for the random discursive threads from that experience that have become "woven into the fabric of dominant structures." While Prakash is seduced by the prospect that the "relocation of subalternity in the operation of dominant discourses leads . . . to the critique of the modern West,"[52] others are appalled by this abandonment of the effort to recover the "subaltern" or colonial subject's experiences. Critics complain that the Derridean turn in postcolonial theory denies agency and autonomy to the colonized, whose struggles against colonial rule and strategies to turn it in their favor are too abundant and abundantly recorded to be dismissed as mere echoes in the chambers of Western discourse.[53] Apart from Prakash, few historians are likely to adopt the stifling stance of the theoretical purists, and there are signs that an increasing number of practitioners of postcolonial studies have begun to back away from it as well. Robert Young concedes in his latest book that the discipline has "reached something of an impasse" growing in part out of a realization that "the homogenization of colonialism does also need to be set against its historical and geographical particularities."[54] And Sara Suleri complains in *The Rhetoric of English India* that postcolonial theory "names the other in order that it need not be further known," and that its practitioners "wrest the rhetoric of otherness into a postmodern substitute for the very Orientalism that they seek to dismantle."[55] Even Edward Said has recently warned against viewing the West and the rest as essentialized dichotomies. He has retreated from his earlier position regarding the pervasiveness of Western power by examining the work of Yeats, Fanon, and other voices of cultural resistance to that power.[56]

Whether figures such as Yeats and Fanon are entirely representative of colonized peoples' reactions to colonial rule, however, is open to question. What Said's use of them signifies is postcolonial theory's residual obeisance to its literary studies roots, with its privileging of canonical authors. Hence the almost ritualistic re-examination of Charlotte Bronte, Kipling, Conrad, Forster, and the like in volume after volume of postcolonial scholarship. While recent efforts to extend the postcolonial inquiry to non-Western writers should be regarded as an important step forward, it remains the case that attention tends to focus on those Westernized authors who have obtained at least provisional admission into the Western canon, such as Achebe, Naipaul, and Rushdie (though Naipaul's status, in particular, is questioned by some postcolonial theorists because of his contrarian political views). It would be useful if postcolonial scholarship made more effort to situate these writers within the class structure of their home societies and the cultural context of a transnational intelligentsia so as to avoid simplistic generalizations that their work embodies some nationalist or "Third World" essence.[57] It would be even more useful if it freed itself from the constraints of a canon altogether. The recent upsurge of studies of travel literature can be seen as one of the ways it has sought to do precisely that, but the abiding limitation of this genre is its Eurocentric character.[58] While some practitioners of postcolonial theory have managed to take up topics and texts that are entirely outside the bounds of any Western-derived canon, the most interesting instances generally have come from scholars trained in disciplines other than literature.[59] Thus, one of the challenges that continues to confront postcolonial theory is to open its inquiries to a wider range of voices, especially those from colonial and ex-colonial territories.

* * *

What, then, does postcolonial theory offer to British imperial history? With its mind-numbing jargon, its often crude essentializations of the West and the Other as binary opposites, and, above all, its deeply ingrained suspicion of historical thinking, one might well wonder if it has anything to offer. In John MacKenzie's view, it does not.[60]

Such a conclusion, I suggest, profoundly misjudges the potential of postcolonial theory to enrich the inquiries of imperial historians. For all its faults, this body of scholarship has inspired some valuable insights into the colonial experience, and historians would do well to take notice. It has reoriented and reinvigorated imperial studies, taking it in directions that the conventional historiography of the British Empire has hardly begun to consider. It has raised provocative, often fundamental questions about the epistemological structures of power and the cultural foundations of resistance, about the porous relationship between metropolitan and colonial societies, about the construction of group identities in the context of state formation, even about the nature and uses of historical evidence itself. These preoccupations are in no way limited to the literary proponents of postcolonial theory: similar inquiries have arisen among anthropologists, area studies specialists, feminist scholars, and others whose methods may seem somewhat less inimical to imperial historians, but whose concerns are often no less challenging to their practices. This chapter, however, has focused on the literary scholarship inspired in large measure by Said because it has been the most audacious in its application of poststructuralist theories and the most uncompromising in its relationship to historiographical traditions.

The principal aim of this scholarship has been to reframe and reassess Europe's impact on the rest of the world—and the reciprocal effects on Europe itself—by shifting the focus from the material to the cultural realm. The contribution of postcolonial theory to this effort lies first and foremost in its appreciation of the relationship between knowledge and power. Said's central premise, derived from Foucault and embraced by other postcolonial theorists, holds that the imperial power of the West was bound to and sustained by the epistemological order the West imposed on its subject domains. While imperial historians have attended to the issue of power since the inception of their field of study, and while their inquiries have given rise to a sophisticated body of work that traces the exercise of power from coercion to collaboration, the fact remains that the circumstances that allowed relatively small contingents of Europeans to acquire and maintain authority over vastly larger numbers of Asians, Africans, and others represent one of the most persistent conundrums to arise from the study of Western imperialism. The postcolonial theorists have opened up a new and intriguing avenue of inquiry into this problem by probing the assumptions and intentions that underlay the efforts to give meaning to the colonial encounter. They have argued that these discursive practices were every bit as expressive of power relations as the more conventional manifestations of those relations in politics and other material realms. Heretofore their work has been more successful in suggesting an intent on the part of colonial rulers than in establishing an effect on colonized subjects: this has been a recurrent point of criticism of Said and his student Gauri Viswanathan, for example.[61] However, they have been helped in their endeavors by others, notably historical anthropologists like Bernard Cohn, whose pathbreaking work on British India has demonstrated a direct relationship between the acquisition of knowledge about subject peoples and the imposition of authority over them.[62] The marriage of this research to the insights from postcolonial theory has shown that a fuller understanding of the West's success in imposing itself on the rest of the world requires a deeper appreciation of its cultural and ideological dimensions.

Postcolonial theory's insight into the pervasive nature of Western constructions of the Other has made it clear that much of what we thought we knew about societies that had been subjected to colonial rule was distorted by the discursive designs of the colonizers. This realization has compelled scholars to reexamine the circumstances under which particular peoples became identified as members of particular tribes, castes, races, faiths, nations, and other culturally defined collectivities. Once again, the theoretical positions advanced by the postcolonial contingent have converged with the empirical researches of others, particularly specialists in the anthropology and history of ex-colonial societies. An exceptionally lively and important body of scholarship has arisen that examines the colonial construction of collective identities. What had long been thought to be the primordial affiliations of tribe and caste, for example, are now seen to have assumed much of their modern shape as a result of contestatory processes arising from the efforts of colonial authorities to impose order over subject peoples who sought to resist those demands. Similarly, religious communalism and other markers of group identity such as race and ethnicity appear to have taken new and more virulent forms under colonialism as a result of its determination to classify and categorize.[63] The influence of postcolonial theory has been felt in studies of peasant consciousness,[64] of gender and sexuality,[65] of the body and disease,[66] and of imperial ideology.[67] Our understanding of the nature and impact of colonialism has been profoundly reconfigured as a result of these and other works, and at the heart of this reconfiguration lies the postcolonial premise that the categories of identity that gave meaning to colonizers and colonized alike cannot be taken for granted: they must be problematized and presented in the context of power.

The final point is that this problematizing of identity has provided an opportunity to overcome what D. K. Fieldhouse described a decade ago as the Humpty-Dumpty syndrome in British imperial history.[68] Since decolonization, the study of the British Empire has shattered into a multitude of separate fragments, with the most significant break occurring between the imperial experience as it has been portrayed from the metropole and from the periphery. By presenting a case for understanding the construction of cultural difference as a binary process—we define ourselves in the context of how we define others—postcolonial theory has insisted that the metropole has no meaning apart from the periphery, the West apart from the Orient, the colonizer apart from the colonized. The dominant party in these parings has its own character shaped as a consequence of the shape it gives the character of the other. This is almost certainly the most significant contribution that postcolonial theory has made to the study of colonial practice. Sometimes, as in Edward Said's effort to read plantation exploitation in Antigua as the silent referent in Jane Austen's *Mansfield Park*, the case for a connection between imperial periphery and center seems strained.[69] But just as often it has worked, supplying fresh insights into the imperial experience and its impact on Britain. Javed Majeed has made a persuasive case for viewing the development of Philosophic Radicalism in the context of colonial India in the early nineteenth century.[70] Moira Ferguson has shown that the abolitionist-inspired debate about colonial slavery helped to shape Mary Wollstonecraft's critique of gender relations in British society.[71] Robert Young has exposed the importance of mid-nineteenth-century racial theory on the development of Matthew Arnold's famous notion of culture.[72] More generally, postcolonial theorists have shown that the "languages of class, gender, and race [were] often used interchangeably,"[73] connecting imperial metropole and colonial periphery in surprising and significant ways. Evidence that historians have begun to take heed of the insights advanced by postcolonial scholarship can be found in works such as Antoinette Burton's provocative analysis of the efforts by British feminists to appropriate the ideology of humanitarian imperialism to their cause and Lynn Zastoupil's careful study of the influence of John Stuart Mill's career in the India Office on the development of his ideas.[74] Postcolonial theory, then, has contributed to the task of restoring the relationship between center and periphery, of recovering the connection between the history of Britain and the history of its imperial dependencies—in effect, of putting Humpty-Dumpty back together again.[75] It has done so by demonstrating that imperialism was a process of mutual interaction, of point and counterpoint that inscribed itself on the dominant partner as well as the dominated one. And it has made it clear that any assessment of this interaction which ignores the cultural dimension—that is, the realm of mutual representations of the self and the other—is one that misses what may well be the most persistent and profound legacy of the imperial experience.

* * *

I began this chapter with a rather polemical metaphor that portrayed postcolonial theory as a colonizing discipline, subjecting a province of historical studies to its alien rule. Insofar as this metaphor resonated with readers, it did so because it pandered to the widespread perception that disciplinary boundaries are akin to ethnic or national ones, abstract entities that must be patrolled and protected at all costs against outsiders. I intend now to denounce this metaphor as misleading and even destructive. It connotes a defensive mentality that hinders rather than advances scholarship and knowledge. While I have argued that there is a great deal wrong with postcolonial theory, I have also suggested that it offers interesting and useful avenues of inquiry that imperial historians would do well to examine. What we need at this stage is a full-fledged critical dialogue between the two parties, a dialogue that exposes areas of difference and delineates points of convergence. There are, in fact, some signs that this has begun to occur.[76] John MacKenzie has made a vigorous, albeit defensive, intervention that has already stimulated debate.[77] My intent has been to push this dialogue in a direction that will encourage imperial historians to rethink their practices in response to postcolonial theory. Whatever the outcome of such a rethinking, it promises to take the historiography of imperialism in fruitful, if unfamiliar, directions.

2

The Boundaries of Oxford's Empire

While mainstream historians of the British Empire continued to work within the conventional confines of the field, its boundaries were being expanded and disrupted by postcolonial studies, subaltern studies, the new imperial history, and other approaches to the imperial past. The publication of the five-volume Oxford History of the British Empire *in 1998–9 was intended to show that a broad consensus had been reached about that past, but instead it exposed the gulf that had arisen between its understanding of imperial history and the approaches adopted by dissident schools of thought. The following review essay, which focuses on the last three volumes of the* Oxford History, *appeared in* The International History Review *in 2001. It acknowledges that the project has much to offer, but it also points out that it suffers from some serious limitations and it urges imperial historians to actively engage with those whose scholarship turned their subject in new and unfamiliar directions.*

The appearance of the *Oxford History of the British Empire* marks the first large-scale collaborative effort to take stock of the British imperial experience since the now dated and dusty *Cambridge History of the British Empire*. Whereas the latter's nine volumes made their leisurely appearance under various editors over thirty-four years between 1929 and 1963, the impresario of the *Oxford History's* five volumes, Editor in Chief Wm. Roger Louis, guided them off the press in a break-neck two years, giving the project an editorial cohesion and sense of common purpose its predecessor decidedly lacked. The first two volumes—*The Origins of Empire*, edited by Nicholas Canny, and *The Eighteenth Century,* edited by Peter J. Marshall—were published in 1998; the final three appeared in 1999. In its entirety, the *Oxford History* runs to more than 3,000 pages, divided into nearly 150 chapters by some of the leading authorities in their fields. The logistics alone make the project a remarkable achievement, but the consistently high quality of the contributions and their cumulative insights ensure that it will be consulted and valued for years to come.

Any enterprise as ambitious and imposing as this one raises intriguing questions about intentions and effects, questions that in turn open an avenue to consideration of the contending purposes that have infused new life into imperial history. This chapter will use an examination of the last three volumes of the *Oxford History of the British Empire* to ask: Why undertake such a sweeping summing up of the British Empire at this time? What does the work seek to tell us about the empire's historical significance and lasting legacy? And what impact is it likely to have on the future direction of scholarship in the field? Although the size of the three volumes and the wide range of their contributions make it difficult to generalize about such an important collaborative undertaking, they also compel one to do so.

Why does the work appear now? Louis states in the foreword to each volume that, with the passing of the British Empire and "the passions [it] aroused ... we are now better placed than ever before to see the course of the Empire steadily and to see it whole" (vols. 1–5, vii). He has repeated elsewhere the claim that we can now "arrive at a balanced answer" to the question of the empire's impact because the emotions it aroused have died down.[1] Perhaps, though the controversy that swirled around Louis's appointment as editor in chief suggests otherwise. The choice provoked highly public complaints from some British historians that Louis, as an American, would work from an anti-British slant.[2] Lord Beloff, the most vocal critic, caused a stir during his plenary address to the Anglo-American Conference at the Institute of Historical Research in 1995, devoted that year to the British Empire, when he associated Louis, who had helped to organize the conference, with what he decried as a tendency for "imperial history [to] become anti-imperial history."[3] Well, Louis may not be a second Sir John Seeley, but neither is he Edward Said's secret-sharer. His large and distinguished body of work on British imperial policy in the twentieth century is noted for its traditional narrative style, meticulous trawling of official archives to tell its tales of imperial policy, and determined reluctance to engage in theoretical discussion or apply moral judgments to his subjects. With a doctorate from Oxford supervised by A. J. P. Taylor and Margery Perham, and a second home there as a fellow of St Antony's College, Louis is hardly an outsider in the English academy.[4] He and his colleagues as editors selected a list of contributors so clearly weighted in favor of English-, and especially Oxford- and Cambridge-trained scholars, that no one can seriously doubt the project's primal loyalties. In the three volumes under review, twenty-five of the contributors received their degrees from Oxford, twenty-one from Cambridge, and nineteen from the University of London, accounting for two-thirds of the total.[5] Louis's respect for the Oxford and Cambridge tradition of imperial history is evident in his lengthy introduction to the historiography volume, where he traces its lineage from Edward Gibbon through Seeley to Ronald Robinson and John Gallagher. In light of these facts, the xenophobic consternation at Louis's appointment is noteworthy not only for proving so absurdly misplaced, but also for revealing the extent to which the imperial past and the interpretive meanings it elicits continue to stir strong feelings.[6]

Indeed, if we wish to understand why such a monumental project came to fruition at this time, we would do well to recognize the fact that even though the British Empire may be effectively dead and gone as a political entity, it continues to thrive as an emotional force; a memory that resonates at various levels among various parties. This chapter is not the place to examine the ways the British and American entertainment and retail industries have marketed imperial nostalgia, nor the ways African and Asian rulers have blamed the colonial heritage for their countries' problems.[7] But it is the place to remark that scholarly interest in the empire has revived after what Robin W. Winks suggests were several decades of decline in the 1960s and 1970s (vol. 5, 13). In recent years, we have seen a deluge of books on the subject, with no sign of diminishment in the foreseeable future.[8]

It will not suffice to explain the revival in terms of the disinterested desire to provide a "balanced" account of the recent past. There is nothing disinterested about the raucous range of voices that seek to be heard on the matter of the empire and its legacy: they are, in fact, motivated by highly charged, contending convictions about the relationship between the imperial experience and the contemporary condition. Without this ferment and the interest it has generated, the financial and scholarly resources needed to realize so ambitious an enterprise might not have been mobilized. And yet in some sense, the project runs directly counter to the intellectual environment that spawned it. As the *Oxford History* imprimatur suggests, its purpose is to present an authoritative account of its subject, a claim for consensus implicit in Louis's opening assertion that the time has come to "see [the empire] whole."

Much the same impulse inspired the production of the *Cambridge History of the British Empire*, and we can better situate its successor by comparing the two. Despite the lengthy genesis of the earlier work, it told a broadly consistent story of the empire as the spread of British political, legal, and constitutional institutions across the globe. For this reason, the project was heavily weighted in favor of the colonies of British settlement, with separate volumes devoted to Canada, Australia, New Zealand, and South Africa, as well as three chronological volumes, and two on India. It applied the test of historical significance that Seeley had sketched out in his *Expansion of England* (1883).[9]

With the end of the empire and the collapse of the institutional structures and political myths it supported, this interpretation carries less authority than it once did; much of it has been jettisoned here. A few contributions, to be sure, show their intellectual obeisance to the older tradition, but the anachronism of examples such as W. David McIntyre's chapters on Australasia and the Commonwealth in volume 4 (667–702), and again on the Commonwealth in volume 5 (558–70), makes for dreary reading. The triumphalist narrative of political progress within the empire is scarcely discernible elsewhere; the emphasis once placed on the colonies of settlement has given way to a broader definition of the subject, both geographical and thematic. Some historians, Phillip Buckner for one, have lamented the diminished attention given to the settler colonies, insisting that it undervalues the importance of their economic, institutional, and, above all, emotional ties to Britain.[10] But the editors—to my mind, quite rightly—have taken the position that their purview should extend beyond the limits accepted by imperial historians in the first half of the twentieth century. Not only have they given more attention than the *Cambridge History* to the other elements of the dependent empire, but they have also shown more appreciation for the multiple levels of engagement between the British and those they colonized. The *Oxford History* examines the social and cultural as well as the political and economic dimensions of the imperial experience, touching on issues that scarcely entered the consciousness of the contributors to its predecessor. It examines the connections across the empire made by trade and finance, free and forced migration, and the exchange of ideas and beliefs. It examines the varied initiatives undertaken by colonized peoples both to accommodate themselves to the British presence and to drive them out. It examines the informal influence the British wielded in Latin America and China as well as the territories they colored red on the map. And it examines Ireland, which the *Cambridge History* conspicuously ignored. Louis asserts the "centrality of Ireland in the Empire" (vol. 4, xii), both as a quasi-colonial territory and as a contributor to colonial expansion elsewhere. The chapters on Ireland support his contention: David Fitzpatrick (vol. 3, 495–521); Deirdre McMahon (vol. 4, 138–62); and David Harkness (vol. 5, 114–33). Oddly, however, Anthony Clayton, writing on imperial defense (vol. 4, 280–305), ignores Ireland in his discussion of British counterinsurgency campaigns.[11]

What remains to be answered is whether the *Oxford History of the British Empire* offers a master narrative in place of the one it discards. At first glance, it would seem that it does not. Louis himself insists on the "pluralistic" composition of the volumes, and the efforts to achieve something close to comprehensive coverage fit uneasily—much like the empire itself—with the goal of narrative unity.[12] All three volumes consist of chapters devoted to a wide array of regional or thematic topics. The regionally oriented chapters touch on almost every corner of the empire's reach, from Auckland to the Yukon and Antigua to Shanghai. The thematic ones address subjects ranging from trade, migration, and defense to religion, architecture, and disease. The sheer variety gives rise to all sorts of disjunctions.

These cut through the work at various levels. Take periodization. Many of the contributors to volume 3 carry their stories to 1914, while their counterparts in volume 4 generally establish 1900 as their point of departure. Or take methodology. D. A. Washbrook's chapter on India from 1818 to 1860 (vol. 3, 395–421), for example, integrates social, economic, political, military, and intellectual history in a nuanced analysis of the shifting boundaries of modernity and traditionalism under British rule, whereas the following chapter by Robin Moore on India from 1858 to 1914 (vol. 3, 422–46) offers a narrowly conceived, traditional account of high politics in the Raj. Most notable, however, are the conflicting interpretations that different contributors apply to the same historical forces. Whereas P. J. Cain ignores the Industrial Revolution in his finance-oriented account of economics and empire (vol. 3, 31–52), B. R. Tomlinson claims that it transformed Britain's economic relationship with its tropical colonies (vol. 3, 53–74). E. H. H. Green places the "constructive imperialism" of Joseph Chamberlain at the center of Edwardian preoccupations (vol. 3, 346–68), while Ronald Hyam insists that the Edwardians were never much interested in the empire (vol. 4, 47–63). Elsewhere, Hyam's (vol. 4, 255–79) praise for the Colonial Office's policy of trusteeship as a progressive force contrasts starkly with John Cell's (vol. 4, 232–54) emphasis on its conservative effects on colonial societies. Whereas Washbrook, Susan Bayly in her account of colonial cultures in South Asia (vol. 3, 447–69), and several other contributors share Cell's conviction that British colonial policy tended to bolster traditionalist elements among subject peoples, John Lonsdale calls colonialism in East Africa a "forcing house" of "modernization" (vol. 4, 530).

Volume 5, on historiography, has its own distinctive sorts of disjunctions, characterized by its contributors' varying understandings of what falls within the purview of historiographical analysis. In his chapter on exploration (290–302), Robert Strafford, who perhaps exhausted his energy on his fine contribution to volume 3, does little more than string together summary accounts of works in the field, presented in order of publication. Robert Frykenberg's chapter on India until 1858 (194–213) is so padded with references to his own writings, including book reviews, that one might suppose that no one else has written anything of importance on the subject. Most contributors take a more sophisticated and less self-absorbed view of their task, though they differ over whether to employ an internalist analysis organized around the historical problems the scholarship in the field has addressed, or an externalist one stressing how particular historical moments have given rise to particular historical concerns. Gad Heuman on the slave trade and abolition (315–26) provides a good example of the former, C. A. Bayly on the Second British Empire (54–72) of the latter. Differences also arise over what place indigenous peoples should have in the historiography on empire. James Belich's incisive and original chapter on New Zealand

(182–93) includes consideration of Maori historiographical traditions, whereas Douglas Owram's chapter on Canada (146–62) is so Euro-centered that one is left to wonder whether any historians, indigenous or otherwise, have examined the colonial experiences of the country's first nations. The point is not simply that the thrust and quality of the contributions vary, but that their variety reflects disagreement about what should be included under the rubric of British imperial history.

Yet, for all the diversity that appears to course through this collaborative enterprise, the *Oxford History of the British Empire* is, in fact, informed by a master narrative, a vision of the story of the empire resting on a broad consensus about how that story should be told. It would be naïve, of course, to suppose that everyone involved shares the same understanding of the historical significance of the British imperial experience. But it is not unreasonable to suppose that a cohort of historians linked by generation and education would embrace a common set of assumptions about how to approach and interpret the past. Many of the contributors belong to a cohort whose intellectually formative years were shaped by a particular place and time—Oxford and Cambridge in the era of decolonization and the Cold War—with discernible consequences for their understanding of the empire.

One way to unpack the portmanteau of ideas carried by this cohort is to turn to that protean pair, Ronald Robinson and John Gallagher, who are in many respects the main avatars of the work's master narrative. Several decades ago, Louis edited a book on the historiographical debate their work provoked,[13] and he concludes his introductory essay on the historiography of the British Empire with a tribute to the "revolution" they caused, insisting that "we live today in the shadow of the reshaping of Imperial history by Robinson and Gallagher" (vol. 5, 39, 41). Winks, too, stresses their contribution in his essay at the end of volume 5 (653–8); elsewhere he has pronounced their work to be "the most influential contribution to British imperial history in the last two decades."[14] As Trevor Lloyd notes,[15] they are cited in the index more often than any other historians, and it is clear that the citations are not empty gestures. They reveal the remarkable intellectual influence Robinson and Gallagher have had on the historians who dominate the project.

What accounts for Robinson and Gallagher's long shadow? For the generation of imperial historians trained at Oxford and Cambridge from the early 1960s, they offered liberation from the increasingly stale story of the political evolution of an imperial state system bound by blood and custom; the story laid down by Seeley and enshrined in orthodoxy by the *Cambridge History*. Their own approach to the imperial past seemed to speak with greater relevance to the global political and ideological forces then at work. As Patrick Wolfe observes, their argument that events on the periphery often precipitated the scramble for colonial possessions carried particular conviction in light of the nationalist initiatives that were forcing the pace of decolonization in Africa and Asia, while their claim that British imperial actions were motivated by political and strategic rather than economic interests resonated well in the Cold War, challenging as it did the then-influential Marxist interpretations of imperialism.[16]

If, however, Robinson and Gallagher's impact was simply attributable to their ability to pitch to a particular Zeitgeist, it would be hard to explain the influence they continue to exert on British imperial history forty years later. Even if we allow for the fact that many of the historians currently active in the field trained under their tutelage, their enduring influence must also be credited, at least in part, to the exceptionally handy and heterogeneous tool kit of ideas they handed out about the dynamics of imperial expansion.

One of the most familiar of Robinson and Gallagher's contributions to the conceptual apparatus of imperial historiography is the "official mind," so pliable an abstraction that it has been employed for any number of purposes, both subtle and trite. In some hands, the "official mind" becomes little more than superficial shorthand for the aims of the imperial state, implying an aloof independence of intent that more often than not has obscured rather than revealed the objects of imperial diplomacy and colonial rule. For others, however, the "official mind" has been the basis for probing investigations into the social and ideological underpinnings of policy and administration, pointing to the complex interplay between aims and action. Perhaps the most interesting variation on the "official mind" in recent years has been P. J. Cain and A. G. Hopkins's (both contributors to the *Oxford History*) claim that the ethos and interests of what they identify as a "gentlemanly capitalist" elite determined the character of British imperialism.[17] The more narrowly construed use of the "official mind" as the loosely defined ideological intentions of a governmental elite continues, nonetheless, to predominate. It is explicitly endorsed by Hyam in his chapter on the Colonial Office (vol. 4, 255–80) and implicitly applied in other chapters dealing with British policy in particular colonies.

A second term that Robinson and Gallagher stamped into the imperial historian's vocabulary is "informal empire." The uses to which the term is put here suggest that the debate about its merits remains very much alive. The editors' decision to commission chapters on Latin America and China for all three volumes, as well as one on trade and informal empire in volume 3, attests to the value they place on the term as a heuristic device for charting the outer limits of British imperial power. The contributors, however, reach no consensus about what "informal empire" means or how its scope and impact can be measured. Jurgen Osterhammel makes a forceful case for "informal empire" as a tool for understanding British relations with China (vol. 3, 146–69; vol. 4, 643–66). Alan Knight, more qualified in his assessment of its relevance to Latin America, draws numerous chronological and geographical distinctions regarding the scale of British influence (vol. 3, 122–45; vol. 4, 623–42). In a historiographical survey of relations with Latin America, Rory Miller implicates the term in the agenda of a discredited dependency theory (vol. 5, 437–49), and Martin Lynn questions its validity in an examination of British foreign policy and trade in the nineteenth century (vol. 3, 101–21). Conversely, both Cain (vol. 3, 31–52) and Tomlinson (vol. 3, 53–74) make productive use of the term in their chapters on economics and the empire.[18] Regardless of these differences of opinion, the fact that "informal empire" still stirs such debate demonstrates the remarkable hold Robinson and Gallagher retain over their successors.

Their influence can also be discerned in the periodization of the project. They overturned the standard view that British imperial policy changed course around 1870, replacing it with a new consensus in favor of continuity across the nineteenth century. This perspective is so deeply embedded in the editorial organization of volume 3 that the issue of a late-Victorian rupture scarcely arises. Only four of the thirty chapters take the late nineteenth century as a point of departure, and two of these are concerned with the scramble for Africa. Similarly, the thematic emphasis volume 4 gives to the British Empire's ability to deflect the challenges that colonial nationalists and expansionist states posed to its global reach can be traced to Robinson and Gallagher. Reacting against a kind of inverted Whiggism that regarded the British imperial experience in the twentieth century as a story of inexorable decline,[19] Gallagher proposed in his posthumously published Ford lectures that the retreat from empire was reversed during the Second World War and for some time thereafter.[20] Robinson fleshed out the postwar lineaments of the revival in an article coauthored with Louis.[21] Not surprisingly, Louis takes a similar stance here, arguing in the foreword to volume 4 that "the British Empire experienced a renewal of the colonial mission after both world wars" (vol. 4, viii). He also contributes a chapter misleadingly titled "The Dissolution of the British Empire," in which he deploys a wealth of archival evidence to demonstrate that the British fought hard to reconstitute their empire in the aftermath of the Second World War (vol. 4, 329–57). Other contributors, including D. K. Fieldhouse (88–113), Hyam (255–79), Judith Brown (421–46), and A. J. Stockwell (465–89), present much the same scenario in their assessments of the endgame of the empire. The insistence that the imperial will did not fail, that the determination to cling to global power continued well into the 1950s, is traceable in large measure to the challenge that Gallagher, and then Robinson and Louis, posed to the conventional chronology of the empire's decline.[22]

Finally, the argument that stood at the heart of Robinson and Gallagher's classic study with Alice Denny of *Africa and the Victorians*—that crises on the colonial periphery provoked the scramble for Africa—is credited by Louis with laying the groundwork for the reorienting of imperial history away from a Eurocentric perspective.[23] "From Robinson and Gallagher onwards," he declares, "the history of British imperialism would be the history of the interaction between the British and indigenous peoples" (vol. 5, 40). *The Oxford History of the British Empire* reflects the influence of the reorientation: half of the chapters in volumes 3, 4, and 5 are devoted to the imperial encounter in particular regions and colonies, and most of them (though, regrettably, not all) acknowledge the important role that local elites and other native peoples played in determining the specific shape and trajectory of colonialism in their territories.

It would be misleading, however, to associate this historiographical concern for indigenous agency too closely with Robinson and Gallagher: they were less interested in the motives and actions of the peoples their analysis highlighted than might be supposed. Their gestures in that direction coincided, however, with the rise in the 1960s of a new interdisciplinary initiative, area studies, which were unequivocally interested in the indigenous side of the story. Responding to the pressing need in the polarized Cold War environment to know more about the nations and societies that were breaking free from European domination, area studies programs provided the linguistic training and other skills needed by scholars who sought to understand the experiences and ambitions of the new states and their inhabitants. Some imperial historians saw area studies as a threat that fragmented their subject into discrete national and regional histories.[24] But it also gave a new dimension to the understanding of the colonial experience, opening the door to the kind of social history or "history from below" that was making its mark on British historiography owing to the work of E. P. Thompson and others. The influence of area studies was especially apparent in the torrent of research on colonial resistance and collaboration that appeared in the 1970s and 1980s.[25] Some of the contributors who work in this tradition bring a perspective that is not only compatible with Robinson and Gallagher's emphasis on events on the periphery, but also provide the local grounding crucial to its claims for attention.

What we have here, then, is a scholarly enterprise that draws much of its intellectual inspiration from scholars and methodologies that broke onto the scene in the late 1950s and 1960s and that is informed in particular by the work of Robinson and Gallagher. While their vision of the meaning of the empire is certainly not shared by all of the contributors, the lineaments of a master narrative are discernible nonetheless. The emphasis on the concepts, themes, and concerns raised by Robinson and Gallagher, along with the methodological contributions of area studies, gives new polish to the old silver that has done much to advance our understanding of the empire over the past forty years. *The Oxford History of the British Empire* is an imposing monument to an important historiographical tradition.

***

This tradition appears increasingly unable, however, to supply the historical perspective we need on the world we currently inhabit. With the collapse of the Soviet Union and the end of the Cold War, area studies programs have seen their institutional support shrink and their intellectual premises brought into question.[26] At the same time, the economic and cultural forces commonly referred to as globalization have assumed unprecedented momentum, driving the integrative and exclusionary ambitions of imperialism into areas uncharted by the paradigm personified in Robinson and Gallagher. The new generation of scholars who have turned to the study of imperialism and colonialism have found inspiration from different, often unexpected, sources. The most visible and remarked-upon of these is postcolonial theory, which stands in stark contrast with the concerns of the established historiography of empire.[27] Disregarding the materialist issues of war, trade, and rule, it focuses on imperialism's epistemological foundations and representational practices. And in place of empiricism, it has introduced a raft of poststructuralist principles. Postcolonial theory appears so profoundly at odds with the aims and assumptions of traditional imperial history that its incursions have caused considerable alarm. Prominent imperial historians have drawn lines in the sand against what they see as postcolonial theory's jargon-ridden, antihistorical, and irredeemably French-inflected influence.[28]

Louis makes a half-hearted effort to steer clear of such discord by remarking that imperial history "can only benefit" from the contributions of "literary criticism and cultural studies" (vol. 5, x). And, indeed, their influence is apparent in the chapters in volume 5 that address the cultural and epistemological subjects that preoccupy postcolonial theory. These include chapters by Jeffrey Auerbach on art, Richard Drayton on science and medicine, Thomas Metcalf on architecture, and Diana Wylie on gender and disease. But the postcolonial influence is less visible in the preceding two volumes, owing both to the topics addressed and to the treatment they receive. Moreover, the general essays that open and close volume 5, providing the framework used to assess the field's accomplishments, either ignore or denounce postcolonial scholarship. Hopkins, in "Development and the Utopian Ideal," dismisses it as the latest in a long line of futile exercises in utopian thinking, "an indulgence of affluence" (vol. 5, 649). C. A. Bayly, while assessing the historiography on "The Second British Empire," also takes it to task, calling it "retrogressive" and lamenting its "faddishness" (vol. 5, 70). Winks, writing on "The Future of Imperial History," sees no place there for postcolonial scholarship practiced by people who "often kn[o]w little hard history" (vol. 5, 659). Peter J. Marshall on "The First British Empire" (vol. 5, 43–53) and A. P. Thornton on "The Shaping of Imperial History" (vol. 5, 612–34) ignore it altogether. So does Louis, whose introductory historiographical survey reaches its apotheosis with Robinson and Gallagher, who are presumed to have influenced everything written since. Postcolonial theory can perhaps take small comfort from the fact that its influence is considered pernicious enough to merit a chapter devoted entirely to exposing its errors. Though Washbrook's critique (vol. 5, 596–611) is well reasoned and forcefully argued, its inclusion reveals far more than Louis's passing remark about the *Oxford History of the British Empire*'s programmatic orientation.

So, for that matter, does the fact that volume 5 offers no systematic treatment of the major schools of thought that have sought to establish the theoretical foundation of imperialism. The capitalist interpretation that runs from Adam Smith through Joseph Schumpeter is ignored; likewise the Marxist tradition, including Karl Marx himself, V. I. Lenin, and Rosa Luxemburg. The psychoanalytic approaches of Octave Mannoni, Franz Fanon, Ashis Nandy, and others also are absent. The liberal critic J. A. Hobson and his successors earn a few passing remarks, but no sustained attention. The unease the volume exhibits toward postcolonial theory must be seen as the latest manifestation of a distrust of theory long felt by orthodox imperial historians.

This stance is troubling in part because it deflects attention away from the theoretical underpinnings of its own practices. It presents history and theory as adversaries, stigmatizing historical works that draw on theoretical insights as suspect. Yet even the most rigorously empirical scholarship rests on assumptions that amount to an inchoate theory. Imperial historians who have drawn inspiration from the ideas of Robinson and Gallagher have been influenced by theory: Robinson once was daring enough to brandish it in an article on collaboration.[29] In this light, the issue is not history versus theory, but the relative merits of one theory over another for the purposes of historical inquiry. Traditional imperial historians tend to lump together a variety of theoretically informed approaches as simply so many manifestations of the current theoretical bete noire, postcolonial theory. In fact, the intellectual flood that has altered the imperial landscape draws its inspiration from a range of sources, including critical anthropology, cultural studies, gender studies, subaltern studies, environmental studies, discourse theory, and, more broadly, both neo-Marxist and poststructuralist theory. And the uses made of these various theories and methodologies are so multifarious that it is difficult to apply a single set of attributes to them or neatly summarize their contributions, apart from pointing out their shared determination to break through the boundaries that have traditionally defined imperial history as a field of study. No doubt this is precisely why they upset so many historians of the empire.

One of the most influential assaults on the field's boundaries is the growing body of work that seeks to understand the empire as something that did not simply happen to others overseas, but to the British at home as well. As Ann Laura Stoler and Frederick Cooper remark, "Europe was made by its imperial projects, as much as colonial encounters were shaped by conflicts within Europe itself."[30] Interest in the imperial exchange has taken various forms. The empire shaped the understanding of what it meant to be British by producing an array of rivals and subjects against whom a common identity could be forged.[31] This identity was not restricted to the British Isles: it stretched across the Atlantic to North America with the first empire, and further afield as British immigrants in Australia and New Zealand embraced what in their own minds was a Greater Britain.[32] Within Great Britain itself, the influence of the empire has been discerned in the imagination of some of the country's intellectual and cultural giants, John Stuart Mill and Jane Austen among them.[33] The empire threaded through the social and political fabric of London and other cities, where pockets of people of color could be found—lascars and other laborers, students, entertainers, elites seeking audiences with imperial authorities, and various others, whose presence and experiences have only recently begun to be recovered.[34] Little wonder that Antoinette Burton, among others, has challenged the traditional narrative of Britain as the "Island Story."[35]

It would be unfair to suggest that the *Oxford History of the British Empire* ignores the impact of the empire on Britain. John MacKenzie reprises his pathbreaking work on imperial propaganda and popular culture in two valuable chapters (vol. 3, 270–93; vol. 4, 212–31).[36] Green traces the influence of imperial enthusiasts on the late-Victorian and Edwardian political scene (vol. 3, 346–68); Nicholas Owen considers their opponents, the "Critics of Empire in Britain" (vol. 4, 188–211); and Drayton makes a plea for the "inclusion of Britain . . . into the space of Imperial history" in an essay on "Science, Medicine, and the British Empire" (vol. 5, 274). Nonetheless, the overall thrust of the volumes reinforces the view that the imperial experience was essentially unilateral, with Britain imposing its will on large parts of the world without itself undergoing any significant transformation.

A related encroachment across the conventional boundaries of imperial history comes from cultural studies' holy trinity of race, class, and gender. One of its principal aims is to show that these categories, far from being fixed and separate realms of experience, were fluid and mutually reinforcing, engaging with many of the same tropes for many of the same ends, and inextricably entwined with the construction of the empire. Here I can mention only a few areas of inquiry by way of example. The subaltern studies collective has used class to highlight the agency of Indian peasants, jute workers, and others.[37] Other works show how British and colonial women constructed their claims for equality, sometimes seeking to transcend the boundaries of place and power by advocating a universal sisterhood, though more often pursuing divergent paths by emphasizing their contributions either to the imperial project or to colonial nationalism.[38] Parallel studies of the social and political construction of masculinity in the service of empire show how it was used as a marker of racial and ethnic difference.[39] Many of these works explore the efforts of British bourgeois culture to impose its social practices on peoples embedded within their own ideational worlds, resulting in the interplay of multiple identities constructed out of religion, caste, and sexuality as well as race, class, and gender. Each interacted with the others in ways that sometimes sustained, sometimes challenged imperial authority.[40]

Although the *Oxford History of the British Empire* deserves credit for devoting several chapters to some of these subjects, they remain marginalized. Rosalind O'Hanlon, in an essay on gender in the empire (vol. 4, 379–97), gives a glimpse of how far feminist scholars have forced a rethinking of the imperial encounter by highlighting the importance of gender to the workings of colonial economies, the rhetoric of colonial nationalism, and much more. Few other contributors, though, take notice of women or gender. Even more egregious is the failure to devote systematic attention to race, arguably the key category of imperial identity. The editors found room for chapters on British humanitarianism and trusteeship (Porter in vol. 3, 198–221; Hyam in vol. 4, 255–79), but none for the racial ideologies and policies that helped to essentialize the unequal distribution of imperial power and privilege.

Religion, as might be expected, is better served: Christian missionaries are the subjects of two chapters (Porter in vol. 3, 222–46; Norman Etherington in vol. 5, 222–46). In addition, Susan Bayly (vol. 3, 447–69) and Frances Robinson (vol. 4, 398–420) provide richly textured studies of the consequences of the collision between British colonial modernity and traditional Asian culture for Hindu and Muslim religious identity. Given the historical and cultural particularities of the construction of racial, gendered, and religious identities, a compelling case could be made for integrating them into the geographically oriented chapters, but this happens all too rarely. Perhaps the most telling evidence of the failure to find an effective way to integrate this literature is the historiographical chapter on "Disease, Diet, and Gender" (vol. 5, 277–89). Despite Wylie's valiant effort to draw together such disparate topics, her intellectually dubious assignment makes gender (and the chapter's other topics) seem like an afterthought.

Wylie points to yet another challenge to the conventional boundaries of imperial history: the empire as an important intersection of the social, scientific, and natural worlds. Here, too, scholarship has taken various directions. One line of inquiry shows how the British altered the colonial landscape's physical form, at times unwittingly but often with intent. Settler societies in temperate zones were prone to large-scale environmental interventions, ranging from the introduction of alien plant and animal species to the redirection of rivers and the destruction of forest canopies.[41] Tropical colonies suffered some of the same effects, owing especially to the increase in plantation agriculture,[42] but there the effects of climate and disease overshadowed other aspects of nature for the British. Although the struggle to "tame" the tropics was regarded as a struggle against its physical maladies, colonial doctors and others who took up the task tended to "situate disease, especially epidemic disease, within a wider physical and cultural landscape" that associated their endeavors with the social and political agenda of the colonial state.[43] The influence of British scientific institutions and the systems of knowledge they promulgated cannot be understood without reference to their relationship with imperial power. The connection seems unequivocal in the case of nineteenth-century disciplines such as geography and anthropology, which established their claims to scientific legitimacy in the service of the empire.[44] But some postcolonial scholars make the more far-reaching claim that all Western knowledge—including historical knowledge—is complicit in the imperial enterprise.[45]

It is hardly surprising that the *Oxford History of the British Empire* does not share the subversive views of postcolonial critics about its own intellectual premises and practices. More to the point, however, it does not show much interest in such epistemological and environmental issues. Tomlinson's chapters on the imperial economy (vol. 3, 53–74; vol. 4, 357–78), which stand alone in acknowledging the environment's influence, draw on Alfred Crosby's neologism, "neo-Europes," to explain the differential patterns of economic development in the empire. Few of the chapters on settler colonies show a similar interest, though Ged Martin makes some mention of the role of geography and climate in his survey of Canada since 1815 (vol. 3, 522–45). The only chapters to pay serious attention to the relationship between scientific knowledge and imperial power are Strafford's on exploration (vol. 3, 294–319) and Drayton's on science and medicine (vol. 5, 264–76).

If the matter at hand were merely one of inclusiveness, a judgment about the amount of attention to be given to such issues, any quarrel one might have with the editors' choices and the contributors' emphases would turn on little more than personal preference. In fact, the choices reveal a fundamental fissure over the meanings we attach to the past and, more particularly, the associations we draw between the heritage of the empire and present circumstances. The single issue most obviously separating the *Oxford History*'s interpretation of the imperial past from that of the new imperial studies is the importance it gives to the state as an autonomous agent of historical change, with the implication this carries for understanding the significance and outcome of imperialism. For the *Oxford History of the British Empire*, the modern nation-state is both the product of the empire and the repudiation of its purposes: the dialectical relationship between the two makes the past meaningful to the present. The new imperial history is interested in the transformation of imperialism into what we now refer to as globalization: it stresses the erosion of national autonomy, the proliferation of hybrid identities, and the intensification of racial, ethnic, and religious divisions. All of these developments are the result of the fevered movement of peoples, goods, and ideas across the globe by way of routes and mechanisms that had their origins in the world system established by the British Empire and its counterparts. The issue that divides the two parties, then, is whether they place the state at the center of their understanding of empire and its influence on the present, or at the margins of global processes.

Perhaps the most compelling criticism of new studies of imperialism is that they focus mainly on the cultural dimensions of the empire. Critics have rightly objected to their neglect of the material manifestations of imperial power, the economic, political, and military might the British wielded and their enemies envied. Hopkins, for one, accuses the culturally oriented scholarship on empire of failing to ask the "hard political and economic questions" that he demands of imperial history. The most striking feature of his recommendations for the direction the field should take, however, is its resemblance to the aims of the new imperial studies. He, too, rejects the state as the centerpiece of analysis. He, too, insists that historians need to turn their attention to the transnational and multiethnic forces that have shaped the contemporary world. He, too, proposes to cut across traditional boundaries, arguing that the study of imperialism can serve as the fulcrum for "a fundamental reappraisal of world history."[46] Thus, he advocates an approach that makes common cause with another body of literature that reaches beyond the conventional confines of British imperial history, but has relevance for it. World historians' research into the integration of the international economic system, the interaction of different modes of production, and the transmission of technologies of power and governance contributes plenty of insights into the workings of imperialism.[47]

It would be impossible for the *Oxford History of the British Empire* to satisfy everyone. Its task is made more problematic, however, by its determination to see the British Empire "whole" at a time when there is less agreement than ever about its dimensions and, indeed, its content and meaning as a discrete subject. The new imperial studies have compelled us to consider the influence of the empire in new ways, opening up a wider range of experiences and peoples to investigation and probing more deeply into the cultural and mental processes that extended the British model of modernity across the globe. For all its good intentions and generosity of scale, the *Oxford History of the British Empire* remains wedded to an interpretation that offers only partial insight into the imperial origins of our current condition. Though the project is an impressive logistical and intellectual achievement that will serve as the essential work of reference on the British Empire for both scholars and students for decades to come, it is more a monument to a particular generation of scholarship than a signpost pointing toward the future.

3

Imperial History and Postcolonial Studies Revisited

The interpretive and methodological disputes I examined in the first two chapters of this book began to diminish over time as more historians became more receptive to the insights offered by postcolonial studies and related perspectives on the past. An invitation to contribute to The Oxford Handbook of Postcolonial Studies *gave me an opportunity in 2013 to chart the changes that imperial historiography had undergone since the mid-1990s, making the case that the remarkable resurgence of scholarship in the field can be attributed in substantial measure to the influence of postcolonial studies. I also stress, however, that its contributions need qualification—it has been marred by elisions and constraints, and intellectual inspiration has come from other sources as well. The question we are left with is this: where now?*

Introduction

For more than a few historians, the advent of postcolonial studies, with its strange language and theoretical promiscuity, appeared akin to an invasion by a barbarian horde. These historians manned the barricades, determined to defend their discipline against the alien invaders. Some patrol the parapets still, though their redoubt is now much diminished. Postcolonialism has managed over time to infiltrate the borders of history and mix with the natives. While important pockets of resistance and points of disagreement remain, the discipline's stance toward this alien interloper has for the most part shifted from suspicion and antagonism to tolerance and even fraternization.

Perhaps nowhere has this change of attitude been more dramatic than in British imperial history, a field that was once among the most hidebound in its insistence on an austere empiricism that stressed the official archive and the political, military, and economic concerns of the state. The gulf between this historiography and postcolonial studies was so great in the first decade of their encounter that it seemed all but unbridgeable. From the mid-1990s onward, however, it became increasingly apparent that postcolonialism had struck a chord with a cohort of scholars for whom imperial history as it was then constituted had ceased to address issues they found meaningful. Others who remained skeptical of postcolonial studies' merits found it necessary nonetheless to rethink and reframe their own aims in response to its challenge. The result has been a remarkable revival of imperial history, transforming it into one of the most active and intellectually invigorating fields of study within the profession at present. The hybridization of British imperial history provides us with an especially striking example of the broader impact of postcolonialism on the historical discipline.[1]

Border crossings

Postcolonial studies found several distinct avenues of entry to history as a discipline. One important source of intercession came from subaltern studies. This group of historians of India was frustrated with a historiography that seemed incapable in its then dominant schools of thought—the hagiographic approach adopted by nationalist historians, Marxist historians' preoccupation with the proletariat, and the Cambridge school's Namier-like analysis of interest-based politics—of coming to grips with the experience and consciousness of the vast majority of the Indian populace, that is to say the illiterate peasantry as well as other subjugated or "subaltern" parties. This frustration extended to the archives that supplied the evidence most historians relied upon, since these products of the colonial and postcolonial state seemed to have left frustratingly few traces of subaltern voices. Ranajit Guha, the founder of subaltern studies, devised a different approach in his seminal study, *Elementary Aspects of Peasant Insurgency in Colonial India*, which made use of semiotic analysis, seeking out verbal clues, physical signs, and other symbols that might give insights into peasant grievances and political aims.[2] Contributors to the early subaltern studies volumes, which Guha edited, drew on a wide array of analytical strategies and theoretical influences, ranging from the cultural Marxism of Antonio Gramsci and E. P. Thompson to the linguistic and poststructuralist approaches associated with Ferdinand de Saussure, Jacques Derrida, and Michel Foucault. Its intellectual trajectory gradually passed from investigations of the social world of the subalterns to a critique of historical practices and historicism, drawing it ever closer to key concerns of postcolonial studies.[3] The publication in 1988 of *Selected Subaltern Studies*, with an introduction by Gayatri Chakravorty Spivak (who also coedited the volume with Guha), was simultaneously an important marker of the collective's turn toward a more avowedly postcolonial perspective, one that entailed a self-reflexive preoccupation with the politics of knowledge, and its highly successful coming out on the international intellectual stage.

Many feminist historians also found established historical practices increasingly unsatisfactory. In their determination to examine the social construction of women's roles, the cultural formation of gendered identities, and the political regulation of sexuality and gender relations, they had to confront the evidentiary limitations of public archives and the methodological limitations of conventional modes of historical analysis. Joan Wallach Scott, Judith Butler, and other feminist critics exposed some of the problems with existing scholarly practices and pointed the way to new approaches. Perhaps because gender difference intersected with racial difference in such striking and revealing ways in the colonial realm, this became a particularly productive area of inquiry. A number of feminist historians began to explore the discursive and institutional interactions of gender, race, and sexuality in the colonial context, initiating what would become one of the most influential areas of engagement with postcolonial studies.[4]

Border crossings by postcolonial studies into history occurred at various other locations as well, including the work of historical anthropologists such as Bernard Cohn, Talal Asad, and Jean and John Comaroff, and historical geographers like J. B. Harley and David Harvey.[5] The intellectual influences, then, were complex, multifarious and impossible to trace to a single lineage. This is a point worth stressing, especially in light of the reputation that Edward Said's *Orientalism* enjoys as the founding text for postcolonial studies. While Said's work certainly influenced much of the newer historical scholarship on empire, it is all too often allowed to serve as a placeholder for many other sources of inspiration. Indeed, Said's impact was in many respects a negative one, serving as a lightning rod for criticism by historians suspicious of literary studies' prominence in the postcolonial turn.[6] What Graham Huggan has referred to as the "slipperiness" of postcolonialism as a school of thought is abundantly apparent in its multiple routes of access to imperial history.[7]

To understand the appeal that postcolonialism exerted with a certain cohort of historians we should also consider the role played by the sociology of knowledge. A disproportionate number of postcolonialism's initial proponents within the discipline were female scholars and scholars of color, most of them either Americans or émigrés from non-Western countries.[8] This was especially true for those who ventured into British imperial history, a field then dominated by white male British historians who remained for the most part wedded to the concerns and methods that John Gallagher and Ronald Robinson had introduced in the 1950s and early 1960s.[9] For women and men who felt professionally marginalized because of their backgrounds or interests, postcolonial studies provided them with an instrument to remake the study of imperialism and colonialism for their own purposes.

How they did so is the subject of this chapter. In it, I will divide imperial history's engagement with postcolonial studies into three thematic categories—identities, geographies, and epistemologies. Attention will be directed toward some of the leading scholarship in each category, indicating its main themes and arguments and noting objections that have been and can be lodged against it. The unevenness of postcolonialism's influence on historians specializing in different regions of the world will receive notice as well, highlighted in the contrast between its transformative effect on colonial Indian historiography and African scholars' much more muted response. Finally, I will speculate on the future of this association between postcolonial studies and imperial history.

Identities

One of the principal ways in which postcolonialism gained purchase among historians engaged in the study of British imperialism, especially those who saw themselves as historiographical outsiders, was as a result of its approach to the problem of identity, particularly racial and gender identity. A key component of its contribution to the "cultural turn" in the humanities was the emphasis it placed on the intersection of culture and power and the determinative role it gave to difference, which served to delineate categories of identity—race, gender, class, religion, and so forth—and to embody them in individuals and groups.[10] These categories were seen as cultural constructs, not primordial instincts, and it was stressed that they served specific social and political interests. Identity, then, was understood as enmeshed within structures of power and susceptible to shifts as those structures altered or collapsed. These insights gave impetus to several important lines of historical inquiry.

One issue that attracted a great deal of interest was the colonial state's use of its classificatory powers to define and differentiate subject peoples, imposing on them much more rigid and mutually exclusive categories of identity than they might have acknowledged or embraced in the past. Bernard Cohn laid much of the analytical groundwork for this analysis with his influential series of essays on the colonial census and other state projects that sought to count and classify Indian peoples. Among those who developed this line of analysis was Cohn's student, Nicholas Dirks, whose *Castes of Mind* argued that the Indian caste system as the British presented it was largely a construct of their own, distorting and simplifying a complex, shifting set of social relationships in order to divide and subjugate Indians.[11] Others argued that Indian communal tensions were made much worse, if not caused, by British policies that institutionalized and politicized distinctions between Hindus and Muslims.[12] Africanists noted similar patterns in that continent's colonial experience, observing that so-called tribal identities were far more fluid in precolonial Africa than they would later become under colonial rule, which they credited in many instances with actually creating tribalism and its attendant conflicts. Although some of those who pursued this line of analysis adopted an avowedly postcolonial perspective, as did David William Cohen and Atieno Odhiambo in their coauthored work, most did not. Leroy Vail and his contributors, for example, relied on the standard tools of social history and cultural anthropology to trace the role that colonial regimes played in *The Creation of Tribalism in Southern Africa*.[13]

Some of the most interesting work on identity focused on the cultural uses of gender, race, and sexuality. Lata Mani's influential essay on the early-nineteenth-century debate about *sati*, the Hindu practice of burning widows on their husbands' funeral pyres, opened the door to a number of studies of colonial gender discourse, many of them expanding on Mani's argument that collusion occurred between male colonizers and colonized elites to speak for and subordinate colonized females.[14] Some African historians came to similar conclusions about the patriarchal politics of colonialism, though once again they did so for the most part without recourse to postcolonial theories or methods. The South Asian debate about gender also took an important turn with Mrinalini Sinha's *Colonial Masculinity*, which showed that both British officials and Indian nationalists deployed competing notions of masculinity and effeminacy, the former by casting the latter as lacking the manliness to govern themselves, the latter by conceding their effeminacy but attributing it to colonial dependency. Sinha stressed the historical particularities of this debate, avoiding any appeal to an overarching discursive framework such as Said's *Orientalism* and grounding her study instead in a specific set of political struggles that exposed the connection between assertions of masculinity and claims to power.[15]

Another scholar who did important work on gender and sexuality in the colonial context was the historian/anthropologist Ann Laura Stoler, who wrote a series of groundbreaking essays and books on the management of the intimate domain in the colonial context, comparing British, Dutch, and other European colonizers' practices. Stoler demonstrated that debates about concubinage, poor whites, miscegenation, child-rearing practices, and other issues associated with personal conduct revealed that gender, race, and sexuality were inextricably woven together and that the policies meant to regulate such conduct were integral to colonial regimes' strategies of rule. Drawing on Foucault's concept of biopower, which concerned the state's regulation of sexuality, she exposed the political stakes invested in the control of intimate behavior.[16] Philippa Levine made a similar point in her ambitious comparative study of the regulation of prostitution in four British colonies—India, the Straits Settlements, Hong Kong, and Queensland.[17] Historians of Africa took up these issues as well, examining the social significance of "white peril panics" and other manifestations of colonial sexuality's racialized politics.[18]

The body itself came to be seen as a culturally pliant indicator of identity. As David Arnold, Warwick Anderson, and Megan Vaughan among others have shown, British medicine encoded racial differences in the classification and treatment of the diseases that afflicted the bodies of both colonizers and colonized.[19] Elizabeth Collingham's examination of "imperial bodies" in British India revealed that even such seemingly mundane matters as style of dress, food preferences, and personal hygiene were important—and shifting—markers of difference, establishing gender and racial distinctions as well as moral judgments about the bodies of both colonizers and colonized. Similarly, Timothy Burke's fascinating study of soap, domesticity, and bodily discipline in colonial and postcolonial Zimbabwe pointed to some of the contested meanings that a commodity culture attached to the African body.[20]

Some of the historians mentioned above came to be identified with the new imperial history, which sought to place "metropole and colony in a single analytic field."[21] Its main intent was to bring the British Isles back into the story of empire, showing how the domestic realm was itself shaped by its imperial interests and colonial dependencies. This line of inquiry shed new light on what it meant to be British. Here was an identity that transcended the ethnic particularisms of the home islands' various peoples and found its most meaningful frame of reference in the context of the larger world, especially the empire. Postcolonial studies, it should be stressed, was hardly the only avenue of entry into this subject. Once again, mainstream social and cultural history provided another option, as John MacKenzie demonstrated in his own pioneering work and in the book series he edited for Manchester University Press, "Studies in Imperialism."[22] Linda Colley's *Britons* was in many ways as responsible as any work in recent decades for the renewed interest in the historical construction of a British identity, and although Colley identified the empire as an important aspect of that identity, postcolonialism had little if any influence on her approach to the subject. J. G. A. Pocock's earlier plea for a more expansive understanding of British history that acknowledged the connections with and contributions of British communities overseas provided another important antecedent to the recent interest in the imperial dimensions of Britishness.[23]

Still, most of the scholars who took up the new imperial history banner embraced the aims and methods of postcolonialism. This was especially true of certain feminist historians, whose interest in issues of gender increasingly drew their attention to the wider set of discursive practices and institutional structures that informed women's roles and opportunities. Antoinette Burton led the way with her provocative challenge to the celebratory historiography on Victorian and Edwardian feminists, showing that these mainly middle-class women made their bid for rights by constructing an identity for themselves as imperial citizens whose moral authority was deemed essential to the British civilizing mission abroad, and especially to the task of saving seemingly degraded and helpless Indian women from their own oppressive society.[24] Catherine Hall, whose earlier work had examined women in British middle-class culture, produced a richly documented study of the Baptist missionaries from Birmingham who sought to transform the lives of ex-slaves in post-emancipation Jamaica, revealing the ways that race, gender, religion, and other categories of identity were formed and reformed through the mutually constitutive constructions of difference in imperial metropolis and colony.[25] Among the most forceful advocates of the view that "empire was . . . the frontier of the nation" was Kathleen Wilson, who sought to show that Britain's worldwide reach informed its sense of self as early as the eighteenth century.[26]

If British identity was constituted at least in part through its connections to empire, what about the identities of settlers and their offspring in places like Canada, Australia, and New Zealand? Reacting against several decades of historical scholarship that had focused on the development of separate and insular national identities in these settler dominions, a new cohort of historians, many of them associated with the "British World" conferences that took place between 1998 and 2007, insisted on settlers' enduring allegiance to a broader British imperial identity.[27] Some of the impetus behind this "British World" scholarship was generated by an antagonism to postcolonial studies, both on methodological grounds and because of the undue emphasis it was said to place on the dependent empire of non-Western peoples. Yet the British Worlders' preoccupation with the problem of identity was itself indicative of the shift of orientation that postcolonialism had helped to produce in imperial history. And it soon became apparent that any analysis of a pan-British imperial identity had to confront the issue of race, which manifested itself most visibly in privileged claims to "whiteness" that marginalized indigenous peoples within these settler states and restricted entry into the colonies by nonwhite immigrants. It is here that historians informed by a postcolonial perspective were especially influential in shaping research into British settler societies. They gave new analytical rigor to the study of race relations between white settlers and indigenous peoples, identifying their various terms of interaction, which ranged from miscegenation and assimilation to segregation and extermination, and assessing their implications for the construction of racial difference.[28] In addition to the numerous case studies of race and identity in particular settler states, the groundwork for a broader comparative analysis was laid by Patrick Wolfe in his brilliant work on the different criteria that Australia, the United States, and Brazil employed to delineate racial categories, revealing the strategic nature of these notions of difference.[29] Others, like Marilyn Lake and Henry Reynolds, have traced the transnational construction of "whiteness" as the source of a greater British identity.[30]

Critics of this postcolonial-inflected body of work on the imperial construction of identities adopted several distinct lines of attack. Bernard Porter took to task the new imperial historians' methodological practices and challenged their claims that empire had a significant influence on the national consciousness of the British public. Although Porter marshaled an impressive body of evidence in support of his argument, it ultimately rested on too narrow a definition of imperialism to be persuasive.[31] David Cannadine was more sympathetic to the view that the British sense of self was shaped by empire, but he objected to the new imperial historians' emphasis on racial identity, which he believed obscured the importance of class and status as categories of difference within the empire. Yet the case he made for them was sketchy and at least as selective as the one he objected to regarding race.[32] A far more penetrating critique came from Frederick Cooper, who had helped inspire the new imperial history. He insisted that historians were using the term "identity" in so many different and often contradictory ways that it had lost all analytical value. He was particularly critical of the tendency in postcolonial scholarship to refer to the fragmented and fluid nature of identity, which seems to subvert the term's nominal associations with sameness, connection, or fixity.[33]

This problem derives in some respects from the tendency to apply "identity" both to individual consciousness and group allegiance, corresponding respectively to what Cooper in his critique referred to as "soft" and "hard" identities. While group allegiance is grounded in conformity to a prescribed set of cultural norms and presumes a sameness and stability in identity, individual consciousness implies far greater pliability and often entails shifting or multiple identities. Quite apart from complaints about the divergent implications of these two conceptions of identity, questions can be raised about whether either of them has inspired as much genuinely new and original scholarship as their proponents have trumpeted. The interest so many postcolonial-inspired historians have shown in the construction of group identity is hardly new, as evidenced by previously mentioned work by various Africanists, as well as Colley, Mackenzie, and other British historians. Insofar as these historians have suggested that categories of identity such as race, tribe, caste, and religion hardened in the colonial period, are they really telling us much more than social historians had already revealed? And insofar as they attribute that hardening almost exclusively to the actions of the colonial state, are not they denying the agency of those peoples who embraced and mobilized around identities that promised them some form of security or power?

Meanwhile, much of the recent scholarship on individual identity, which stresses the subjective self, has perhaps unavoidably taken on a biographical thrust. Though this work rarely assumes the form of a conventional biography that narrates a single life from birth to death, it often relies on serial or group biographical sketches. Catherine Hall's *Civilizing Subjects* opens with a lengthy prologue on the imperial career of Edward Eyre, and biographical accounts of its other protagonists are central to the book's narrative structure. Antoinette Burton has framed many of her books around the lives, experiences, and perceptions of a select group of individuals, and one of her recent studies focuses entirely on what she calls the "postcolonial careers" of Santha Rama Rao. My own work took a biographical turn with an intellectual study of Richard Burton. Indicative of what may be taken as a trend is the collection of essays edited by David Lambert and Alan Lester, *Colonial Lives Across the British Empire*, which consists of a series of essay-length biographical studies. There is surely some irony in the fact that so many practitioners of the *new* imperial history have been drawn to biography, one of the most old-fashioned ways of telling stories about the past.[34] As yet, no one seems to have seriously grappled with the significance or implications of this development. Does this postcolonial preoccupation with individual consciousness risk recapitulating conventional biography's limitation as a mode of historical analysis, a limitation that lies in its being subject in many respects to its own subject's subjectivity? Does it confirm the complaint of critics who suggest that postcolonialism's rejection of master narratives leaves historians with little more than a fragmentary array of singular lives to investigate and interpret?[35] These remain open questions.

Geographies

A second important aspect of postcolonialism's influence on history arose from its challenge to the spatial assumptions or geographies that informed how most historians plied their trade. This challenge took at least two distinct forms. One derived from Edward Said's analysis of the "imaginative geographies" that differentiated the West from the rest. Said showed that the territorial spaces with which these binary categories were associated became imbued with contrasting cultural meanings and political significance, making them discursive repositories of imperial efforts to exert power.[36] The other aspect of postcolonialism's approach to the issue of geographical space was provoked by frustrations with the way the nation was privileged as the primary locus of historical scholarship.[37] It launched a sustained critique of the limitations of national historiographies and provided at least some of the intellectual impetus for a heightened interest in mobility, migration, and the multiple circuits through which peoples, practices, and ideas moved across space.

The Saidian concern with imperial representations of space generated a huge scholarly industry, bringing historians into dialogue with historical geographers, literary specialists, art historians, and others. A large body of work directed attention to the ways European explorers, officials, missionaries, and others imbued strange and exotic environments with meanings. Some of these meanings derived from traditional European aesthetic models like the picturesque, the pastoral, and the sublime, which supplied a familiar frame of reference for unfamiliar landscapes.[38] But other meanings carried connotations of difference, often expressed in terms of danger and desire, as Said demonstrated in his study of the "Orient" in Western thought and as others observed about the "tropics," "darkest Africa," and other morally freighted geographical categories. David Arnold showed how India came to be conceived as part of the tropics after the mid-nineteenth century, a designation that carried connotations of decay and degeneration. Medical theories, botanical categories, and other aspects of British scientific knowledge were colored by this preoccupation with geographical difference.[39] Timothy Mitchell's *Colonizing Egypt* portrayed that country as succumbing to a European disciplinary order that "inscribe[d] in the social world a new conception of space," one that differentiated between reality and representation and created a "world-as-exhibition."[40] Works such as these exposed the culturally constructed character of Europeans' notions of space and place, which came into correspondence with their notions of time by equating other lands with an earlier stage in their own historical development. Among the more intriguing lines of inquiry in recent years is one that focuses on the intentions and assumptions embedded in British scientific mapping of colonial territories. Thought-provoking studies of Captain Cook's naval surveys of the Pacific, the Great Trigonometric Survey of India and various other cartographic endeavors have shown that these scientific practices operated in discursive contexts that served to legitimate imperial ambitions.[41]

Space also assumed importance for postcolonial historians of the British colonial world because of their frustrations with the influence exerted by nation-centered histories, which they came to view as arbitrary and ideologically imposed constraints on the spatial scope of their inquiries. Subaltern studies arose in large measure as a challenge to those historians who saw India as their sovereign subject, and similar objections were raised by historians of Britain and its empire, with Antoinette Burton, for example, pointedly asking, "Who Needs the Nation?"[42] In both instances, this discontent came to a head in the context of political crises that shook the foundations of the two nations, evidenced in India by the state of emergency and the Sikh separatist campaign and in Britain by civil war in Northern Ireland and demands for devolution in Scotland and Wales. Those historians who adopted a postcolonial approach to the problem of the nation pursued two distinct strategies. One was to direct attention, as we have already seen, to those subaltern peoples whose interests and identities seemed divorced from the state within which they resided, thereby disaggregating the nation into what Partha Chatterjee referred to as "its fragments."[43] The other response was to shift attention to diasporas and other transnational processes that lay beyond the grasp of national histories. One of the most interesting examples of this line of inquiry comes from the Pacific historian Tracey Banivanua Mar, whose study of indigenous islanders' struggle against colonial rule highlights the "massive displacement and scattering" they experienced and the "stateless forms of decolonisation" they pursued.[44] Postcolonial historians were certainly not the only ones to move in this direction, as was evident from the preoccupations of the "British World" contingent, as well as the increasing attention economic historians gave to the imperial engines of globalization.[45] But the contribution made by those who shared postcolonialism's interest in the cultural and epistemological dimensions of imperialism was distinctive and important.

This turn to the transcolonial-cum-transnational aspects of British imperialism stirred new interest in the cultural plaiting that tied the various strands of empire together. Social and demographic historians had, to be sure, produced a large and distinguished body of work that tracked the movements of particular groups of peoples—British settlers, African slaves, Indian indentured laborers, and so forth—from their homelands to foreign shores, and economic historians had done much the same for capital and commodities. Surprisingly little attention had been given, however, to the transnational networks that made the movement of these peoples and products possible, and their equally important service in circulating ideas, institutions, and cultural practices around the globe had gone all but unnoticed. This began to change with Paul Gilroy's *The Black Atlantic*, which examined the transnational cultural ramifications of the African diaspora. Among historians of the British colonial world, Alan Lester and Tony Ballantyne became two of the leading proponents of the idea that a network or web (their respective metonyms) supplied a more flexible and productive analytical framework for understanding imperial processes than the nation-state, with its unilateral limits, or the bilateral binary of metropole and colony. Ballantyne in particular showed in his first book how an idea (Aryanism) and in his second a people (Sikhs) circulated through the empire, their meanings or identities shifting as they moved from place to place.[46] Others have directed attention to the technological lineaments of these networks—steamships, railways, telegraphs, the press—and observed the influence they exerted on the idea of empire and the contending uses to which it was put by colonized peoples.[47]

As a consequence of this reconceptualization of space, some standard assumptions about the unidirectional flow of imperial power were challenged, resulting in what has been termed the "decentring" of empire.[48] This was not simply an assertion of the limits of imperial power, but an acknowledgment of its dispersal across multiple locations. Jessica Harland-Jacobs traced the transnational and transracial imperial bonds forged by Freemasonry. Thomas Metcalf examined the sub-imperial system that operated out of India and extended across the Indian Ocean to Southeast Asia, Arabia, and Africa. Similarly, Eve Troutt Powell showed that Egypt pursued imperial ambitions of its own in the Sudan both before and after it came under British control.[49] Other historians made the important point that the circuits of empire also aided in the circulation of anticolonial agents and ideas, expanding their influence and establishing common ground with opponents of British rule elsewhere.[50]

Various objections can be made to these interpretations of imperial space. The sheer range of imaginative geographies that scholars have attached to

European representations of various parts of the non-European world at various points in time has raised questions about whether the dichotomies between the West and the Orient (or the tropics or "darkest Africa" or such like) were quite as clear, categorical, and enduring as the Saidians have drawn them. The turn toward a decentered approach to empire that traces its circuits of exchange and disaggregates its drive for expansion can be seen in some sense as an effort to overcome the essentializing tendencies of the imaginative geographies model. But it runs risks of its own, most notably as a result of its tendency to downplay the importance of power. Unlike the standard view of empire that sees it projecting outward from a metropolitan center, a decentered empire is one where power is in some sense diffused and geographically dispersed. It has been noted, too, that the networks this empire creates also facilitate connections between the anticolonial forces arrayed against it, thereby equalizing or neutralizing their power effects.

Finally, the postcolonial critique of nation-centered histories can be criticized for being itself too Western-centered in its orientation. The title of an essay by the Australian historian Ann Curthoys aptly illustrates the problem: "We're just starting making national histories, and you want us to stop already?"[51] While nation-centered histories may have established a stranglehold on historiographical practices in Britain and powerful postcolonial states such as India, it is doubtful whether the same can be said of the many small, fragile countries in Africa and elsewhere that emerged from colonial rule without the institutional means to propagate a strong sense of national pride or consciousness among their populations. This may help to explain why Africanists have been less susceptible than South Asianists to postcolonial critique—its objections seem misdirected if not meaningless for their subject, given the limited influence that most African states exert over historical memory and the production of historical knowledge. More broadly, much of the weight of contemporary concern about the nation-state has shifted from anxiety about its strength to worries about its weakness, with Afghanistan, Pakistan, Somalia, and most recently, some of the countries of North Africa and the Middle East serving as examples. In this regard, the postcolonial challenge to histories that privilege the nation can be seen as very much a privilege of its own.

Epistemologies

A third contribution that postcolonial studies made to the new histories of British imperialism came about as a result of its critique of the intellectual underpinnings of the West's claims to power. This epistemological inquiry encouraged some historians to reevaluate the ideological rationales offered on behalf of British imperial rule and to expose their own discipline's complicity in the consolidation of its practices. Postcolonial theorists placed particular importance on the universalist ambitions of European thought, especially as manifested in the Enlightenment, which was charged with having advanced its own standard of rationality and model of modernity as templates for other peoples. Its teleological conviction that all societies passed through uniform stages of development provided Europeans, who saw themselves as leading the way in this march to progress, with the justification to impose their will on those they considered less civilized.

While the ideological origins of the British Empire have been traced by David Armitage and others to the composite monarchy that arose in Britain in the sixteenth and seventeenth centuries, most of the postcolonial-inflected studies of British imperial ideology have focused on the period from the late eighteenth century onward, with particular attention being paid to how nineteenth-century liberal theorists rationalized autocratic rule in India. Thomas Metcalf's masterful *Ideologies of the Raj* traced the tension within imperial thought between notions of similarity and notions of difference with respect to Indians, showing how British attitudes and policies oscillated from one position to the other as the circumstances of their rule changed over time.[52] Although Metcalf's analysis owed something to postcolonial insights, the scholar who brought its influence most directly to bear on the question of imperial ideology was Uday Mehta, a historian of political theory, who argued in *Liberalism and Empire* that the leading lights of liberalism, James and John Stuart Mill foremost among them, defended imperial polices that thwarted freedom for Indians by equating them to children who required the tutelage of adults—or, in this context, the British.[53] Mehta presented Edmund Burke as the main exponent of an alternative liberal tradition, an abortive one that opposed empire and its universalist premises. More recently, however, Burke has been portrayed by Nicholas Dirks as the true progenitor of liberal imperialism, rescuing Britain from a sense of complicity in the scandals that arose out of East India Company rule in late-eighteenth-century India. In Dirks's view, Burke laid the foundations for Britain's subsequent sense of mission to bring the benefits of Western civilization to the subcontinent.[54] Either way, most scholars agree that nineteenth-century liberalism accommodated itself to empire.[55] Although much of the empirical evidence for this accommodation had already been marshaled by mainstream historians,[56] the postcolonial perspective brought a new urgency to the inquiry into liberal imperialism, not least because its nineteenth-century proponents could be characterized as the direct antecedents of the neoliberalism that has informed recent US foreign policy.

A related measure of the postcolonial influence on historical inquiries into British imperialism's epistemological premises can be discerned in the attention it has given to the relationship between empire and modernity. Most defenders of the British Empire portrayed it as the agent of modernity, which they understood to entail civil society, free trade, the rule of law, private property, monogamy, science and technology, and so on—that is to say, those characteristics that were credited with having contributed to Britain's success on the world stage. The conviction that this model of modernity was universally applicable informed British colonial policies in India, Africa, and elsewhere, and its traces lingered on in Western aid and development projects following decolonization.[57] For historians inspired by postcolonial theory, it became important to expose these universalist claims for what they were, the particularistic products of a European cultural and intellectual tradition. The aim, as Dipesh Chakrabarty provocatively put it, was to "provincialize" Europe. Chakrabarty did not reject the idea of modernity per se, but he sought to show that Bengalis negotiated their own distinctive agreement with what Anne McClintock has characterized as "the angel of progress."[58] Other historians of India, as well as many of their Southeast Asian and East Asian counterparts, pursued a similar line of inquiry, creating a cottage industry concerning the indigenous sources of colonial and postcolonial modernity across the region.[59]

Given the remarkable economic and political progress that Asian nations have experienced in recent decades, this scholarly interest in the culturally variable origins of modernity is understandable. The lack of any equivalent progress in most of Africa and the Middle East may help to explain the very different tack that historians of those regions have taken toward this issue. Long before postcolonial studies entered the arena, Africanists in particular felt a need to explain why their continent was so politically troubled and economically enfeebled. What the postcolonial turn produced was a move away from explanations that stressed material forces, such as the sway of the military on politics or the constraints of global systems of trade on wealth production, toward those that highlighted cultural and ideological factors. Mahmood Mamdani, for example, argued that the British reliance on indirect rule in Africa institutionalized the authority of local chiefs, whose powers derived from their ability to maintain and reinforce a sense of tribal identity. This "decentralized despotism" survived decolonization and sustained the polarizing ethnic rivalries that have continued to plague the African pursuit of modernity. Similar charges were made about Britain's reliance on princely rule in the Middle East, though Priya Satia has taken this critique a step further with her analysis of the British agents who laid the foundations for that rule, suggesting that they themselves forsook modernity and its assertion of rationality in favor of an intuitive ethos that embraced the very primitivism they attributed to the "Arab mind."[60]

Lastly, the postcolonial challenge led historians to question the epistemological foundations of their own discipline. Some gave scrutiny to the archive, rejecting the view that it was a neutral repository of information about the past that made objective historical knowledge possible. The charges that postcolonial scholars had issued against colonial information-gathering practices and institutions like the census, the cadastral survey, and the museum were equally applicable to the archive—that it was the creation and instrument of the state, reflecting its interests and concerns.[61] Antoinette

Burton gave this critique a feminist thrust, arguing that even though the state's panoptic ambitions were manifested in this "archive fever," it failed to take into account women's historical perspectives, which were usually private and passed on through memory.[62]

Others focused on what they saw as the failure of the discipline to extricate itself from a mode of historical reasoning arising from the Enlightenment, which posited Europe's past as the master narrative against which all other societies' histories could be measured. This historicist tradition, Chakrabarty argued, "enabled European domination of the world in the nineteenth century" by establishing the premise that its own historical experience provided the roadmap for all other societies, a roadmap that only Europeans were qualified to read.[63] Even if historians can overcome historicism, according to Chakrabarty, they can never reconcile their understanding of the past with the enchanted version found in many traditional peasant communities, which made no room for reason or evidentiary rules. He also concedes, however, that modern historiography, for all its limitations, remains indispensable. Ranajit Guha, by contrast, seems in a recent work to reject it altogether. Identifying Western-style history as an innately imperial system of thought that originated with Hegel, Guha urges its rejection in favor of stories that recovered some of the wonder evoked by traditional epics like the Mahabharata.[64]

It is hardly surprising that Guha's radical recommendations, which could dismantle historical practices as they are currently constituted, have had few takers within the discipline. The more nuanced stance adopted by Chakrabarty has generated greater interest and admiration, though it too has stirred uneasiness and even bafflement in some circles. And almost every aspect of the critique advanced by a number of postcolonial scholars about the intellectual framework that sustained British (and, more broadly, European) imperialism has provoked criticism. The charges it has lodged against the Enlightenment as the nursery of modern imperial ideologies and their universalist doctrines have been challenged by scholars who have demonstrated that many of the leading *philosophes*—Bentham, Condorcet, Diderot, Herder, Kant, Smith—were outspoken in their objections to European imperial expansion.[65] Even as the Enlightenment descended into nineteenth-century liberalism, it continued to harbor far more varied views on imperialism than the preoccupation with James and John Stuart Mill would suggest.[66]

A similar objection has been raised against the preoccupation with modernity as the principal manifestation of the liberal imperial project. Given the range of alternative modernities that historians working from a postcolonial perspective have identified as emerging across much of the colonial and postcolonial world, Frederick Cooper has rightly asked whether the term retains any serviceable meaning.[67] Adding to the confusion is the countervailing argument associated with Mamdani, Satia, and others, which attributes to the British an antimodern attitude and agenda in certain parts of their empire. Is there, then, any instrumental association between modernity and imperialism?

As for the postcolonial critique of the historical discipline and its practices, this is a stance that seems open to objection on two grounds—its derivativeness and its exaggeration. There are few if any historians active today who are naïve enough to suppose that the historical records housed in government archives provide full and objective insight into the past. The profession has been cognizant for decades of the need to seek out other sources of information, ranging from archaeological artifacts to visual records such as painting and photographs to oral traditions and interviews. And the postcolonial charge that subaltern peoples have been rendered invisible in the archives is seriously exaggerated, a point that Ricardo Roque and Kim Wagner have made with persuasive power.[68] Resourceful historians have frequently found ways to extract from the archives a great deal of information and insight about women, peasants, and other subordinated and marginalized groups. To take only one of many examples, Durba Ghosh's *Sex and the Family in Colonial India* has drawn from court records, church registers, personal papers, and other archival sources a remarkably rich body of evidence about the lives of the indigenous women who married or were mistresses of British officials in late-eighteenth-century and early-nineteenth-century India.[69]

Future directions

What does the future hold for the postcolonial turn in British imperial history (and in history more generally)? It is always risky to predict scholarly tastes and trends, and that risk seems especially great at this juncture, when the global forces that do so much to shape the kinds of questions academics ask seem in such flux. That said, the number of noteworthy books cited in this chapter suggests that postcolonial approaches to the history of empire are far from flagging. To appreciate how prevalent they have become, one need only consider Patrick Kelley's *Imperial Secrets* (2008), a postcolonial critique of the limitations of imperial intelligence, written by a US army major and published by the National Defense Intelligence College! With so many new imperial historians, subaltern studies scholars, and other postcolonial-inflected historians of imperialism and colonialism now ensconced in secure and often prominent places in the academy, we can expect much more scholarship to build upon their already substantial body of work.

But will historians' relationship to postcolonial studies remain the same? The inspiration that the early proponents of a postcolonial approach to the history of imperialism and colonialism drew from theorists and critics in other disciplines—figures such as Michel Foucault, Edward Said, and Gayatri Spivak—has likely run its course. Arguably the most influential voice within postcolonial circles in recent years has been a historian, Dipesh

Chakrabarty, while the work of other historians interested in aspects of the British imperial world has become essential reading among the broader community of postcolonial scholars as well. Insofar as a cross-disciplinary dialogue continues to characterize the postcolonial enterprise, much of its energy and insight seems likely to come from history itself.

What remains to be seen is whether this work will retain the same edge and sense of purpose that made its intellectual interventions so compelling and influential during the past few decades. Recent events may have precipitated a rupture in the way historians approach the problem of empire. The American invasions of Afghanistan and Iraq have reminded us of the role that naked military force, with its desire to induce "shock and awe," still exerts in world affairs, while the subsequent insurgencies in those countries have reminded us of the limits of imperial power, as well as the resourcefulness—and often ruthlessness—of those who resist it. Postcolonial studies and its allies in history are not well suited to addressing the military and political manifestations of empire. And the sudden collapse of the global economic system in 2008–9 has alerted us to the fact that capitalism itself remains a far more vital and volatile factor in shaping our future than the recent bland pronouncements about globalization and its decentering effects would have had us believe. Michael Hardt and Antonio Negri's *Empire*, acclaimed not so long ago for its analysis of the new post-national imperialism of globalization, now reads like an artifact from a bygone era.[70]

Will we return, then, to the pre-postcolonial version of imperial history, with its emphasis on the military, economic, and political manifestations of empire? It seems more likely that historians of empire will adopt strategies that integrate the material, cultural, and epistemological dimensions of imperialism into a post-postcolonial synthesis. The growing interest in the history of consumerism, commodities, and material culture may be one indication of such a move.[71] Still another is the renewed attention being given to the ideological lineaments of the imperial state.[72] Even the surge of scholarship that has recently appeared on the violence that accompanied imperial conquest, rule, and collapse is a far cry in its aims and methods from traditional histories of imperial wars.[73] The collaboration between postcolonial studies and imperial history may be waning, but its contribution to the renewal of the latter field over the past two decades cannot be gainsaid. It has helped to create a richer and more nuanced understanding of the effects of imperialism, exposing its manifold cultural and epistemological implications, not least on historical practice itself.

4

Exploration and Empire

Exploration was frequently the founding undertaking of empire, yet it attracted surprisingly little attention from imperial historians for decades after decolonization. When I began research for what would become my book The Last Blank Spaces: Exploring Africa and Australia *(2013), I found that the richest, most illuminating scholarship on exploration came from historical geographers, historians of science, and literary scholars. The original version of this essay, which appeared in* History Compass *in 2007, sought to synthesize this multidisciplinary scholarship and identify themes that seemed especially relevant to my own foray into the subject. The revised version that appears here acknowledges the renewed attention the history of exploration has received in recent years.*

Exploration, as it is commonly understood, is a product of a particular historical legacy. According to the Oxford English Dictionary, "exploration" first came to refer to arduous journeys to strange lands in the mid- to late eighteenth century, while the word "explorer" was coined in the early nineteenth century. Felipe Fernández-Armesto and others have pointed out that most societies in the past have engaged in what can be broadly construed as exploration.[1] Even so, the practice assumed a particular set of cultural, social, and political valences for Europeans as they extended their reach around the globe. Exploration came to connote a combination of scientific and technological achievement, state power, and national prestige—connotations that persist to the present day, perhaps most notably in space exploration. Expeditions to the far corners of the earth helped to bolster Europeans' sense of exceptionalism. Explorers served to embody the enterprise, tenacity, and thirst for knowledge that Europeans saw as some of the key characteristics that set them apart from other peoples.[2]

From the mid-eighteenth century onward, Britain was at the forefront of this endeavor to explore the world. The voyages of Captain James Cook gave unprecedented prestige to exploration as an instrument of national wealth, knowledge, and power. Intellectual curiosity—the desire to advance scientific understanding of the natural world and acquire information about the diverse species that inhabit it—supplied an important impetus for many expeditions into unfamiliar lands. This inquisitiveness was accompanied by the acquisitiveness of capitalism. Explorers sought out new routes, new markets, and new resources, ranging from plants to minerals and more. These efforts were tied in turn to imperial ambitions. The British sent out expeditions to gather intelligence on their rivals and claim strategically valuable territory. No country made more expansive use of exploration to advance its economic and political interests than Britain, which dispatched naval expeditions across the seven seas and to the ice-bound poles, as well as territorial expeditions into the interiors of Australia, Southeast and Central Asia, sub-Saharan Africa, Latin America, and other regions of the world.

Contemporaries were not coy about acknowledging the purposes of exploration. They praised its role in Britain's rise to preeminence on the international stage, which they associated in turn with progress and civilization.[3] Their pride in the empire provided them with an appreciation of the intertwined roles that scientific inquiry, economic enterprise, and political interest played in exploratory endeavors. Chroniclers of exploration, however, began to decouple these connections as the empire itself started to come under assault. For botany, geography, anthropology, and other fields of study that had served as the handmaids of empire, its deteriorating reputation provided a powerful incentive to declare their independence as disinterested scientific disciplines, detached from political or economic agendas. Insofar as they acknowledged that exploration had helped to shape their professional genealogies, they portrayed it as a purely scientific enterprise, undertaken to advance knowledge of the natural world. A decoupling of a different sort occurred in the way exploration was represented in popular narratives. These tales of adventure were increasingly drained of their chauvinistic emphasis on imperial achievement, concentrating instead on the personal stories of the explorers themselves. Biography, then, became the main genre through which the history of exploration was recounted: it concentrated on the personal courage and psychological compulsions of the explorer.[4]

Starting in the 1960s, exploration lost much of its appeal as an academic research subject. To be sure, the subject remained popular with the public, but not with professional historians. Two notable works about the British encounter with Africa published in the 1960s make the point. In *The Image of Africa*, the pioneering African historian Philip Curtin relied heavily on British explorers' accounts of West Africa to trace British perceptions of Africa and Africans between 1780 and 1850, but he paid virtually no attention to the enterprise of exploration itself.[5] A few years later, Robert Rotberg, another historian of Africa, tried to integrate exploration and explorers into an

African-centered history in his edited volume *Africa and Its Explorers*, but it failed to kindle new interest in the subject among Africanists.[6] While the general reader's appetite for stories of exploration remained strong, it fed on popular narratives that highlighted intrepid explorers' feats of derring-do.[7]

Academic interest in exploration began to revive as a consequence of the intellectual crisis that spread through the humanities and social sciences in the 1970s and 1980s as a result of poststructuralism's entry on the intellectual scene. Challenged by poststructuralist critics to examine their own epistemological premises, a host of academic disciplines became more self-reflexive, probing the assumptions that underwrote their intellectual practices and exposing their heritage of collusion with empire. Anthropology was perhaps the first discipline to carry out this auto-critique, with Talal Asad editing an influential volume on anthropology's associations with colonialism, followed by important critical and historical studies by Johannes Fabian, George Stocking Jr., and others.[8] Similarly, the historical origins of geography as a discipline came under interrogation by David N. Livingstone, among others, while the influential critique of "metageography" by Martin Lewis and Kären Wigen questioned the very categories that geographers used to identify and differentiate territorial spaces.[9] This sort of self-scrutiny brought new attention to the explorers who played such an important role in the ethnographic and cartographic practices these disciplines had been founded on. Even the natural and experimental sciences began to come under critical scrutiny, with historians of science revisiting their formative practices and finding that exploration and travel were far more important to their development than previously appreciated.[10]

The same spirit of epistemological inquiry transformed literary studies, where one of the key texts was Edward Said's *Orientalism* (1979), an immensely influential reassessment of Europeans' intellectual engagement with the peoples and cultures of the Middle East and North Africa. Although Said was not concerned with exploration per se, he drew on the experiences and accounts of explorers in his analysis of European perceptions of the "Orient" and he used the term "imaginative geography" to connote the constructed nature of those perceptions.[11] Above all, he reaffirmed the largely neglected fact that Europeans' relentless pursuit of knowledge about other lands, not least the knowledge they gained through exploration, was integral to their imperial ambitions. Moreover, he insisted that its influence continued to be felt long after the colonial era had come to an end; hence the appearance of the term postcolonial theory to refer to his and kindred scholars' efforts to establish an analytical framework for understanding colonialism's lasting effects. The epistemological implications of Said's appreciation of the relationship between knowledge and power were not lost on other students of literature, who began to turn their attention to exploration and travel writing.

The most influential works to follow up on Said's insights were Paul Carter's *The Road to Botany Bay* and Mary Louise Pratt's *Imperial Eyes*.

While these two works employed rather different methodological strategies, they shared many of the same objectives. Both addressed aspects of European exploration—Carter's book focusing on Australia, Pratt's on South America and Africa—but neither told conventional stories of explorers' personal exploits or scientific achievements. Instead, they gave sharp scrutiny to the ways in which Europeans' written accounts of their journeys characterized the unfamiliar lands and peoples they encountered and observed. At the heart of both studies was the analysis of Western discursive practices, which led in turn to a postcolonial critique of Western epistemological premises. Carter opened his book by declaring that history as it was commonly written in the West was intended "not to understand or to interpret," but "to legitimate": it was, he declared, an "imperial history." He sought to replace it with a new "spatial history" that examined how language was used to symbolically transform space into place, by which he meant a location imbued with a meaning.[12] Pratt, too, asserted that her purpose was to "decolonize knowledge," to deconstruct the "planetary consciousness" that she argued the West had produced as a result of the explorations its representatives had conducted across the globe. Unlike Carter, however, who was concerned exclusively with the West's efforts to impose its own categories of meaning on other places and peoples, Pratt offered glimpses of a counter-discourse that opposed the totalizing claims of this planetary consciousness, detecting its traces in the "contact zones" of cross-cultural interactions where some measure of "transculturation" occurred.[13]

Taken together, the postcolonial perspective adopted by Said, Carter, and Pratt had a profound influence on subsequent scholarship on exploration. That influence derived in the first instance from their success in exposing and discrediting the premises that informed so much of the prior literature on the subject. They presented explorers' feats of heroic individualism and exploration's contributions to scientific knowledge as culturally constructed claims that both obscured and legitimated the imperial interests these endeavors invariably advanced. It was not, however, the purpose of Said, Carter, and Pratt to foreground the political and economic dimensions of imperial power; rather, they sought to show how explorers constructed claims about the objects of their inquiries that revealed a far more insidious and enduring form of power, the power to determine the way we view the world, its regions, and their inhabitants. This discursive power and its epistemological underpinnings have become one of the primary themes of recent scholarship on exploration.

The influence of Said, Carter, and Pratt was felt most directly in literary studies, where it directed increased attention to the genre of travel writing. By integrating explorers' narratives into the broader category of travelers' tales, this scholarship demonstrated that explorers gave voice to the modes of representation, ethnocentric assumptions, and other cultural conventions of their countrymen. From the late 1980s through the early 2000s, a steady stream of studies appeared that enriched our understanding of the strategies, sensibilities, and aesthetic traditions that shaped narratives of travel and exploration.[14]

This approach soon reached an impasse, however. Its preoccupation with textuality and representation produced increasingly insular and repetitive scholarship. Too often it adopted a predictable rhetorical stance that characterized all travel narratives as generating the same baleful colonizing "gaze." It failed to recognize that exploration came to be constructed as a distinct enterprise, with its own scientific protocols, its own trained practitioners, and its own unique partnerships with scientific societies, the state, and the public. It also neglected the social and political forces that shaped exploration in the field, confronting explorers with conditions that undermined their authority and destabilized their culturally determined certainties. Few literary scholars paid heed to Pratt's insistence on the importance of the "contact zone." The discursive approach, with its reliance on published texts by Western writers, was simply not suited to such a line of inquiry.

One strategy for escaping this impasse came from the art historian Bernard Smith, whose most important work was published long before the rise of postcolonial studies. In *European Vision and the South Pacific*, his seminal study of early European artistic representations of the Antipodes and its inhabitants, Smith argued that Enlightenment science's demand for precise empirical observation of the natural world and the man-on-the-spot's difficulties placing the region's strange lands, plants, animals, and peoples within conventional biological categories and aesthetic traditions converged to cause a radical disjuncture in European art and thought.[15] While not denying that Europeans sought to contain this new world within the confines of their own cultural preconceptions and discursive practices, Smith stressed the limits of these efforts and the transformative effects of the encounter itself.

Smith's book went almost unnoticed outside his native Australia until a second edition appeared in 1985, when it struck a chord with a wider scholarly audience, now attentive to the issues it raised. Art historians began to reassess the paintings and other images (botanic prints, photographs, topographical drawings, etc.) that gave glimpses of lands and peoples unfamiliar to Europeans, acknowledging that the traditional aesthetic criteria used to evaluate "high" art were inadequate in addressing the challenges and innovations that characterized these works.[16] Visual representations of environments deemed exotic by European travelers attracted the attention of historians and others engaged in the examination of exploration and its cultural consequences.[17]

The phenomenological approach employed by Smith had its parallels in the increasing attention anthropologists gave to the dynamics of the cultural encounter between Europeans and indigenous peoples. They were particularly insistent on understanding this encounter as an exchange—an uneven one, to be sure, but an exchange that altered European as well as non-European perceptions and practices. Some of the best work along these lines followed Smith into the South Pacific, though other richly nuanced analyses of encounters—Jean and John Comaroff's study of British missionaries and their Tswana interlocutors in southern Africa was a notable early example—appeared elsewhere.[18] Anthropologists also produced insightful applications and critiques of postcolonial theory, as well as lively debates about what we can actually know about the perceptions and intentions of indigenous peoples in their initial encounters with Europeans.[19]

The intellectual currents that stirred fresh interest in exploration among anthropologists, cultural geographers, literary scholars, and others were slow to attract the attention of historians, as I have pointed out in previous chapters. The end of empire in the 1960s had eliminated much of the incentive to revisit its origins in exploration. The rise of social history, with its emphasis on the poor and the powerless, and the spread of area studies, with its conviction that non-Western societies deserved their own histories, took the discipline in different directions, with imperial history increasingly marginalized. While some good historical studies of exploration appeared over the next few decades, they were outliers in a field that focused mainly on colonial rule and its aftermath. When historians of empire rediscovered exploration as a subject meriting study, they did so by way of the scholarship that had already come from anthropologists, literary critics, and others. Far more than many areas of historical inquiry, then, the new histories of exploration have proven to be highly interdisciplinary.

In the remainder of this chapter, I intend to sketch out the two main themes that run through the recent historiography on British exploration from the late eighteenth through the nineteenth century. One concerns the various forces within Britain that supported and shaped exploration as a distinct, organized enterprise. Underwriting these forces, which included political, economic, social, and scientific considerations, were an important set of epistemological premises. The second theme concerns the actions and attitudes of explorers in the field, where expectations often collided with experience, causing a disjunction between premises and practices, representations and reality. The conflicts and accommodations that arose between explorers and indigenous peoples would shape the courses and outcomes of expeditions in profound and unexpected ways.

* * *

British exploration from the mid-eighteenth century onward invariably occurred at the behest of institutional sponsors, who imposed their own expectations on the explorers. The Admiralty was responsible for dispatching a series of naval expeditions to distant seas in the second half of the eighteenth century, the most famous being Captain Cook's three voyages through the Pacific in the 1760s and 1770s, which were responsible, a new book argues, for "a significant shift in how Europeans could know the world."[20] Cook was instructed to conduct careful astronomical observations, test the reliability of new navigational instruments, determine whether a southern continent existed, and seek out a northwest passage between the Atlantic and the Pacific Oceans. The remarkable skill and daring with which he carried out his tasks established a new standard for scientific exploration, one that Vancouver, Bligh, Flinders, and other British naval explorers following Cook sought to emulate.[21]

The Admiralty continued to contribute to the expansion of geographical knowledge through much of the nineteenth century. With the Pacific and other oceans yielding fewer secrets, its attention turned to two other areas of investigation. A series of high-profile expeditions were dispatched to the Arctic and Antarctic, making national heroes of James Clark Ross, William Parry, John Ross, and others. The disappearance of the John Franklin expedition in the 1840s generated immense public interest in the exploration of the Arctic. Yet the Admiralty's less celebrated hydrographic surveys of the coastlines of Africa, Australia, and other large landmasses, along with the probes it sent up the Congo, the Niger, and other rivers, may have had a more lasting impact.[22] These initiatives operated at the boundary between land and sea, and their significance lay in the closing of the great age of seaborne exploration and the opening of a new era of continental exploration.

The founding figure of this new era was Alexander von Humboldt, the German naturalist whose exhaustive tour of Central and South America (1799–1804) transferred to terra firma the meticulous methods of scientific investigation that Cook had embodied at sea.[23] His achievements would inspire several generations of adventurous young men to seek out similar challenges in other lands. As attention shifted from oceans to continents, the Admiralty's standing as the directing agency for British exploration diminished.

What institution replaced it? Given the widely acknowledged association between land exploration and imperial expansion, the British Army was a likely candidate. Its American and Russian counterparts leaped at the opportunity to organize expeditions, which promised professional rewards and territorial annexation. But the British Army never assumed a similar role, a fact that has not received the attention it deserves. Perhaps it can be explained in part by Britons' longstanding distrust of a powerful standing army; perhaps, too, the reduction in armed forces after the Napoleonic Wars and the rise of the fiscally frugal Victorian state limited its ability to participate in such matters. In any case, the army provided surprisingly little institutional support for British exploration in the nineteenth century.

The Colonial Office and the Foreign Office each sponsored a few expeditions, but no branch of the British government assumed the leading role in land exploration that the Admiralty asserted over sea exploration. The state institution that was most active in promoting exploration was a quasi-private one, the British East India Company. It had economic and strategic reasons of its own to gain greater knowledge of South and Central Asia. After conducting maritime surveys of India's coastline and major rivers in the mid- to late eighteenth century, the Company turned its attention to the lands that bordered British India, sending expeditions to places like Tibet and Persia.[24] The scope of its investigations soon extended from Southeast Asia through Central Asia to Arabia and even East Africa.[25] It also sent out parties to survey the territories it had conquered, culminating in the Great Trigonometrical Survey, the decades-long enterprise that mapped the entire subcontinent and, in the view of Matthew Edney, established a "legitimating conception of empire" for the British in India.[26] Other colonial states sponsored exploratory endeavors as well. Much of the impetus behind the surveys of the Canadian West came from Ottawa, acting at the behest of land-hungry settlers. And the colonial governments of New South Wales, South Australia, Victoria, Queensland, and Western Australia sponsored a series of competing expeditions across the Australian outback, motivated by civic pride and the search for pastures, minerals, and other resources.[27]

In Britain itself, various individuals and voluntary societies filled the void left by an inattentive state. They usually cast exploration in terms of the advancement of scientific knowledge and the pursuit of commercial opportunities, with less emphasis placed on strategic considerations. Joseph Banks, the patrician naturalist on Cook's first voyage and president of the Royal Society, was the leading impresario of exploration until his death in 1820. He used his social and institutional connections to the royal family and prominent politicians to lobby on behalf of various expeditionary projects. He helped found the African Association (1788), which sponsored a series of expeditions by Mungo Park and other explorers of North and West Africa.[28] He turned Kew Gardens from a royal estate to a botanical clearinghouse for exotic plants collected by explorers and other overseas visitors. Banks's tireless efforts to gather botanical specimens from around the world reflected the broader ambitions of Enlightenment science to observe, classify, and utilize the products of the natural world.[29] Richard Drayton has shown that Banks and his contemporaries were deeply influenced by an ideology of agrarian improvement that connected their botanical endeavors to one of the key rationales of territorial conquest, the compulsion to bring untilled land into productive use.[30] This understanding of scientific inquiry was related in turn to their status as landed gentlemen: the African Association, for example, was intended by its genteel founders, at least, to advance their moral authority and social prestige.[31]

Scientific considerations continued to intersect with other interests in shaping the institutional environment that fostered exploration. The Royal Geographical Society (RGS) became the leading institutional advocate of British exploration after its founding in 1830, and it would remain so through the nineteenth century. It was simultaneously a sober scientific institution, a shrewd promoter of the explorer as national hero, an active lobby for

British economic and political interests abroad, and a stuffy gentleman's club.[32] While its roster of members included prominent aristocrats and other landed gentlemen, the largest single category of members consisted of navy and army officers, and the list of fellows included a number of scientists, most notably Charles Darwin and Thomas Huxley. Women, while enthusiastic consumers of exploration narratives, were excluded from the society until 1904.[33] Roderick Murchison, who made the RGS into a "key national institution," had originally established his reputation as a geologist, and his conception of scientific exploration gave new emphasis to stratigraphic mapping and the search for mineral deposits.[34] This agenda reflected the fact that Britain's booming industrial economy was generating a growing demand for minerals, oils, fibers, and other natural resources.

Other scientific institutions benefited from exploration as well. The British Association for the Advancement of Science, founded in 1831, became a popular venue for explorers to report on—and quarrel with one another over—the discoveries they had made.[35] Kew Gardens established itself as an important research center under the aegis of William Hooker and his son Joseph, classifying, cultivating, and disseminating cinchona, rubber, sisal, and other commercially useful plants that had been collected by explorers.[36] The British Museum acquired great quantities of ethnographic, archaeological, and zoological material from expeditions; the London Zoo displayed some of the live animals these expeditions had brought back from strange lands; the Royal College of Mines classified and assessed the value of the geological samples they had gathered; the Royal College of Surgeons became the repository for the skulls of "savage" peoples that explorers avidly collected. The British Natural History Museum, which opened in South Kensington in 1881, was stuffed with plants and animals that explorers had plucked and pressed, caught and pickled, shot and stuffed. By the end of the nineteenth century, specimens and artifacts from expeditions filled thousands of cases in the hundreds of natural history and ethnographic museums that had sprung up in Britain, India, Australia, and elsewhere across the empire.[37] Taken together, these museums, societies, and related organizations supplied much of the institutional support and intellectual rationale for nineteenth-century exploration.[38]

They also saddled explorers with a set of protocols that governed their activities in the field. Expeditions invariably set out with written instructions from the RGS and other sponsoring agencies, defining their objectives and detailing the procedures they were expected to follow. It became obligatory for explorers to keep daily journals, calculate latitude and longitude, draw maps and sketch scenery, measure rainfall and wind direction, collect botanical specimens and geological samples, gather ethnographic artifacts and word lists from indigenous populations, and more. Naval and army officers possessed more of these skills than most travelers, which is one reason so many explorers came from their ranks. (Another reason, of course, was that the "long peace" of the nineteenth century constricted conventional avenues of career advancement for military men.)

Scientific exploration required the use of precision instruments such as sextants, chronometers, barometers, thermometers, pedometers, and artificial horizons. Historians of science have noted that the primary purpose of these instruments was to establish a system of "standardisation and accountability," providing "forms of equivalence and modes of comparison" for the information explorers brought back to Britain.[39] We catch a glimpse of their importance to explorers' sense of themselves as men of science in a studio photograph of John Hanning Speke, the famed East African explorer, who poses for the camera with a pocket watch in one hand and a sextant at his feet.[40]

Even the explorers' gaze, that highly subjective act of observation, came to be seen as an exercise that could be regulated and made scientifically valid by establishing ground rules about where and how it was to be directed in the field.[41] J. R. Jackson's *What to Observe; or, the Traveller's Remembrancer* was just one of a number of publications in the nineteenth century that sought to systematize what the explorers observed and how they recorded those observations.[42] When photography became a viable technology, metropolitan sponsors of expeditions eagerly embraced it as another way to overcome the subjectivity of observation. Most explorers, however, found it too cumbersome and fragile to be of much use until the closing decades of the century.[43]

The emphasis that the directors of the RGS and other institutions that sponsored expeditions placed on scientific protocols and instrumentation cannot be separated from their struggle to impose their own social and intellectual authority over the men who ventured into new lands. Many of the precision instruments that became increasingly obligatory components of the explorer's kit were so costly that they usually came on loan from sponsoring agencies, thereby strengthening these agencies' control over the expedition and their claims to the data it collected. The gentlemen who oversaw this global enterprise from their cozy London boardrooms and clubs "carved out a niche for themselves as regulators of measurements," self-proclaimed authorities who insisted that they alone possessed the technical expertise and breadth of vision to interpret the mass of raw information that had been brought back from the field.[44] These were the so-called "armchair geographers" (and their equivalents in other nascent scientific disciplines), men like Francis Galton, who as head of the RGS's Expeditions Committee and author of its "Hints for Travellers" (1854) wielded a great deal of power.[45] Their administrative oversight of expeditions and power to assess the contributions these expeditions made to geographical and other branches of knowledge provoked intense resentment among explorers, who often raged against the not-so-subtle message that their role was "to see and not to think," as Burton acidly put it.[46]

We now know that explorers' field notes and journals went through multiple emendations prior to the publication of the books and articles that purportedly provided direct, unmediated accounts of expeditions. Both the explorers themselves and their editors and other figures made these changes. Their purpose was not merely to smooth grammatical and rhetorical rough edges, but to eliminate embarrassing revelations and infuse narratives with greater dramatic power. In so doing, explorers' accounts of their experiences were often distorted in important ways.[47] The engravings and other visual representations of expeditions were similarly massaged and modified to ensure that they accorded more fully with popular tastes and expectations.[48] How these works were received by audiences and, especially, how they were read and made meaningful by readers is more difficult to determine, though scholars have begun to grapple with this important issue.[49]

Some explorers found ways to free themselves from the shackles placed on them by publishers, armchair geographers, and other experts at home, especially in the second half of the nineteenth century. David Livingstone, the missionary-explorer of Central Africa, paved the way in the 1850s with his unprecedented public celebrity, which derived from his saintly persona and success in communicating a moral rationale for exploration—the redemptive power of commerce and Christianity for Africa's slave-ridden peoples—in an immensely popular series of books and lecture tours. This celebrity gave him a certain degree of autonomy in his dealings with the RGS and other sponsoring agencies, and the mythmaking that shaped his posthumous reputation would influence the attitudes and agendas of other African explorers.[50] The most deliberate attempt to don Livingstone's mantle was made by Henry Morton Stanley, the journalist-explorer who first gained fame by finding Livingstone, his whereabouts then unknown, on the shores of Lake Tanganyika in 1871. While Stanley was no saint, he was a shrewd exemplar of the new press who used his formidable journalistic skills to acquire fame, freeing him in large measure from the grasp of the geographical fraternity with whom he had chilly relations.[51] But perhaps the most striking indicator of the erosion of the institutional constraints on who could be an explorer and how exploration should be conducted was evidenced with the entry of women into the fraternity. While the category of traveler had been open to women for some time, it was only around the turn of the century that women like Mary Kingsley and Gertrude Bell came to be seen as explorers.[52]

The RGS and other organizations that promoted scientific exploration bore some responsibility for the public's increasing interest in explorers and exploration. Roderick Murchison and his fellow geographers did their best to burnish explorers' reputations by sponsoring the public lectures they gave, publishing their reports, awarding them gold medals, and honoring their achievements in various other ways, figuring that the attention would redound to the benefit of the RGS and its agenda. Institutions as varied as the British Museum, Kew Gardens, and the London Zoo, all of which were deeply dependent on the material gains of expeditions, catered increasingly in the second half of the nineteenth century to the patronage of the general public, which was granted unprecedented glimpses into the unfamiliar worlds that explorers had brought to light. Historians have given increasing attention in recent years to the role of "spectacle" in shaping British attitudes toward Africans and other peoples. Toward the end of the century, audiences in London and other British cities flocked to various commercial exhibitions that supplied dramatic renderings of clashes between representatives of British civilization and agents of local primitivism. The highly successful Stanley and African Exhibition (1890) cast Stanley in a heroic light, showing his expeditions into Central Africa as an effort to bring enlightenment and liberty to a dark and dangerous land.[53] Like many of these exhibitions, the display included indigenous peoples—in this case, two African boys—who served, as Felix Driver has observed, to represent "cultural and racial difference through the display of native bodies."[54] By the end of the century, then, exploration had entirely broken through the dike the scientific societies, publishers, and government agencies had built to contain it, operating instead as an impetus for personal fame, public entertainment, commercial profit, ethnographic education, and much more.

* * *

The other main theme of recent scholarship on exploration concerns the actions, experiences, and perceptions of explorers in the field. There is no doubt that explorers served as an advance guard for imperial expansion—sometimes unwittingly, but often with conscious intent. They played an active role in promoting the aims of settler colonization in Australia, Canada, and other lands that attracted large numbers of British immigrants. Even in places like North and West Africa, Central Asia, and the Amazon basin, where the pressure from settlers was limited or nonexistent, explorers invariably understood that their efforts were intended to serve British economic and political interests, opening the doors to commerce, preempting the designs of rivals, and, when required, laying formal claim to territory. By the late nineteenth century, the connection between exploration and empire was often direct and institutionalized. Henry Morton Stanley, for example, worked actively in his later expeditions on behalf of parties with imperial ambitions in Central Africa, and the caravans he organized and led resembled invading armies in their size and use of violence.[55]

Some scholarship, drawing in part on the insights of Carter and Pratt, has sought to show that the epistemology of exploration was inherently imperial, contributing to the mental construction of distant lands as alien and savage, a characterization that allowed the British to cast themselves as agents of a civilizing mission. Particular attention has been paid in recent years to the ways in which the category of the tropical was applied to certain regions of the world.[56] David Arnold argues that the European "traveling gaze" transformed India from a land of antiquity, rich in culture, into a realm of nature, divorced from history and defined as part of the tropics, a category of alterity that legitimated its imperial appropriation.[57] The same trope had already been applied to the West Indies, the South Pacific, and Central and South America, where Alexander von Humboldt played an important role in its construction as a geographical category of radical otherness to the temperate world.[58] It would be extended in the nineteenth century to other parts of the globe, most notably to sub-Saharan Africa, which explorers like Stanley would represent as the "dark continent," a primitive land where nature ran rampant. While the term tropical was applied only to the northernmost reaches of Australia, explorers of the continent's great outback were no less intent than their counterparts in Africa to establish what Simon Ryan, who examines their discursive practices, refers to as "an anchorage for a mythological justification of possession."[59]

Cartography was crucial to this assertion of possession, as Ryan and many others have noted. The explorer's ability to map his course on the abstract grid of latitude and longitude was what set him apart from a mere traveler. It laid the groundwork for claiming the territory. It is important not to push this argument too far, however. Most explorers did not assert possession of the territory they passed through, and, indeed, their cartographic practices were in many respects unsuited to such designs. A distinction needs to be drawn here between the Trigonometrical and the traverse survey. The trigonometrical survey was a slow, systematic, labor-intensive enterprise that could only be carried out *after* a territory was under effective colonial control, as was the case with the Great Trigonometrical Survey of India, which required decades to complete.[60] Explorers, by contrast, usually conducted more rough-and-ready traverse surveys, which simply supplied the geographical coordinates for the routes they had taken. The traverse survey, as Graham Burnett has observed in his illuminating study of the mapping of British Guiana by Robert Schomburgk, was "*useless* for the geographical construction of the colony." That task, which required some measure of political power, was one of "boundary-making," whereas explorers were more often engaged in "boundary-crossing."[61]

These boundary-crossings often obliged explorers to make adjustments, compromises, and concessions in the field that were strikingly at odds with their public reputations as white gods, cowing the denizens of the dark lands and exposing them to the light of civilization. Explorers' vulnerabilities and dependence on the goodwill of indigenous inhabitants have only recently received serious attention. Explorers relied on local peoples to grant them passage through their lands, to supply them with food and shelter, and to provide them with guides, translators, and porters. When these peoples were uncooperative, expeditions could stall, or worse: plenty of explorers lost their lives by stirring suspicion and hostility. It behooved African explorers to appeal for warrants of safe passage from rulers like the khedive of Egypt and the sultan of Zanzibar, whose reach extended into the interior of the continent, though this often came at a price: the British government paid Tripoli's pasha £25,000 to protect Dixon Dehman and Hugh Clapperton on their journey south across the Sahara.[62] Explorers also relied on existing trade networks to gain access to unfamiliar territory. The famed series of expeditions that Richard Burton, John Hanning Speke, David Livingstone, Verney Lovett Cameron, and Henry Morton Stanley carried out in East and Central Africa from the 1850s to the 1870s followed the well-developed caravan routes that ran through the region, operated by African, Arab, and Indian traders and sustained by a professionalized corps of Nyamwezi and other African porters (essential to a region where the tsetse fly prevented the use of pack animals). Stephen Rockel has shown that explorers relied extensively on this caravan trade's routes, resources, and modes of operation to accomplish their missions.[63]

Indigenous intermediaries' crucial contributions to expeditions have attracted increased attention in recent years.[64] While individuals like Tupaia, the Tahitian who helped Cook navigate his course across the South Pacific during the first voyage, or Sidi Bombay, the East African who oversaw the caravan operations for Burton, Speke, Stanley, Cameron, and other explorers, are well known to historians and, indeed, were well known—and celebrated—in their day, we have begun to recognize that almost every expedition of note was dependent to some degree on indigenous intermediaries. Even in the Australian outback, where explorers seemed especially self-sufficient, those who shunned the advice and assistance of indigenous peoples did so at their peril. Water was *the* key determinant for survival in this arid environment, and the Aborigines knew where to find it. They also knew how to live off the land, a skill that could be crucial to explorers who ran low on supplies. The Burke and Wills expedition met with disaster because it disdained local knowledge, even though the area where its leaders starved to death supported a local Aboriginal community.[65] Most successful explorers, whether in Australia or elsewhere, took care to recruit indigenous intermediaries, and some of these intermediaries managed to make careers for themselves by serving a succession of expeditions.[66]

What Mary Louise Pratt has termed the process of "transculturation," which alludes to the cultural and psychological effects of encounters in the "contact zone," posed particular challenges for explorers. Studies of early European travelers to the South Seas have shown how susceptible many of them were to the islands' exotic attractions. Those who went "native" and embraced the life of the "beachcomber" served as cautionary tales, exposing the instability of the self and the seductive appeal of the "other."[67] The public in Britain often turned against explorers who appeared to embrace indigenous practices with too much gusto—examples included James Bruce and, later, Mansfield Parkyns in Ethiopia.[68] Despite the disciplining effects of domestic opinion, however, some accommodation to local custom was useful and in certain circumstances even necessary. Explorers in North Africa, the Middle East, and South Asia often found it useful to don the dress of the peoples whose lands they passed through, and the more audacious ones sought to impersonate "natives" by acquiring fluency in local languages and expertise in their religious beliefs and cultural practices. Richard Burton famously assumed the guise of a Sufi pilgrim of Pathan origin in order to gain entry to Mecca and Medina, a feat that brought him great acclaim in Britain. But Burton also exemplified the risk entailed in such cultural cross-dressing; it easily evolved into a real affection for the society being penetrated and a corresponding ambivalence toward British society, posing troubling questions about the loyalties and identity of the explorer.[69]

Even in those circumstances where explorers were able to operate without much need to accommodate the cultural sensitivities of indigenous communities, their sense of self often underwent profound changes in the course of the expedition. Johannes Fabian's study of Belgian and German explorers in Central Africa offers a perceptive analysis of this process of destabilization. He shows that the physical and emotional strains of the journey, supplemented by the psychotropic effects of drugs and fever, tended to break down explorers' guise of scientific rationality and give rise to an alternative state of consciousness, a realm beyond reason that he terms "ecstasis."[70] The phenomenon he describes is equally applicable to British explorers of Africa, Australia, and elsewhere. Though most were understandably reluctant to discuss this aspect of their experience in published accounts of their expeditions, they would sometimes reveal its transformative effects in private journals and correspondence. It helps us make sense of behavior that otherwise appears inexplicable.

* * *

The great age of British exploration came to a close in the early twentieth century. Its final frontier was Antarctica, where the absence of any indigenous inhabitants allowed the explorers Robert Scott and Ernest Shackleton to pit themselves and their parties against that continent's harsh environment without the mediation of local informants. This goes some way to explain why both men's efforts eventually met with disaster, but it also helps to account for the enduring appeal their stories hold for the British public. As Siobhan Carroll has shown, the "atopic" environments of ice, air, and water—spaces where permanent human habitation is impossible—have long exerted a powerful appeal to the British imagination.[71] The "conquest" of the atopic Mount Everest by the New Zealander Edmund Hillary in 1953 supplied a simulacrum of exploration's earlier triumphs. Hillary's achievement, however, was purely symbolic, a last gasp of imperial pride, and even then, it was tempered by the need to acknowledge the contribution of his Sherpa guide Tenzing Norgay, a sign of the shifting sands of power.[72] British exploration as it had come to be understood in the nineteenth century had ceased to be a viable enterprise, and its demise was sealed with the loss of empire.

It is now possible to see exploration as a central and perhaps defining feature of Britain's encounters with the rest of the world, laying the groundwork for imperial expansion, setting in motion the great engine of globalization, and making an important contribution to the rise of modern scientific knowledge, as well as to ideas of difference. For all these reasons, scholars have shown renewed interest in exploration. Rather than rehearsing the tired old themes of exploration as the expression of individual heroism and national prestige, however, they have focused attention on the ideological construction of a Western sense of exceptionalism and the experiential engagement with other peoples.[73] Although modern exploration as a distinct practice was very much a Western-driven enterprise, it was aided, altered, and remade by the non-Western peoples who engaged with the explorers.

This recent resurgence of academic interest in the story of exploration, I have suggested, is bound up with several broader intellectual trends. One is the endeavor to examine the epistemological foundations of the imperial project and expose the lingering influence it has had on our mental map of the world. Another is the desire to understand the dynamics of cultural encounter and exchange, which has become such a prominent feature of what we now call globalization. Both of these agendas speak of issues that are in some sense traceable to exploration as their point of origin. The idea and practice of empire arose out of the initial impetus to discover new lands. And the primal scene of cultural encounter was the first contact between explorer and indigene. As historians and others work to craft an integrated narrative of our intersecting pasts as a human community, it is hardly surprising that they have rediscovered the theme of exploration, since it supplies a particularly effective avenue of entry into these concerns.

5

The White Man's World

One of the most important developments in British imperial historiography over the past decade or so has been the renewed interest in the so-called white settler colonies. These colonies and their inhabitants have become the subject of two distinct schools of historical scholarship—one identified with the British World conferences that were held between 1998 and 2007, the other with a body of work that has come to be known as settler colonial studies. Although they examine much the same places and peoples, they do so in such strikingly different ways that they seem to address entirely different realms of historical experience. Why this is so, I argue in this previously unpublished essay, has nearly as much to do with current political concerns as it does with the questions they ask about the past.

When in 1868 the Liberal politician Charles Dilke published *Greater Britain*, an account of his journey through much of the English-speaking world over the previous two years, he touched a public nerve, jolting his countrymen into greater appreciation of their overseas cousins' colonizing prowess and popularizing a phrase—Greater Britain—that gave a sense of collective purpose to their diaspora.[1] The promise of Greater Britain would inspire several generations of imperial advocates of closer political and economic union between Britain and its settler colonies or, as they would come to be known in the twentieth century, the white dominions.[2] Even now, it retains a nostalgic appeal for some British Conservatives, who have dusted it off as a possible alternative to the European Union in the aftermath of Brexit.[3]

What made Greater Britain seem possible for so long was the dispersal of peoples of British heritage across the globe in the nineteenth and early twentieth centuries. Between 1815 and 1914, nearly 23 million people left the British Isles for overseas destinations. Most went to the United States, but significant numbers also settled in Canada, Australia, New Zealand, and other parts of the empire, and imperial destinations became especially popular in the closing decades of the nineteenth century, a pattern that persisted through the first half of the twentieth century. The enhanced opportunities these new lands afforded immigrants spurred high fertility rates. As James Belich puts it, they "bred like rabbits," leading to the "explosive colonization" of North America, Australia, New Zealand, and other lands.[4] This dramatic demographic growth and sweeping geographic dispersal of peoples of British heritage were the most striking manifestations of a Europe-wide phenomenon that led to large enclaves of European settlers in Latin America's Southern Cone, North Africa, Siberia, and elsewhere. Time's arrow seemed to be arching unerringly in the direction of a white man's world. Various other peoples were duly dismissed as "dying," the inevitable losers in the Darwinian struggle for survival, the future fossils of history.[5] Meanwhile, "lost white tribes" were being discovered in the most remote and improbable corners of the earth.[6] Although skeptics like Charles Henry Pearson issued warnings from the late nineteenth century on that the "yellow races" in particular posed a growing threat to this white man's world—a theme that seems to be experiencing something of a revival in some circles—they too regarded its global dominance as an established fact.[7]

This subject has inspired two highly influential bodies of historical scholarship over the last two decades.[8] One goes by the title of the British World; the other is known as settler colonial studies. Both focus mainly on those countries that were colonized by large numbers of Anglophone settlers—above all Australia, Canada, New Zealand, and South Africa, with the United States included in some studies. Both seek to explain the shared characteristics of these countries and the special circumstances that made them so successful. Yet neither engages with the other's work. British World and settler colonial studies scholars follow very different paths toward what is arguably the same destination. Why this is so and what it tells us about both bodies of scholarship and about the subject they share are the issues I aim to address in this chapter.

* * *

The British World project got its start at a conference held at the University of London's Institute of Commonwealth Studies in 1998. The historians who launched the project—a veritable old Commonwealth in miniature, which consisted of the Australian Carl Bridge, the Canadian Phillip Buckner, the New Zealander James Belich, the South African Bill Nasson, and the Britons John Darwin and Robert Holland—shared a sense of frustration at what they saw as the neglect of white settler colonies in the mainstream literature on the British Empire. They were especially dismayed by the direction the field had taken as a result of the siren calls of Edward Said, subaltern studies, and related practitioners of postcolonial theory. They objected not merely to the methods of these outsiders, but to their tendency to equate the empire almost entirely with Africa, India, and other regions where colonized populations heavily outnumbered the colonizers. They also were disappointed by how little attention the white settler colonies received in the new *Oxford History of the British Empire*, the first two volumes of which appeared the same year as the inaugural British World conference. They drew inspiration from J. G. A. Pocock's and Linda Colley's works on the imperial dimensions of British identity and they found parallels to their own objectives in the new imperial history's insistence on the imbricated nature of Britain's domestic and imperial realms.[9]

The British World project gathered momentum with a quick succession of conferences in Cape Town (2002), Calgary (2003), Melbourne (2004), Auckland (2005), and Bristol (2007). A series of edited volumes followed from the conferences.[10] James Belich, one of the project's original proponents, contributed a major historical study of his own to this growing body of scholarship. In addition, the editor in chief of the *Oxford History of the British Empire* responded to his British World critics by commissioning *Companion Series* volumes on Australia, Canada, British North America in the seventeenth and eighteenth centuries, and imperial migration. Still others hitched their wagons to the British World, giving the project further range and depth. It has consequently become a significant force in the current imperial historiographical scene.

So what is the British World project? I am unaware of any programmatic statement by its founders. Carl Bridge and Kent Fedorowich's introduction to the volume that arose from the first conference probably comes as close to such a statement as we are likely to get. They offer a summary of themes that run through much of the British World scholarship: the migration of millions of people from the British Isles to the settler colonies, the efforts to forge a shared sense of Britishness among these migrants, and the eventual erosion of those bonds in the second half of the twentieth century. At "the heart of the imperial enterprise," Bridge and Fedorowich conclude, was "the peopling and building of the trans-oceanic British world."[11]

The "British world," however, begs for definitional clarity. For starters, where was it? What places did it include? The sites of the British World conferences offer one clue to its territorial range: they were held in Britain and those countries that were once known as the white dominions, that is, Australia, Canada, New Zealand, and South Africa. The essays in the Bridge and Fedorowich volume focused entirely on these territories. The contributors to a later conference volume ranged more widely, however, and its editors conceded that the British World's boundaries are "open to interpretation."[12] James Belich include the United States in his ambitious study, a decision that required a crucial change in nomenclature: he rechristened the British World the "Anglo-World." More recently, its reach has been broadened to include India, China, the Caribbean, West Africa, and even the Ottoman Empire, blurring the boundaries between places settled by peoples of British heritage and places where such peoples were merely expatriate sojourners—or in some cases where the ostensible agents of the British World had no British heritage at all.[13]

Scholarship on the British World is troubled as well by lacunae and inconsistencies. The only attention it gives to Ireland is as a source of emigrants. This is despite the fact that Ireland was Britain's first settler colony and held dominion status from 1922 to 1937, when it kept company with Canada, Australia, New Zealand, and South Africa. The last of these countries creates another conundrum. How sizeable a settler population is required to gain entry to the British World? Does it need to exceed the indigenous population? Australia, Canada, and New Zealand (along with the United States) meet that demographic standard, but South Africa does not: its African inhabitants outnumber whites by five to one. Yet if South Africa is granted entry to the British World, why not Southern Rhodesia or Kenya? Granted, the settler populations of these two colonies were smaller than South Africa's, but they were certainly substantial, sought permanence, and wielded outsized political power. Southern Rhodesia even enjoyed quasi-dominion status, with its affairs overseen by the Dominions Office. Yet neither Southern Rhodesia nor Kenya figures in the literature on the British World.[14]

The second definitional challenge for the British World project can be summed up in the question: who counts as British? Bridge and Fedorowich associate Britishness with emigrants from the British Isles or their descendants. But the notion of a British identity looks much more problematic if you trace migrants back to their roots in the British Isles. Scottish, Irish, English, and Welsh identities, not to mention Cornish and other regional affiliations, loomed a lot larger in these places of origin than did an overarching sense of Britishness. Some British World historians not only concede this point; they insist on it, arguing that a shared British identity was a product of the colonial experience itself. But if Britishness was not something most migrants brought with them from Britain's shores, but something they acquired *after* they arrived elsewhere, then the questions multiply. What did Britishness entail in the colonial context? Who could claim membership? What purposes did such an affiliation serve?[15]

Historians associated with the British World project have for the most part characterized Britishness as a set of cultural characteristics that could be acquired, including language, religion, and codes of behavior. Phillip Buckner and Douglas Francis assert, for example, that Britishness arose as a result of the assimilation of Irish, Scottish, and Welsh immigrants into an English-majority culture in settler colonies. Vivian Bickford-Smith makes much the same argument in an essay on Anglicization in the Cape Colony. Pushing back against this position, John MacKenzie has insisted that Scots retained a strong sense of themselves *as* Scots in South Africa. Other contributors to the British World debate have pointed, in turn, to the persistence of Welsh, Irish, and other regionally rooted ethno-cultural identities among colonists.[16] While there is no reason to believe that these same colonists could not simultaneously consider themselves British, it does leave unanswered the question of what that identity actually entailed.

This question becomes even more difficult to answer when we turn from colonists of British heritage to French Canadians, South African Boers, and other non-British colonist communities. Could these groups be considered members of the British World? If membership meant embracing the ruling majority's language or religion or other cultural practices, then the answer must be "no" given these ethnic minorities' determined efforts to defend their own distinct cultural heritages. Some historians have argued that non-British settlers who affirmed their allegiance to crown and empire thereby claimed their place in the British World.[17] This may be true in the civic sense that they saw themselves as British imperial subjects and the British monarchy as their sovereign, but this is hardly the same thing as embracing British cultural norms. Cultural identities cannot be so easily flattened out and fused together, especially in colonial societies where so many different groups came into contact—and often collision—with one another. Even where differences were overcome, they did not disappear, as this description of a small community in the Canadian West in the early twentieth century indicates: "There were the Englishmen, representatives of old families; the Indian woman, 'Stoney,' the American, a scarlet-coated policeman, a native of Denmark, a man from Edinburgh, a Frenchman from old Quebec, and 'the Sheriff,' a native-born son."[18]

Further complicating efforts to determine the parameters of Britishness in the British World is the fact that some colonized peoples sought admission to its privileged precincts. They did so strategically, recognizing, as Bill Schwarz has observed, that "Britishness was, largely, the only game in town."[19] Across the British Empire, missionary-educated and other Westernized indigenous elites made the case that they were British by virtue of their embrace of Christianity, their use of English, their adoption of Western dress and customs, and the like, and that they therefore could claim its rights and privileges. How the colonizers who patrolled the boundaries of Britishness responded to such efforts exposes the hollowness of the liberal promise that its doors were open to all who espoused its cultural values. Color, not culture, proved to be the crucial criterion for admission to the British World.

To speak of Britishness in the British World was in large measure to mean whiteness. Those who possessed its phenotypical markers invariably lorded over those who did not. Charles Dilke's notion of a Greater Britain rested on race. To be sure, his mid-Victorian version of racial thinking took the form of Anglo-Saxonism, which was not strictly a category of color: it considered the Irish an inferior race as well. But a more encompassing, color-coded conception of race became far more prevalent as a marker of difference in the British Empire by the late nineteenth century. It is no accident that the British World's main settler colonies came to be known as the *white dominions*.

Yet the historians most closely associated with the British World project have had surprisingly little to say about race in the making of that world. For all the attention the conference volumes have given to the colonial construction of Britishness, only a few contributors have addressed its associations with ideas of race. To understand what whiteness meant to the British World, one must turn elsewhere. Among the recent works that offer insight into this issue are Marilyn Lake and Henry Reynold's *Drawing the Global Colour Line*, which shows how a heightened sense of racial anxiety in Australia and other Anglo settler societies—they too include the United States—drew them together on behalf of a self-proclaimed white man's world. Also noteworthy is Bill Schwarz's *Memories of Empire,* which follows the feedback loop that caused this colonial project to inform notions of race and memories of empire back in Britain.[20] Both books show that the construction of Britishness as a racial category was above all a political project, designed to control access to power. Despite the British World founders' declared indebtedness to Linda Colley's *Britons*, they lose sight of its insistence that political objectives propelled the formation of British national identity. By consigning the British World's Britishness to the realm of cultural identity, they obscure its exclusionary agenda and accept its comforting myths of assimilation, opportunity, and transnational brotherhood.

It is telling that the most substantive and successful works to come out of the British World project have largely bypassed the quagmire of cultural identity. They have shifted attention instead to the demographic and economic dynamism of Anglophone settler societies. This is the shared focus of James Belich's *Replenishing the Earth* and Gary Magee and Andrew Thompson's *Empire and Globalization*. Both of these ambitious books examine settler societies' critical contributions to the growth of global capitalism in the nineteenth and twentieth centuries, the same issue that inspired an important comparative study by Donald Denoon decades earlier.[21] They pose much the same question: what explains the rapid economic growth of these societies? Their answers, however, follow very different trajectories.

Belich's big, ambitious book seeks to explain how the Anglo-World, by which he means the main British settler colonies and the United States, achieved such an outsized influence on the modern world. Crucial to this outcome, he argues, was the large-scale emigration from the British Isles to these territories and the rapid reproduction of their settler populations. This resulted in explosive growth, evident in the rise of "instant" cities like Chicago and Melbourne, and a cycle of booms and busts. While Belich gives a richly detailed, highly compelling account of these developments, his causal explanation minimizes the forces that made this Anglo-World an interconnected whole, arguing instead that its various settler societies followed parallel but independent paths. He insists that the vigorous but volatile growth of these settler societies was largely self-generating, with

Britain only belatedly bringing them into association with its own industrial export economy through a process he terms "recolonization." (The northeast United States' industrial hub, he argues, would serve the same role in relation to the American West.) This argument makes the concurrent success of these sites of settlement more coincidental than causally connected. It poses a further complication: how to account for the fact that British (or Anglo) peoples were more successful at colonizing other lands and "replenishing the earth" than their European rivals? Belich rightly rejects a racial explanation, but it is not clear what alternative he offers. The result is a work that tells us a great detail about what happened, but disappointingly little about why.

Magee and Thompson are more helpful in explaining why the British world was so successful. Like Belich, they regard the demographic and economic growth of the settler colonies as profoundly important to the making of the contemporary world. Unlike Belich, however, they offer a causal explanation that emphasizes the "networks of people, goods and capital" (the subtitle of their book) that were forged between the settler colonies and Britain. These networks, they argue, acted as key drivers of globalization in the second half of the long nineteenth century. The time frame of their study, it should be acknowledged, is narrower than Belich's, corresponding in certain respects to the stage he refers to as "recolonization." But this periodization permits them to probe more deeply into the importance and implications of these networks. First, they restore Britain to a relevancy that is missing from Belich's analysis. Indeed, Britain's role as the imperial metropolis places it at the hub of this world system. Second, the United States becomes less relevant. While Magee and Thompson acknowledge that the United States played a part in these economic networks, they also insist that its protectionist policies, broader pool of immigrants, and other factors made its connections more inconsistent and tenuous. Third, they offer an explanation for the economic success of the British World that brings culture back into the story in a meaningful way. In their telling, the British World economy was bound together not merely by market interests, but by its participants' shared heritage, their self-identification as British, which proved instrumental in creating and maintaining those interests. This sense of Britishness drew on a common language, religion, laws, and other cultural markers, but it also increasingly drew on racial markers. Magee and Thompson are unequivocal in their view that "participation in imperial networks was racially defined."[22] Taken together, these identifying attributes enhanced economic exchange among globally dispersed settler communities, making "culture and ethnicity key determinants of economic behaviour and performance."[23] Their work points to one of the most promising avenues of investigation made possible by the British World project.

* * *

One topic that has received scarcely any attention in the scholarship on the British World is the encounter between settlers and indigenes. Wherever settlers established themselves, they came in contact with native peoples. The ensuing clashes over land and other resources left a lasting imprint on settler societies. Yet the leading lights of the British World have had little to say on the subject. Even Belich, whose weighty tome covers a wide range of topics, devotes no more than a few pages here and there to the indigenous peoples whose lands were occupied by settlers. Moreover, his theme in these passages is the "resilience and adaptability" of these peoples, highlighting their resourcefulness in conducting campaigns of resistance.[24] While this is a worthwhile corrective to settler triumphalism, it stands at odds with Belich's main argument that the explosive growth of the British World or Anglo-World was unprecedented, sweeping away every obstacle in its path. It also entirely ignores the impact that the subjugation of indigenous peoples and expropriation of their lands had on the character of settler societies themselves.

These issues lie at the heart of a second body of scholarship, commonly referred to as settler colonial studies. Like the British World project, its founding moment came at the end of the twentieth century, though in this instance it was the publication of a single book—Patrick Wolfe's *Settler Colonialism and the Transformation of Anthropology* (1999)—that provided the initial impetus for its creation. This book sketched out some of the key concerns of settler colonial studies and its author became its most prominent proponent. A British expatriate in Australia, Wolfe wrote an intellectual history of anthropology, focusing on its treatment of Aborigines, but he placed his study in the context of Australian settler colonialism, which sought, as he put it, "the elimination of native societies."[25] Australia subsequently became the main intellectual breeding ground for settler colonial studies, though its influence quickly spread among scholars in the United States, Canada, and a number of other countries.

The fullest explanation of settler colonial studies' aims can be found in a brief but densely argued book by Lorenzo Veracini, another Australia-based historian, who cofounded the journal *Settler Colonial Studies*. Veracini insists that settler colonialism is "structurally distinct" from other forms of colonialism, above all in terms of its treatment of indigenous peoples. Instead of exploiting the labor of the native inhabitants, settlers seek their physical and/or psychic removal from colonial society. This objective takes multiple forms: Veracini identifies over two dozen distinct strategies for the "transfer" or elimination of indigenous peoples, including the ultimate sanction, genocide.[26] While grounded in history, Veracini's approach to settler colonialism as an analytical category is openly interdisciplinary, drawing on literary theory, psychoanalytic theory, and other modes of inquiry. This engagement across disciplines has in fact become one of the distinguishing characteristics of settler colonial studies, setting it apart from British World scholarship in methodology as well as subject matter.

For all the theoretical rigor and interdisciplinary range of his analysis, Veracini is no less vague about the historical parameters of his subject than are some of his British World counterparts. His work draws mainly on Australia, Canada, New Zealand, South Africa, and the United States as case studies of settler colonialism, but it also makes reference to various other examples, most notably Israel. And although Veracini insists that settler colonialism is "antithetical" to other forms of colonialism, he argues that in places like Algeria, Angola, Kenya, and Korea, "settler projects can also operate as a *function* of enabling colonial regimes" that have stressed the exploitation of indigenous labor, not the elimination of the indigenous presence.[27] Indeed, settler colonialism manifests itself in so many contexts in Veracini's book that the structural distinctiveness he claims for it runs the risk of melting into a shapeless mass.

This widening remit has become characteristic of settler colonial studies as a whole. It has come to address an ever-expanding array of places and topics. The field was "initially viewed in terms of British, and to some extent European, settler endeavour," according to Penelope Edmonds and Jane Carey, *Settler Colonial Studies*' current editors, but it has since pursued a more diverse range of subjects, not to mention a more interdisciplinary pool of contributors. It is true that attention continues to focus mainly on Australia, Canada, New Zealand, and the United States, along with Israel, but articles have also appeared on Taiwan, Botswana, New Caledonia, and other places. Furthermore, historical perspectives on settler colonialism have increasingly been counterbalanced in the journal by studies of gender and sexuality, art and design, law and politics, popular culture, and more. Above all, emphasis has been placed, in the words of Edmonds and Carey, on the "operation of settler colonial polities past and present," a point accentuated by two other proponents of settler colonial studies, who insist that "it is misleading to refer to settler colonialism in the past tense." These statements indicate how integral to settler colonial studies are such contemporary concerns as the rights of Aborigines in Australia and the plight of Palestinians in Israel.[28]

This insistence on establishing a connection between the past and the present is readily apparent in two edited volumes. In *Genocide and Settler Society*, Dirk Moses and his contributors confront the controversial issues of whether the violence perpetrated against Aborigines by colonial settlers and the removal of Aboriginal children from their families by the Australian state qualify as genocide. In his introduction, Moses points out that the answer depends on whether genocide is understood to require intentionality on the part of its perpetrators or whether the outcome itself suffices. And in the case of "stolen" children, there is the added complication of whether assimilation qualifies as cultural genocide. Not surprisingly, the contributors provide a range of responses to these issues.[29] Another volume addresses the enduring impact of the settler colonial past through an examination of historical monuments, museums, and memory in Australia, Canada, New Zealand, and South Africa. Its editor, Annie Coombes, declares: "One of the main aims of this collection is to insist that an understanding of the political and cultural institutions and practices which shaped these colonial societies in the past can provide important insights into the available means for contesting its legacy of unequal rights by historically marginalized peoples in the present."[30]

It is perhaps fitting that the most important work to arise out of settler colonial studies has come from its founder, Patrick Wolfe. His recently published *Traces of History: Elementary Structures of Race* is a powerful and provocative comparative study of the uses of racial categories and distinctions in Australia, the United States, Brazil, Central Europe, and Israel. In an earlier essay that laid out much of the analytical groundwork for his book, Wolfe argued that the various ways the settler societies of Australia, the United States, and Brazil defined and managed subordinated groups were determined by structural forces, most notably the settlers' need for land and labor.[31] The strikingly different demands of these forces were aptly illustrated in his discussion of the United States, where Native Americans were meant to disappear through extermination, expulsion, or assimilation so that settlers could claim their land, while African Americans were meant to propagate as a racially distinct group through strategies such as the "one drop rule" so that settlers could control their labor. In his book, Wolfe expands on and enriches this line of analysis, offering additional insights into the particular historical conditions that have shaped the racial categorization of Aborigines in Australia, Native Americans and African Americans in the United States, and Native Brazilians and African Brazilians in Brazil.[32] At the same time, he enlarges the scope of his inquiry by adding case studies of post-emancipation Jews in Central Europe, where he argues that the rise of modern anti-Semitism amounted to the racialization of its victims, and Jews and Palestinians in Israel, where he argues that its Zionist founders forged a settler colonial state that sought the dispossession of Palestinians exclusively through expulsion.

By expanding his study to Jews in Central Europe and Jews and Palestinians in Israel, Wolfe enriches his analysis in some respects, but muddies it in others. The first and most obvious difficulty is that Central Europe is not a settler colony and its Jewish population can be classified neither as Aboriginal landowners nor enslaved laborers. His rationale for this case study is that "the discourse of race is a distinctly European phenomenon," traceable to a tension in Enlightenment thought between its promise of equal rights and its insistence on natural taxonomies. This led to the construction of racial categories that ensured Jews, Africans, and others would continue to be set apart and subordinated even after their emancipation.[33] Yet this argument hinges on ideological rationales for inclusion and exclusion, not structuralist pressures for land and labor.

When Wolfe turns to the creation of Israel, he further complicates matters. Zionists, unlike most other settler groups, arrive in Palestine with a preestablished conception of themselves as a distinct race, formed in the crucible of European anti-Semitism rather than arising from the colonial conditions they confront. Also, they are unique among settlers in justifying their occupation as a return to a long-lost homeland. In these and other ways they stand apart from the other cases examined in the book. The Israeli example, then, is in many respects an anomalous case of settler colonialism.

Furthermore, Wolfe's analysis of Israel as a settler society offers insight into an issue that is otherwise all but absent from his work, as it is from settler colonial studies more generally. In an intriguing final chapter, he argues that the Ashkenazi Jews who came to Palestine from Europe recruited Mizrahi Jews from the Arab world to replace Palestinian Arabs as a labor underclass, an endeavor that required Zionists to reframe race in terms of religion rather than culture or ethnicity or place of origin. Whatever the merits of this argument, it exposes an absence in his analysis of other settler societies. They too consisted of various groups, differentiated by their places of origin, forms of faith, modes of speech, and the like, and they too often occupied separate niches in the settler economy. Yet over time they assumed a shared identity, a process neatly captured in the title of Noel Ignatiev's book about Irish immigrants to the United States—*How the Irish Became White*.[34] It is revealing that Wolfe and the other scholars who have contributed to settler colonial studies have given almost no attention to this process or to the peoples it drew together. For them, settlers are already and always a homogeneous group whose sole significance lies in their oppression of other peoples. In this respect, then, settler colonial studies stands in stark contrast to the British World historians' preoccupation with settlers' diverse origins and development of a common British identity.

* * *

If there is a point of convergence between British World scholarship and its settler colonial studies counterpart, it is their shared preoccupation with the relationship between settler societies past and present. Yet here too they approach the subject in strikingly different ways. For the British World contingent, the central theme is one of rupture; for the settler colonial studies crowd, it is one of continuity. This contrast has its source in their answers to the question: is settler colonialism subject to decolonization?

The answer is yes for those who work within the British World framework. Their raison d'etre is to recover the history of settler communities' commitment to Dilke's Greater Britain, an idea and a practice that was forgotten, as they see it, when nationalist sentiments and perspectives supplanted this transnational commitment. But how and when did decolonization take place in these countries? The conventional understanding of decolonization as the transfer of sovereignty to a previously foreign-ruled population fits awkwardly in the case of the white dominions, which gained control over their own political affairs long before they lost their sense of themselves as loyal subjects of the British Empire. Such a sensibility had less to do with their political relationship with Britain, according to the historians of the British

World, than it did with their social, cultural, and economic connections. By these measures, decolonization took place as emigration from the British Isles to the dominions began to shrink, the populations of the dominions became more culturally and ethnically diverse, and imperial trade networks grew less valuable with Britain's entry into the European Union and the United States' rise as a global economic behemoth. The fact that these developments occurred in the same era as the struggles for independence by colonial subjects in Africa, Asia, and elsewhere reinforces the view that this process can be characterized as decolonization.[35] For British World scholars, it marks a fundamental transformation, one that brings settler societies' sense of Britishness and attachment to Britain to an end.

Settler colonial studies' proponents insist, by contrast, that settler societies have been, in the words of Lorenzo Veracini, "resistant to decolonization."[36] From their perspective, the key determinant of decolonization is not whether these societies lost their special connection to Britain, but whether they reconciled themselves to indigenous self-determination. While New Zealand's Waitangi Tribunal and similar initiatives in other settler societies are seen as important steps toward this end, decolonization remains for settler colonial studies an ongoing process, incomplete and at risk of reversal. Israel looms so large in this literature precisely because it stands as proof that settler colonialism remains alive and well.

Underlying these different understandings of the decolonization of settler societies is a difference in the basic orientations of the two bodies of scholarship. The British World is preoccupied with the past, and its concerns are tinged with nostalgia. Settler colonial studies is preoccupied with the present, and its concerns are tinged with advocacy. No wonder they do not engage with one another.

* * *

One of the problems with the preceding survey is that it runs the risk of reducing its subject to a simple binary contrast, consigning all relevant scholarship to either the British World or the settler colonial studies camp. Some fine work in recent years has bypassed this Hobson's choice altogether. I want to conclude by commenting on several examples, highlighting how they either offer points of convergence between the two camps or shift debate to directions not taken by either camp.

Few recent studies of settler colonialism have been more ambitious and original than John Weaver's *The Great Land Rush and the Making of the Modern World*. Like Belich and other British World scholars, Weaver argues that Australia, Canada, New Zealand, South Africa, and the United States were far more successful than other European settler projects. But he also shares the view advanced by settler colonial studies that this success had its source in the settlers' expropriation of land from indigenous peoples. Because this land grab provoked repeated conflicts on colonial frontiers,

Weaver gives sustained attention to the encounter between settlers and indigenes, reinforcing the similarities between his approach and the one advanced by settler colonial studies. At the same time, Weaver shares with many British World historians the view that cultural factors contributed to the success of British settler colonialism, above all "a particular tradition concerning land, property rights, and notions of material improvement."[37] *The Great Land Rush* provides a fresh perspective on settler societies that brings the two leading approaches to the subject into productive association with one another.

Other historians have moved beyond the Anglocentrism that continues to predominate in British World and settler colonial studies circles, pursuing broadly comparative examinations of settler colonialism. Saliha Belmessous and her contributors have charted how various European colonizers, ranging from the Spanish in sixteenth-century America to the British in nineteenth-century New Zealand to the French in twentieth-century Algeria, sought indigenous consent to their rule, notably through land cession treaties, indigenous use of imperial legal systems, and assimilationist promises of equal rights.[38] While these practices rarely generated widespread or lasting consent, they did demonstrate that colonizers were periodically open to efforts to overcome difference, a point neglected by both the British World project and settler colonial studies. In a strikingly different approach, *Settler Colonialism in the Twentieth Century*, a volume of essays edited by Caroline Elkins and Susan Pedersen, narrows its chronological focus to the last century, but expands its geopolitical scope beyond the standard category of European overseas settler colonialism to include the Japanese in Korea and Manchukuo and the Germans in Poland.[39] Elkins and Pedersen point out that, except for the case of the Jews in Palestine, none of these twentieth-century settler projects endured, unlike earlier projects in the Americas and the Antipodes. They propose a typology of these projects that delineates their common characteristics and challenges, and in so doing they cast a new light on the more successful settler societies that have preoccupied the British World and settler colonial studies scholars.

Finally, a nod should be given to Alfred Crosby's now classic *Ecological Imperialism*, which continues to inspire important work on those settler societies he so memorably termed "neo-Europes." Crosby and his successors have argued that the success—or, alternatively, the failure—of a particular settler colonial project had less to do with the factors advanced by the historians we have discussed above than by the environmental opportunities and constraints that existed in the lands they sought to settle.[40] Their work reminds us that the white man's world involved forces that its beneficiaries could scarcely control, or even understand.

6

Debating the End of Empire: Exceptionalism and its Critics

Between 2006 and 2015 I was a member of the faculty that ran the International Decolonization Seminar under the leadership of Wm. Roger Louis. Every July but one during those ten years I got acquainted with 15 talented early career scholars and became familiar with their research projects. Their interests closely tracked—and indeed helped to shape—the rapidly shifting scholarship on decolonization, which has become one of the most dynamic and hotly debated fields of inquiry in imperial history over the past decade. This chapter, which was written for this book, surveys the historiography on decolonization, highlighting the recent rupture between an established body of work that has characterized the British withdrawal from empire as a distinctively peaceful, pragmatic process that left little mark on Britain itself and a new set of studies that stress the violence and trauma it caused in many colonies and the repercussions it had at home.

Britain ceased to be an imperial power about half a century ago. When exactly this happened is open to debate—was it the Suez Crisis of 1956? Macmillan's "Winds of Change" speech in 1960? the withdrawal from "East of Suez" in 1971?—but almost everyone agrees that the end of empire came several decades prior to the last noteworthy transfer of imperial territory, the 1997 handover of Hong Kong to the Chinese. More than a generation has now passed since the British held dominion over palm and pine.

How have historical assessments of British decolonization changed over those decades? Has the passage of time produced any consensus on the subject? Certainly there is broad agreement that the dismantling of the empire was a profoundly important development—not just for the British themselves, who saw their global standing dramatically diminished, but also for the millions of Africans, Asians, and other colonized peoples who achieved political independence. Otherwise, however, historians are arguably more deeply divided in their assessments of the course and consequences of British decolonization than they were just a few decades ago. Their differing stances on the subject are worth examining both because they tell us something about what is conventionally referred to as "the state of the field" and, more importantly, because they highlight the enduring and intractable legacy of Britain's loss of empire.

* * *

Initial attempts to historicize the dissolution of the British Empire came from the generation that had personally observed and in some cases participated in that wrenching upheaval. Many of these early assessments were openly celebratory or overtly accusatory, reflecting their proponents' contending opinions about the costs and benefits of the empire. Some accounts predictably told the story of decolonization as the heroic struggles by subject peoples against imperial oppression. These were mainly nationalist and Marxist histories, written either to instill a sense of pride among ex-colonial peoples in the new nation-states their struggles had produced or to inspire them and their metropolitan supporters by arguing that the system of capitalist exploitation would collapse once its imperial scaffolding was gone. The dominant narrative within Britain, however, was one of loss, and some of its authors attributed that loss to a weakness of will on the part of the British themselves. No one made this case with greater prosecutorial zeal than Correlli Barnett, who blamed evangelical humanitarianism, socialist pacifism, and other forms of naïve idealism for emasculating the governing elites and leaving the country vulnerable to more virile and ruthless powers. This sense of betrayal was tellingly expressed in the title of George Woodcock's 1974 book, *Who Killed the British Empire?*[1] The empire's demise was a crime, and the task of the historian was to prosecute the guilty parties.

A less polemical, more sober assessment of the circumstances that led to the loss of empire gained ground in the 1980s. Led largely by the Cambridge school of imperial history, it characterized decolonization as a transactional process, the product of largely rational calculation by competing political elites. The task of the historian was not to assign blame, but to reveal the structural forces that drove decolonization, along with the political strategies that shaped its trajectory. The question of causation lay at the heart of these inquiries. John Darwin's lucid summary of the state of the field in 1991 delineated four main schools of thought on the subject.[2] One attributed the retreat from empire to political pressures at home, another to the restructuring of the global economy, a third to international political and ideological forces, and a fourth to the challenge posed by colonial nationalists.

Whichever causal forces they credited as the primary ones, these historians agreed on two central points. One was methodological: any explanation of decolonization had to attend first and foremost to the decision-making processes that took place at the highest levels of the British government, characterized in Robinson and Gallagher's memorable phrase as the "official mind." How British authorities *managed* the challenges they faced, whether these were domestic or international, economic or political, was seen as crucial to understanding how the empire came to an end. Some of the impetus for this preoccupation with the "official mind" came from the rolling release of government documents under the thirty-year embargo rule, which was opening up new research opportunities for historians of decolonization. Their investment in the official archive culminated in the publication by Her Majesty's Stationary Office of the *British Documents at the End of Empire* series, a dozen volumes of official memoranda, reports, and other records, each of them edited by a leading expert in the field. Series A documented the policies of successive British governments toward the empire from 1927 to 1971, while Series B dealt with the political and diplomatic processes that culminated in independence for particular colonial territories.[3]

The other point of agreement was interpretive: British officials' responses to the growing threats across the empire, while largely ad hoc and incremental, were informed by a determination to cling to key colonial possessions for as long as they possibly could. John Darwin, Wm. Roger Louis, Robert Holland, and other historians of this cohort provided broadly consistent accounts of British strategies to prevent, postpone, and manipulate the withdrawal from empire in such a way as to minimize its adverse effects on the country's global standing.[4] The work of these historians provided a powerful riposte to earlier critics like Barnett. Far from seeking shelter from the winds of change, the British faced its gusts with a doughty determination that seemed at times almost delusional—for example, the Suez Crisis. Even as Britain's imperial standing rapidly unraveled, its statesmen made the best they could of the situation—or the worst, depending on one's view of the process and its outcome.

Until recently, a broad consensus seemed to exist among historians of empire in favor of this explanation of British decolonization. It offered what can be characterized as a geopolitical narrative. Making meticulous use of official records, it provided a complex, multicausal explanation of the circumstances that caused Britain to retreat from empire. At the same time, it offered a framework for making sense of the new role Britain forged for itself as a postimperial state, most notably in terms of its global partnership with the United States and the neocolonial influence it exerted on various ex-colonial states. For those metropolitan-centered historians who see the dramatic diminishment of Britain's status as a great power as the dominant theme of decolonization, the geopolitical approach taken by Darwin, Louis, and others has proven hugely influential, as is evidenced by the important scholarship it continues to generate.[5]

Over the past decade, however, others have been studying decolonization from very different frames of reference. Few of these newcomers identify themselves as historians of empire. Some are Africanists and other area studies specialists who come to the subject through their work on indigenous societies and nationalist struggles against colonial rule. Others are military historians who work on the British Army and its counterinsurgency campaigns. Still others are British social and cultural historians who are interested in the domestic consequences of the loss of empire. Each group draws on a specialized set of skills and resources. Each in turn addresses a distinct array of questions and concerns. Still, they share several characteristics that set them apart from the geopolitical cohort. For one, they do not view decolonization from the vantage point of imperial policymakers. Rather than channeling the "official mind," they venture into the more complex and contested environs of late-colonial (and postcolonial) practices and perspectives, places where government policies intersected with peoples' lives in direct and visceral ways. These lines of inquiry have led, in turn, to the use of far more varied bodies of evidence than can be found in the *Documents at the End of Empire* project. Interviews and oral histories, court testimonies, personal memoirs, and other, more unconventional sources have been used to supplement and even supplant the government records produced by imperial officials and their local interlocutors.

Those who have adopted these alternative approaches have diverged from conventional historiographical practice in another important respect: they show little interest in explaining *why* the empire came to an end. In short, causation is not their central concern, as it has been for the geopolitical historians. They have focused their attention instead on the quotidian struggles for power in late-colonial societies and the repercussions of those struggles for British society itself.

* * *

The new approaches I have just sketched out are consistent with broader shifts that have occurred in historiographical practice over the past few decades—most notably the turn from political and diplomatic to social and cultural histories. As such, they are not especially distinctive or noteworthy. But there is another difference between these works and the geopolitical scholarship on British decolonization, a difference that is at once more subtle and more profound. It arises out of the obvious fact—so obvious it often goes unstated—that the British Empire's decline and fall occurred in the context of the dissolution of European colonial empires as a whole. The contemporaneous collapse of the French, Dutch, and other empires gives rise to an important question: was the British case different or did it conform to a broader pattern?

There is, of course, no simple either/or answer to this question. The disintegration of the British imperial realm was a messy, multivalent process that resembled the experiences of its European counterparts in some respects, while diverging from them in others. Nonetheless, the issue of exceptionalism exposes one of the deepest fault lines in the current debate about British decolonization. Until recently, most imperial historians seemed to agree that the British abandoned their imperial possessions with relatively little of the *Sturm und Drang* that characterized the retreat from empire by other Europeans. That consensus has broken down over the past decade, with much of the recent scholarship on the subject giving greater weight to the ways in which the British experience resembled that of the other European imperial powers. These contending interpretations demand our attention, not least because they entail moral judgments about the past that speak to the present.

One way to gauge the influence that the exceptionalist interpretation has exerted on the historiography about British decolonization until recently is to examine historical surveys of the subject. A consistent theme of these surveys is that the British gave up their colonies in a planned, peaceful, orderly fashion that left few lasting scars on the contending parties. Britain's experience is placed in contrast—occasionally explicitly, though more often implicitly—to the precipitate, disorderly, often violent disengagements from empire by the Dutch, the Belgians, the Portuguese, and, above all, the French. D. George Boyce concludes *Decolonisation and the British Empire, 1775-1997* (1997) with the pronouncement that "England"—an unexamined but telling placeholder for Britain—"underwent remarkably few traumas as a result of the end of empire."[6] In his survey *British Decolonization, 1946-1997* (1998), W. David McIntyre claimed that "in nearly all cases, decolonization was arranged by orderly transfers of power to democratically elected regimes."[7] Nicholas White adopts a more nuanced stance in *Decolonisation: The British Experience Since 1945* (1999), but he too stresses the point that "the British are generally regarded as more liberal in their approach to colonial nationalism than their European counterparts."[8] This is certainly the view advanced by Ronald Hyam, whose *Britain's Declining Empire* (2006) is the most richly researched political narrative of the subject to have appeared in recent years. "The peaceful divestment of the Empire," he proudly proclaims, "was the most successful political achievement of Our Age."[9]

Such self-congratulatory claims have come under increasing assault. One harbinger of the turn against the exceptionalist consensus appeared a year prior to the appearance of Hyam's book with the publication of two widely reviewed histories of the Mau Mau rebellion in Kenya. The authors of these works, the Africanist historians David Anderson and Caroline Elkins, showed that British imperial authorities dealt with the

Kenyan crisis in a manner starkly at odds with the conventional narrative of "peaceful divestment." The emergency measures instituted by the British to combat Mau Mau produced a police state that subverted the rule of law and committed human rights abuses against Kenyans on a massive scale. Anderson exposed the kangaroo courts that sentenced more than a thousand suspected rebels to death by hanging, while Elkins examined the incarceration of hundreds of thousands of Kikuyu civilians in brutal detention camps, the most notorious being the Hola camp where eleven detainees were beaten to death in 1959.[10] Following on the heels of their pioneering research, other historians have provided further evidence that the British conducted a systematic campaign of terror—a "dirty war"—in Kenya.[11]

This ruthless suppression of the Mau Mau rebellion does not necessarily undermine the broader assertion that the British made a more orderly and graceful exit from empire than other European powers. Exceptions to any historical generalization can be found. And imperial historians had known of the unsavory tactics used in the Kenyan counterinsurgency campaign for some time, even if they were not entirely aware of the scale of the violence that Anderson and Elkins's research unearthed. It remained possible to dismiss the Kenyan case as an aberration.

Or did it? Other historians were simultaneously uncovering similar stories about British conduct in other late-colonial crises. In their aptly titled *Forgotten Wars* (2007), Christopher Bayly and Tim Harper detailed the conflicts and convulsions that accompanied Britain's determined efforts to maintain or restore colonial rule across South Asia and Southeast Asia after the Second World War.[12] Benjamin Grob-Fitzgibbon's meticulous trawling of government records supplied new and unedifying details about the "dirty wars" the British conducted in Palestine, Malaya, Cyprus, Suez, and elsewhere during the "endgame" of empire.[13] The conduct of the police forces, intelligence services, and other agents of imperial coercion that the British used to suppress nationalist movements came under increasing scrutiny from historians.[14] Another body of scholarship placed the Kenyan case in the context of settler colonialism, a system of rule that seemed especially susceptible to violence and disorder when indigenous peoples sought independence.[15] Taken together, these works suggested that what had happened in Kenya was less of an exception than an especially lurid manifestation of a broader pattern of behavior.

In a related development, David Edgerton's *Warfare State* (2006) laid the groundwork for a broader reassessment of the role of militarism in modern British history. Edgerton rejected the view that "as a liberal nation Britain was anti-militaristic," arguing that through much of the twentieth century it was more a "warfare" than a "welfare" state.[16] Strangely, Edgerton himself ignored the empire's role in the development of the warfare state, but other military historians soon drew a connection between the two with their reassessments of British counterinsurgency campaigns in Malaya, Kenya, and other colonies. They noted that the scale of these postwar counterinsurgency operations, combined with the pressures of the Cold War, resulted in the most expensive rearmament program ever undertaken by Britain in "peacetime," as it is conventionally characterized. Simultaneously, the government imposed a National Service requirement from 1948 to 1960, marking the first time the country conscripted able-bodied young men for military service in the absence of a major war.[17] The emergency powers granted to British forces in their counterinsurgency campaigns permitted them to operate outside the bounds of international legal oversight, exerting lethal force with impunity. David French, who has written three important books on the subject, notes the larger significance of his and other historians' findings: "The army," he observed, "has been written out of post-war British history because to admit that it took part in active operations in the empire after 1945 is to admit the hollowness of British claims that their imperial mission was the beneficent one of bringing peace, democracy, and independence to colonial peoples."[18] So much for the exceptionalist argument that Britain's liberal principles made it more accommodating toward those colonial subjects seeking independence than other European imperial powers. This point was hammered home by Huw Bennett in the conclusion to his recent study of the British Army's campaign against Mau Mau: "The belief that Britain waged its decolonization wars with a greater degree of civility than other governments is no longer convincing, if it ever was."[19]

Defenders of the exceptionalist argument might well object that the examples highlighted by the new historians of colonial counterinsurgency campaigns are still outnumbered by the cases where relatively peaceful transitions from colonial rule took place. To concede this point, however, does not diminish the significance of the challenge these works pose to the belief that the British responded in a more positive, conciliatory manner than other Europeans when confronted with colonial nationalists' increasingly forceful demands for independence. The cumulative evidence of the coercive actions undertaken by British authorities in Palestine, Kenya, Malaya, Cyprus, Suez, Aden, and elsewhere casts serious doubt on the exceptionalist claims made by Hyam and others. While Britain did, to be sure, manage to peacefully transfer power in various territories, so did France. The reputation of the French as diehard defenders of their empire rests mainly on the wars of decolonization in Vietnam and Algeria. Elsewhere across Indochina and North Africa, as well as in West Africa and other regions, they granted independence to colonial subjects with far less struggle and trauma. How the French experience is measured against that of the British depends, of course, on the cases selected and the weight given to each. Recent comparative studies, however, have suggested that the British and the French exhibited greater similarities than differences in their use of military force to suppress colonial discontent. In *Fight or Flight*, Martin Thomas shows that both imperial powers oscillated between coercion and conciliation. Although Thomas suggests that the French may have been somewhat more inclined to fight than flee, he provides abundant evidence that the British were prepared to do the same.[20] Fabian Klose, in turn, finds little to distinguish between French and British conduct during their campaigns in Algeria and Kenya. Both empires carried out collective punishments, forced resettlements, systematic torture, mass executions, and other acts of state terror, contravening international law and giving urgency to the United Nation's efforts to codify human rights in the context of colonial rule.[21] At the very least, then, the work that has appeared over the past decade has called into question the complacent conviction that the British were more "liberal" and conciliatory in their conduct toward colonial subjects during the transition to independence than their European counterparts. Indeed, one historian refers to such claims as "the central British myth of decolonization."[22]

* * *

Another feature of the division between the exceptionalist literature on decolonization and recent work on the subject has to do with the ramifications of the loss of empire for the British at home. Historians who see decolonization as the final stomach-churning descent in the "roller-coaster of geopolitical fortune" argue that the domestic parties who experienced this thrill ride were mainly the ruling elites.[23] The British public, according to Bernard Porter and others, never took much notice of the empire, and its loss consequently left little discernable mark on British politics, society, or culture.[24] The standard historiography on the British Isles in the postwar era has largely reinforced this view, casting it as an island story dominated by the rise of the welfare state and the creation of a more egalitarian society. The retreat from empire is relegated to a sidebar. Britain's experience thus stands in stark contrast to the destabilizing domestic crises that afflicted France, Portugal, and other European countries as they lost their colonial possessions.

Recently, however, this historiographical consensus has been fractured, its foundations undermined by the new imperial history's determination to trace the mutually constitutive connections between the domestic and imperial realms, as well as by contemporary British society's manifest racial and cultural diversity, itself an undeniable consequence of empire. It is a testament to the growing body of work on the effects of the withdrawal from empire on Britain itself that it has become the subject of a special volume in the *Oxford Companion to the British Empire* series.[25]

Politics appears at first glance to be a realm where decolonization has exerted little domestic impact, especially in comparison to other European countries. The British demonstrably did not experience the traumatic domestic political upheavals that shook France and Portugal as they disengaged from imperial commitments. For France, the intolerable strains of the Algerian war led to the collapse of the Fourth Republic, the return to power of Charles de Gaulle, and a period of political instability highlighted by right-wing terrorism and the threat of a military coup. For Portugal, the protracted counterinsurgency campaigns against colonial insurgents in Africa precipitated the overthrow of the country's authoritarian regime by army officers, which led in turn to the establishment of a parliamentary democracy. The closest the British came to confronting such a crisis occurred as a result of the 1956 Suez debacle. Prime Minister Anthony Eden was forced to resign in disgrace, but the Tory government did not collapse.

No other event during the relentless retreat from empire caused a comparable political storm in Britain.[26] The postwar Labour government faced criticisms from the Winston Churchill-led opposition for its decision to "scuttle" from South Asia, but the political price paid for that action was minimal, not least because the government simultaneously sought to strengthen the empire elsewhere, particularly in Africa. When the Conservatives returned to office in 1951, the imperial policies they pursued were not dissimilar—maintaining colonial rule where possible, relinquishing it where necessary. A crucial turning point came when Conservative prime minister Harold Macmillan gave his famous "winds of change" speech, declaring that the decolonization of Africa was unavoidable. This continuity and consensus among governments of both parties minimized the domestic repercussions of the loss of empire. The political scientist Miles Kahler concluded in his comparative study of *Decolonization in Britain and France: The Domestic Consequences of International Relations* (1984) that its effects were far less disruptive to British than to French politics.[27]

Some recent works suggest, however, that the loss of empire had a subtle but discernible effect on political institutions and behavior in Britain. It was an especially emotive and divisive force for the Conservative Party.[28] Bill Schwarz makes the case in his *Memories of Empire* (2011) that imperial attachments and postimperial resentments have played a significant, if often neglected, role in British politics. He considers Enoch Powell, the Tory minister whose notorious 1968 speech warned that the influx of peoples of color from ex-colonial territories would lead to "rivers of blood" in Britain, a pivotal figure who gave political expression to public anxieties about the influx of these immigrants and prepared the ground for the rise of Thatcherism and far right parties like the United Kingdom Independence Party (UKIP). Powell gave voice to a reactionary, racist strain of thought in British politics that Schwarz traces in part to the settler colonial experience in southern Africa.[29] A more recent study of Powell stresses the formative impact of the Second World War on his vision of the British nation as an organic, hierarchical polity that had no place for nonwhite immigrants.[30]

The political right's commitment to the empire was also closely connected to the monarchy, which came to embody the ethnic bonds of the Empire/Commonwealth. In a striking metaphor, Philip Murphy describes this reverence for the royal family as "British Shintoism," a faith in duty and sacrifice that found expression in a combination of ancestral and imperial associations. The relentless dismantlement of the empire and the transformation of the Commonwealth into a multiracial organization placed strains on the monarchy and deepened the anguish of its most committed supporters.[31]

Others have drawn a connection between the end of empire and the fragmentation of the UK itself. The now familiar argument, first advanced by Tom Nairn in 1977, is that the shared sense of British identity that connected the English, the Scots, the Welsh, and the Northern Irish derived from their partnership in the imperial project, and that the loss of empire has eroded those bonds of Britishness.[32] This interpretation has generated increased interest in recent years, especially in light of the Scottish Nationalist Party's ongoing efforts to achieve independence from the UK. While historians remain at odds over the nature and scale of the impact of the end of empire on English-Scottish relations, there is a growing consensus that it contributed to the fissiparous forces that have increasingly threatened this union.[33]

Britain's own deepening ambivalence about the European Union, which led to the stunning referendum last year in favor of Brexit, has given rise to a parallel argument. As Benjamin Grob-Fitzgibbon shows in *Continental Drift* (2016), Winston Churchill and other leading proponents of a "United States of Europe" saw it as a natural counterpart to the empire, each essential in its own way to postwar reconstruction and the restoration of British power. The rise of Euroscepticism in recent decades reflects the growing anxiety that postimperial Britain has lost its place in the world.[34] (Some of those Eurosceptics have suggested that Britain could regain its lost glory by establishing an "Anglosphere" alliance with Australia, Canada, New Zealand, and the United States, a nostalgic effort to reinvent an all-white Commonwealth.)[35] The larger significance of these studies is that they forcefully challenge the established view that the British state and its political order withstood the imperial retreat with little if any damage or disturbance.

The social and cultural repercussions of the end of empire are undergoing a similar reassessment. While the exceptionist argument holds that Britain escaped most of the domestic problems that decolonization brought to other postimperial countries,[36] this position has increasingly come into question. Elizabeth Buettner's wide-ranging and deeply researched comparative study of the British, Dutch, French, Belgian, and Portuguese cases highlight the shared challenges these countries confronted in the aftermath of empire. While recognizing that each case was distinctive in many respects, Buettner points out that all of these countries had to cope with a common set of issues, including the repatriation of large numbers of European settlers and other colonists, the immigration of even larger numbers of non-European colonial and ex-colonial subjects, the struggles to reshape notions of national identity and belonging in increasingly multiethnic societies, and, most recently, the demands to confront a painful, often willfully forgotten imperial past.[37] Cast in this light, the impact of decolonization on the British domestic realm looks a good deal less distinctive than it once did.

The exceptionalist island story has also come under assault from Jordanna Bailkin, whose meticulous investigation of social welfare files and policy studies by sociologists, psychologists, and other experts shows that the withdrawal from empire, far from causing little or no consternation at home, gave rise to "a wide range of metropolitan debates about youth, education, marriage, child-rearing, and crime."[38] Bailkin's important study makes it clear that the overseas imperial sphere and its postcolonial "afterlife" were deeply imbricated in the domestic realm of the welfare state. This point is reinforced in an illuminating comparative study of housing policies in postwar Britain and France, which finds an "underlying similarity or convergence in assumptions and outcomes as both countries confronted the process of decolonization and rapidly increasing immigration in a period of housing shortage between 1945 and 1974."[39]

The main impetus for this infiltration of imperial/postimperial issues into domestic policy was the growing influx of West Indian and South Asian immigrants to Britain. Small but vibrant communities of Africans, Indians, and other colonial subjects had lived in London and other British port cities for decades, but their numbers grew rapidly in the postwar years, previewed by the arrival of the 492 West Indian immigrants on the SS *Empire Windrush* in 1948.[40] The growing presence of these racial and ethnic outsiders soon gave rise to a whole host of social and political concerns, leading to race riots, legislation to restrict immigration, and various other repercussions that belie the notion that British society remained untouched by the upheavals of decolonization.[41]

The postwar emigration of ethnic Britons also demonstrates that the imperial and domestic realms intersected in important ways in the era of decolonization. Two and a half million Britons left the British Isles in the two decades after the Second World War (surpassing the number who did so during the interwar decades), and the so-called white dominions, especially Australia and Canada, welcomed about three-fourths of them. Ellen Boucher's recent study of child migration schemes, a controversial aspect of this exodus, shows that it drew inspiration from the imperial idea of Greater Britain, and that it lost favor as the white dominions lost faith in this idea.[42]

The other side of the story is the return to Britain of many postwar migrants, along with the various civil servants, military personnel, technical experts, and other sojourners who were repatriated from colonies as they obtained independence. This remigration certainly does not compare to the sudden and often traumatized waves of refugees who fled to France with Algerian independence in 1962 or to Portugal after its African empire collapsed in 1974 or even to the Netherlands or Belgium when they lost their colonial possessions. Nevertheless, the cumulative effect of this reentry of ethnic Britons from the empire into domestic social and cultural life was not insignificant.[43] Nor was the impact of the one and a half million young men who returned to Britain after fulfilling their National Service obligations, often in colonial hotspots.[44] All of these returnees were shaped by their experiences overseas, acquiring new habits, tastes, interests, perspectives, and convictions, which invariably complicated cultural commitments in Britain.

Charting these and other manifestations of decolonization's destabilizing effects on British culture is a challenging task, and its outcomes are uneven at this stage of research on the subject. There is a large and growing literature on the effects of African, Asian, and West Indian immigrants on "race" relations in postwar Britain. The ethnic Britons who returned from colonial climes have attracted far less attention, though they too must have shaped domestic debates about race.[45] As minority immigrant communities established a larger and more permanent presence in Britain, their proponents coined the term multiculturalism to characterize the contributions they made to their host country. Perhaps the most commonly noted manifestation of this phenomenon is the popularity of South Asian cuisine in Britain, though the most careful and critical studies of the subject have stressed its limits as an expression of multiculturalism.[46]

Other historians have focused their attention on a different aspect of decolonization's impact on British culture—the feelings of anxiety, loss, regret, and nostalgia that so often colored public opinion about postimperial Britain.[47] Recent studies of postwar popular culture in Britain have shown that decolonization's effects were manifested in a range of narratives, some resurrecting war stories of martial masculinity, others expressing anxieties about racial threats to British families, and still others constructing a new sense of "Englishness against empire."[48] A study of James Bond's cultural appeal to the British public characterizes him as a wish fulfillment fantasy: "Bond is the natural, indeed unavoidable, expression of traditional British imperialism—there is no culture he cannot patronize, there is nothing he does not understand, nowhere he does not have access. . . . He has a carte blanche denied to other nationalities."[49] In stark contrast to Bond's appeal, the popularity of the satire boom of the early 1960s rested largely on its mockery of those old elites who maintained pretensions of national greatness. British playwrights grappled with decolonization in critically acclaimed works like Peter Nichols' *Privates on Parade* (1977) and Caryl Churchill's *Cloud 9* (1978). By the 1970s, argues Stuart Ward, the retreat from empire would feed into a broader narrative of British decline and decay that left a lasting scar on civic culture. "It was precisely the imperial context," he declares, "that underpinned contemporary perceptions of national degeneration."[50]

These examples by no means exhaust the range of repercussions that the loss of empire had on British attitudes and practices. But they suffice to cast doubt on the exceptionalist narrative that Britain's domestic realm, unlike its French and other European counterparts, remained essentially untouched by the disorder of decolonization.[51] While every ex-imperial country undoubtedly experienced the rapid diminishment of its power and pride differently, none were immune from the overseas upheavals that caused that outcome.

* * *

Why does it matter that the scholarship on British decolonization has become so diverse and divided over the past decade? What difference does it make whether the British experience was exceptional or not? Some might dismiss the issue as simply a self-promoting controversy driven by historians' compulsion to say something new. But the stakes are in fact far larger than that, and they manifest themselves in a political struggle over public memory about the past, a struggle that carries important implications for Britain's present identity and future trajectory.

This politics of memory takes several forms. One concerns contending judgments about the morality of British conduct during the late colonial era. The challenge that Anderson, Elkins, and others have posed to the previously prevalent view that the British extricated themselves from their colonial possessions without the violence and trauma that accompanied the decolonization of other European empires has gained purchase at present not simply because of the empirical merits of this scholarship, but because it resonates so powerfully with recent events. The Labour government's highly controversial decisions to participate in the invasion and occupation of Afghanistan and Iraq gave greater relevance to these studies, which have exposed the ugly underside of counterinsurgency warfare. And the Afghanistan and Iraq campaigns fostered a heightened distrust of government officials, including suspicions that they harbor shameful secrets, helping to set the stage for the recent revelation that thousands of incriminating documents concerning late-colonial policies had been hidden for half a century in the government's secret intelligence facility at Hanslope Park. With the release of these documents, the colonial past has intruded into the postcolonial present in a politically powerful and morally troubling way.

Another striking manifestation of the politics of memory that informs how the history of decolonization is addressed can be found in the debate about its domestic social and cultural repercussions. Among the most contentious issues the British are grappling with at present is immigration, and its power to provoke anxiety and polarize opinions is rooted in the legacy left by the large-scale influx of West Indians, South Asians, and Africans unsettled by the upheavals of decolonization. As Britain becomes a more multiethnic society, it confronts the increasingly complex challenge of what it actually means to be British. The historical debate about decolonization has thus become bound up with the issue of national identity. This issue has assumed other pressing forms as well, evident above all in the recent referendum in favor of Brexit and the ongoing campaign by Scottish nationalists to leave the British union. The decentered analysis of the British Empire that some historians have argued for in recent years seems increasingly applicable to Britain itself: the center cannot hold at home, not least because the end of empire has left that center so diminished and divided over its composition and its character.

7

On the American Empire from a British Imperial Perspective

The election of George W. Bush as president in 2000 empowered a group of neoconservative foreign policy experts who believed the United States should embrace its imperial destiny. With the invasions of Afghanistan and Iraq in the aftermath of the 9/11 attacks, they sought to realize this goal, and in so doing they set off a fierce, wide-ranging debate about America as an empire. In this updated essay, which originally appeared in The International History Review *in 2007, I trace the roots and course of this debate and set it in the context of British imperial history. With the wars in Afghanistan and Iraq still ongoing and a militaristic new president convinced that America is engaged in a global struggle against "radical Islam," the issues discussed here have, sadly, not lost their relevance.*

To speak of the United States as an empire has become so common that it is easy to forget how recently this characterization entered the nation's discourse. The first murmurings could be detected soon after the collapse of the Soviet Union in 1991, but it took the military invasions of Afghanistan in 2001 and Iraq in 2003 to provoke a full-throated discussion of the issue. Pundits of all political stripes began talking openly about the rise of an American empire. Periodicals devoted special issues to the topic, professional societies organized conferences on it, and publishers issued a veritable flood of books with titles like *Imperial America*. What it meant for America to be an empire stirred a vigorous public debate, and its echoes linger to the present day.

The willingness to attach the tag of empire to the United States is not entirely unprecedented, of course. It also happened during a previous US foreign policy crisis, the Vietnam War. Then, however, the tag's use was limited to the political left, which wielded words like empire and imperialism to condemn American policy.[1] Now the notion of an American empire has its admirers as well as critics, and the debate between the two groups poses a number of intriguing questions. Is an American empire the inevitable outcome of the country's unrivaled global presence and power or is it the opportunistic consequence of decisions taken by particular groups pursuing particular ends? Is it the necessary guardian of international order and prosperity or is it the inexorable engine of global inequality and conflict? Is it sui generis or does it resemble empires of the past? Is its imperial reign the end of history or does it portend America's own end? These are questions about the political purposes and moral consequences of power. They speak to the ambitions, anxieties, and antagonisms that America's engagement with the world arouses. Yet they are questions that hinge on the use of the term empire, a semantic and conceptual issue that historians have long grappled with, and that requires an understanding of causation, chronology, and comparison, modes of analysis that are the stock-in-trade of historians. "People in public life reason by historical analogy," observes Roger Louis.[2] It should be no surprise, then, that historians have played an especially prominent role in the debate about what it means for America to be an empire.

This chapter examines the upsurge of interest in America as an empire and the opportunities it presents to integrate the American experience within the broader historical inquiry into the nature of empires. It begins by tracing the immediate sources of the recent debate about an American empire and the contending stances of its contributors. Next, it examines attempts to give historical context to our understanding of what an American empire might mean. Finally, it compares the American experience with the British Empire. It proceeds from the premise that the United States *is* an empire. While this stance limits certain lines of inquiry, such as the distinction that has been made between a hegemon and an empire, it opens up others too long closed off.[3] The enduring belief among Americans that their country's heritage and ambitions are inimical to empire and imperialism has sustained an exceptionalist view of American history that resists comparative considerations of the consequences of global power.[4] To be sure, the notion of America as an empire can encourage exceptionalism of another sort: the argument that America's empire is so much grander than previous ones as to defy comparison. But empire is a term so variable in its meanings that its value as a conceptual category is contingent on the adoption of a comparative frame of reference. It requires an appreciation of the other contexts, conditions, and countries to which it has been applied. To speak of America as an empire, then, necessitates engaging in comparative historical analysis.

* * *

Irving Kristol, one of the intellectual founding fathers of the neoconservative movement, posed the following question in an interview during the summer of 2000: "What's the point of being the greatest, most powerful nation in the world and not having an imperial role?"[5] Kristol and other neoconservatives believed that the time had come for the United States, which enjoyed unrivaled international supremacy in the aftermath of the Soviet Union's disintegration, to behave like an imperial power, robustly asserting its will on the rest of the world. A blueprint for what they had in mind was "Rebuilding America's Defenses," an influential report prepared during the 2000 election campaign under the aegis of the Project for the New American Century, a Washington think tank founded by William Kristol, Irving Kristol's son and now editor of *The Weekly Standard*, a magazine that purveys conservative political opinion. The report recommended a significant increase in military spending, a restructuring of the armed forces to make them better prepared to carry out foreign interventions and "perform . . . 'constabulary' duties," the repudiation of treaty commitments and international obligations that restrained unilateral action, and other measures designed to ensure that the United States remained "the world's only superpower."[6] Although the report avoided any explicit reference to "empire," its recommendations corresponded closely to Irving Kristol's notion of what an empire should be and do.

With the inauguration of George W. Bush as president of the United States in January 2001, many neoconservatives affiliated with the Project and its objectives were appointed to key roles in the administration, granting wider currency and greater influence to their views. A debate soon broke out in conservative foreign policy circles about whether the United States was an empire and, if so, whether its imperial ambitions should be openly embraced. The chief instigator of the debate was the deputy director of the Project and principal author of "Rebuilding America's Defenses," Thomas Donnelly. He answered both questions with a resounding "yes."[7] Seeking to overcome the evident unease with which many Conservatives responded to the tag "empire"—Bush had declared during the presidential campaign that America was not an empire and the conservative commentator and one-time presidential candidate Patrick Buchanan had written a book arguing that America's political values and traditions were antithetical to empire—Donnelly embraced the term, insisting that empire was the logical and necessary outcome of the United States' rise to global predominance.[8]

While the neoconservatives, then, were singing the praises of American empire from the earliest days of the Bush administration, only an ideologically sympathetic cognoscenti actually heard their siren song prior to al-Qaeda's attacks on New York and Washington. After 9/11, the political climate in the United States was transformed and its military resources mobilized for the invasions of Afghanistan and Iraq. In the heady days that accompanied these campaigns, an increasingly bellicose Bush administration threatened Iran and Syria and announced its ambition to remake the Middle East. The testosterone-charged mood was neatly captured in a remark by a British official who was said to be privy to the US government's thinking at the time: "Everyone wants to go to Baghdad. Real men want to go to Tehran."[9] At this moment, and in this context, intellectual boosters of the administration's actions reached out to a larger audience by producing a flurry of opinion pieces, articles, and books that urged Americans to embrace their imperial destiny.

Those who welcomed the prospect of an imperial America insisted that its standing as the world's sole superpower compelled it to assume the burdens of empire. One of the most prominent proponents of this view was the historian Niall Ferguson, who called on Americans to overcome their traditional distrust of empire, acknowledge its virtues as a stabilizing force in the world, and forthrightly project American power whenever and wherever necessary.[10] Americans might "lack the imperial cast of mind," he declared, but America "always had been an empire."[11] This assessment was shared by Max Boot, a historian by training and a senior fellow at the Council of Foreign Relations, who argued that the United States had fought plenty of "splendid little wars" in the past, imperial interventions that provide models for the projection of force demanded by current circumstances.[12] While the most explicit endorsements of an American empire came from the political right, some liberal interventionists also advocated the exercise of imperial power.[13] Michael Ignatieff, for one, endorsed "empire lite," arguing that humanitarian crises and political disorder justified "imperial policing" measures.[14] At the core of the argument advanced by those who favored the assertion of imperial power by the United States was the premise that empire guarantees order and prosperity, while its absence generates disorder and poverty. Broadening Niall Ferguson's claim that the British Empire brought about "anglobalization," the economist Deepak Lal made the case that empires were essential for the promotion of globalization and economic growth.[15] Thomas P. M. Barnett, a military strategist at the Naval War College, contended that "gaps" in globalization create regions of instability that compelled the United States to play "Leviathan full-time"—an assessment of the nation's obligations that made him a "guru" to officials in the Pentagon.[16] Similarly, the journalist Robert Kaplan insisted that America had an obligation to dispatch its troops—he frankly referred to them as "imperial grunts"—to trouble spots around the globe in order to keep at bay the Hobbesian threat of chaos and violence.[17] How to find a way "to legitimize colonial rule by some other name, and to create institutions that can conduct it" was the main challenge confronting the United States, according to the influential neoconservative foreign policy specialist Eliot Cohen.[18] The National War College in Washington, D.C. began offering its students a lecture and study program on "Empires."[19] Though the Bush administration publicly protested that it had no imperial ambitions, privately it harbored other views: "We're an empire now, and when we act, we create our own reality," one White House official famously told a reporter. "We're history's actors ... and you, all of you, will be left to just study what we do."[20]

The rest of us did indeed study what they did. What this official probably could not have anticipated, however, was how quickly and vociferously the administration's embrace of empire was turned against it. Books soon began to pour from the presses with titles like *The Folly of Empire* and *Imperial Delusions*, signaling their authors' conviction that the administration was pursuing a policy of imperial aggression and hubris that could only come to an unhappy end—as, indeed, it did.[21] The negative connotations that the term empire long carried in American political and popular discourse—consider President Ronald Reagan's charge that the Soviet Union was an "evil empire" or the designation of the villains in the "Star Wars" films as the "Empire"—echo throughout these works. The objections they raised were wide-ranging: an imperial America sustains militarism and endless war; it encourages arrogance and provokes antagonism around the world; it drains the nation's resources and distorts its economy; it undermines the democratic foundations of the republic itself. Much of this literature drew its inspiration from leftist intellectual traditions. Perhaps the most prominent and certainly the most prolific of the leftist critics was Noam Chomsky, the famed linguist and political gadfly, who continued the project he originally launched as an opponent of the Vietnam War, seeking to expose the United States as a rogue state, its imperialist misadventures undermining the freedom and prosperity of peoples around the globe.[22] The geographer David Harvey drew on classical Marxist interpretations of imperialism, arguing that America's actions were driven by the inherent contradictions of modern capitalism.[23] Other important critics, however, came from very different backgrounds and ideological persuasions. Chalmers Johnson, an East Asian specialist, had been one of the leading academic defenders of the American war in Vietnam, while Andrew Bacevich was a retired military officer who had found a new career as a professor of international relations. Both Johnson and Bacevich worried that the rise of an unrivaled, unrestrained military had set the United States on an imperialist course.[24]

Perhaps the most striking feature of this proliferating, polemical literature was that both sides in the debate shared the same basic premise: the United States is an empire. While some commentators continued to insist that the term empire did not accurately characterize America's role in the world, they were a shrinking minority.[25] The principal point of dispute now seemed to come down to a moral question: is the American empire a good or a bad thing? A secondary issue was whether the aggressive assertion of American military power since 9/11 was a sign of strength or of weakness.

As the occupations of Iraq and Afghanistan grew more troubled and costly, the debate at home became more one-sided, with the critics of empire gaining the upper hand.[26] Recognizing that advocacy of empire had become "a losing political issue," its proponents became less assertive, and one prominent neoconservative publicly proclaimed his change of heart.[27] With the election of Barack Obama to the presidency in 2008, those who had promoted and planned the military interventions in Iraq and Afghanistan appeared entirely discredited. Irving Kristol's vision of an America that took pride in its imperial power lost its appeal. Even Niall Ferguson conceded that the costs of American empire seemed to exceed its benefits, though he remained hopeful that "the calculus of power could swing back in its favor tomorrow."[28]

So what did the two sides in this shifting debate mean when they spoke of America as an empire? For some, the designation was assumed to be self-evident, requiring no explanation or analysis. They relied on the word "empire," along with its cognates "imperial" and "imperialism," to do totemic duty, using it in their titles and texts to evoke awe or anger.[29] This was most noticeable among those who were so preoccupied with American foreign policy after 9/11 that they lost sight of earlier American interventions overseas, and of the experiences of previous empires. They tended to regard the present as a moment without parallel, a post–Cold War "unipolar" juncture where the United States enjoyed such unrivaled predominance that it had no equivalent in the past. Whether this was the "end of history," a secular second (or in this case first) coming that announced the universal triumph of American values and institutions, or the era of "endless war," brought on by an unbridled Pentagon determined to assert its power around the world, it was portrayed as a state of affairs that transcended anything any other empire had ever achieved.[30]

Even among the advocates of American exceptionalism, however, there was some incentive to allude to past empires, if only to highlight what differentiated the United States. Glib comparisons to the Roman Empire were common.[31] More meaningful efforts to make sense of America as an empire require, however, more systematic attention to its historical context and counterparts. Empire is a pervasive but elusive historical term. The sheer variety of past polities that have been characterized as empires frustrates efforts to formulate a definition or typology that applies to all cases. While most scholars are likely to agree that an empire refers to the authority exerted by a state or its agents over an ethnically diverse combination of peoples, this understanding of the term is too general to mean very much, accommodating as it does such different phenomena as the continent-wide conquests of the Mongols and the transoceanic extortions of the Portuguese. Moreover, even this definition may not be broad enough to account for the way the term has been used, for example, in reference to that loose affiliation of central European states known as the Holy Roman Empire or to the "shadow empires" that arose along China's steppe frontier.[32] As Dominic Lieven has observed, "to write the history of empire would be close to writing the history of mankind."[33]

How, then, can meaningful comparisons be drawn between the United States and past empires? In the immediate aftermath of the invasions of Afghanistan and Iraq, several volumes took up this question, seeking insights into current events from authorities on past empires and colonies. A collection of essays prepared for a conference sponsored by the Social

Science Research Council and an issue of the American Academy of Arts and Sciences' journal *Daedalus* set the US experience in the context of the Russian, Ottoman, Chinese, French, and other empires. While both these works were rich in insights, they were also riddled with differences in definitions of empire, categories of comparison, and conclusions about whether the United States was an empire, and, if so, of what sort.[34] Other historians focused attention on American involvement in the Middle East and Central Asia, comparing it to past imperial interventions in these regions. While they drew some striking parallels, their studies begged the question of how much could be learned from these cases about the broader character of empires.[35]

Others took up the challenge posed by this question, conducting comparative inquiries into past empires in order to contextualize the existing moment of American global dominance. Especially noteworthy were books written by Charles Maier, Jane Burbank and Frederick Cooper, and Timothy Parsons.[36] As the first of these books and the one that addressed the contemporary moment most directly, Maier's *Among Empires* deserves particular attention. Ranging across a wide span of history, Maier identified the "recurring elements of empires," asking "to what extent the United States shares these attributes." Among the elements he found most common are the maintenance of systems of inequality, tolerance for social and cultural heterogeneity, reliance on governance by collaborative elites, and, above all, persistent problems with frontiers, the "fault lines" that mark the most open manifestations of imperial power and most clearly expose its limits. For Maier, "Rome remains the most compelling imperial model," though his analysis included incisive discussion of other empires. Having produced a typology of empires in the first half of the book, he turned to the United States in the second, providing an illuminating if overly Europe-centered examination of its rise to global predominance. While Maier was reluctant to declare the United States to be an empire, he came close: "The United States reveals many, but not all—at least not yet—of the traits that have distinguished empires."[37]

Maya Jasanoff has observed that empires "build on the structures and policies of their predecessors."[38] The United States' immediate predecessor was the British Empire, and it should be the first case to which we turn for meaningful historical comparisons. The extent to which the United States has drawn on the structures and policies of the British Empire reveals a great deal about its pursuit of imperial power. It came into existence by breaking away from the British Empire, but it retained many of the institutional and doctrinal traditions of its erstwhile sovereign. It marshaled these traditions to new purposes as it expanded across the continent and turned its ambitions abroad. With the British retreat from empire in the second half of the twentieth century, the United States became its most obvious heir, filling the economic and military vacuum that Britain's decline left in the international arena while finding new ways to exert influence over its former colonies.[39] Now the United States finds itself occupying several countries that the British occupied in the past. The length and lingering bonds of this relationship indicate that much can be learned about America as an empire by comparing it to the British Empire.

* * *

A *New Yorker* profile of Douglas Feith, one of the neoconservatives who helped to plan the invasion of Iraq as the Pentagon's undersecretary of defense for policy, noted in passing that his personal library was "weighted disproportionately to the history of the British Empire, and Feith has spent many hours schooling himself in the schemes and follies of the British on the playing fields of the Middle East."[40] Although it is tempting to conclude that Feith either learned nothing from his studies (or drew the wrong lessons), the most intriguing aspect of this anecdote is the fact that he turned to the British imperial experience for historical insights in the first place.

Feith was hardly alone. In the period immediately surrounding the invasions of Afghanistan and Iraq, a flurry of opinion pieces turned for perspective on US policy to Britain's earlier engagements in these countries.[41] Since then there has been a steady stream of commentaries that compare America's actions today to those of Britain in its imperial heyday. Many of them come from historians who have studied either the British Empire itself or some region of the world that was once under its sway. We have two books from Niall Ferguson, one on the British Empire, the other on the American Empire, with the first explicitly offered as a lesson for the second (though that lesson is so starkly divorced from the historical account he provides that it might be better termed a homily).[42] We have had critical cameos from Caroline Elkins, historian of the Mau Mau rebellion in Kenya, who warns that those who urge American strategists in Iraq to emulate the British counterinsurgency campaign in Malaya fail to acknowledge its brutal, repressive nature, and William Dalrymple, historian of British India, who observes that the American overthrow of Saddam Hussein resembles the British destruction of Tipu Sultan in its cynical and ruthless warmongering.[43] We have had cautionary tales from Juan Cole, Rashid Khalidi, and Karl Meyer, each of whom warns that the United States is following in the Middle East and Central Asia in the fateful footsteps of the British, whose failures it was doomed to repeat.[44] We have had a reminder from Linda Colley that America's own origins and ambitions for greatness were conceived in terms of empire and evolved in relationship to the British Empire, which was at once its model, its nemesis, and its ally.[45] And we have had Tony Hopkins weigh in with an assessment of the motives driving "the New American Empire," concluding it was "the product of nationalism rather than of capitalism."[46]

The most sustained reflections on what the British experience can tell us about the current American empire have come from Julian Go, a historical sociologist, and Bernard Porter, a distinguished historian of the

British Empire. The next chapter examines Go's book at length. Here I intend to summarize the argument made by Porter, who offers a sweeping if idiosyncratic consideration of the two states' roles as global powers. Despite his pretense that he has no wish to judge whether the United States is an empire ("'Imperialism' *is* only a word, after all"), the title and content of his book proclaim otherwise: it is not merely an empire, but a "superempire," far surpassing Britain in power and ambition.[47] This distinction is central to his argument, which stresses the differences rather than the similarities between the two empires. Even though he echoes many of the concerns critics voiced about the foreign policy of the George W. Bush administration, he is no more enamored of their efforts to condemn its policies through analogy to the British imperial experiences than of its defenders' efforts to endorse these policies by the same means.

Where Porter stretches credulity is in his determination to downplay the power and influence of the British Empire. It was, he claims, a "cheapskate empire" that only managed to expand as far as and last as long as it did because of "luck," "bluff," and the occasional dose of "repression," which itself was a sign of "fear . . . or of weakness"—although he concedes that it may not have seemed so to those who were being subjugated.[48] Like Ferguson, Porter believes that imperial power is a matter of willpower, but whereas Ferguson asserts that the British had it, Porter is convinced that they did not. Reprising the argument advanced in his previous book, *The Absent-Minded Imperialists*, he asserts that the British had little interest in their empire and lacked any genuine "imperial 'will'." Hence, the British Empire was a troubled, tottering entity, "pre-programmed" to fail.[49]

When a historian brings both chance and fate into his argument, and then caps it off with claims about national character, alarm bells ring. Porter also turns to national character to explain how the United States became a "superempire." Again staking a position in opposition to Ferguson, he insists that Americans have the will for empire that their diffident British cousins lacked. They acquired it, he suggests, in the early colonists' wars against native peoples, which imbued Americans with a "masculinist" mentality that found expression in ruthlessness and a proclivity for violence. This is why US cities are so dangerous and the US military so powerful.[50] As a polemic, this is a rousing read, but as historical analysis it leaves a lot to be desired.

Rather than attempt to adjudicate the argument between Porter and Ferguson about whether the Americans or the British have more of the backbone required of imperialists, we would do better to look for more analytically and historically meaningful ways of measuring the two empires against one another. Michael Mann, a historical sociologist whose critique of current American foreign policy is one of the first and most perceptive of the recent spate of books to view it in terms of empire (albeit an incoherent one, as his provocative title proclaims), suggests that imperial power has four distinct dimensions: political, military, economic, and ideological.[51] While I would broaden the ideological dimension to include cultural power, Mann's four categories provide a useful framework for addressing the question of how the American empire does and does not resemble its British predecessor.

* * *

The most commonly cited difference between the British Empire and its American successor has to do with how each has exerted political power. The British Empire was first and foremost a colonial empire, famously represented in those maps that colored its far-flung possessions in red. At its fullest territorial extent in the aftermath of the First World War, the British Empire held sway over the Indian subcontinent, vast swathes of Africa, large parts of Southeast Asia and the Middle East, as well as Australia, New Zealand, Canada, and countless smaller territories around the globe. Though these disparate lands were ruled in different ways, with the ones populated mainly by peoples of British stock acquiring rights to self-governance that did not extend to the lands inhabited mainly by African, Asian, and other non-Western peoples, all were political dependencies of Britain, acknowledging the Crown as their sovereign.[52]

The United States, by contrast, has shown far less inclination to govern territories as colonial dependencies, even though, from the beginning, it was constantly seeking to expand its borders, acquiring territory previously claimed by Spain, France, Mexico, and Russia while sweeping aside Native American communities in ruthless campaigns of displacement and destruction.[53] As many historians have noted, this westward march across the continent bore striking similarities to settler expansion in South Africa, Canada, Australia, and New Zealand, not least in terms of the settlers' harsh, even exterminationist, policies toward indigenous peoples.[54] It is standard practice to apply the term colonialism to the latter cases, but the term presents problems in the American context: while Native Americans may have been subjected to a form of "internal colonialism," the territories taken from them were not politically subordinated to the conquering state, but incorporated within it.[55]

Once the United States reached the limits of its continental expansion, it did make a sudden bid for the sort of overseas colonial empire that Britain possessed. Starting in 1897, it seized numerous overseas territories, including Hawaii, the Philippines, Puerto Rico, eastern Samoa, Guam, the Panama Canal Zone, and, briefly, Cuba, where the most enduring legacy of its imperial ambitions is the now notorious Guantanamo.[56] Still, this colonial empire was small by British standards (in part because so little of the world remained unclaimed by other empires, forcing the United States to wrest most of its possessions from Spain), and of shorter duration. The Philippines got self-government in 1935 and formal independence in 1945. Hawaii was granted statehood (equivalent, in some ways, to the unrealized ambitions of British imperial federationists, who sought the political incorporation of colonies like Canada and Australia into a Greater Britain) in 1959. Puerto Rico and Guam have remained unincorporated territories, but their residents are US citizens. The United States had become a sharp critic of European colonial rule during the Second World War and the main architect of a postwar international order that was premised on the eventual extension of national sovereignty to all peoples.[57]

For those who equate imperialism with colonialism, this shows that the United States might have had imperial ambitions in the past, but gave them up as it came into its own as a world power. Some of the proponents of an American empire make the same connection, but instead of applauding the fact that most of the US colonial system was dismantled, they urge its revival on a grander scale. Their romantic nostalgia for colonial rule is evident in Max Boot's oft-quoted remark about those "troubled lands" that "cry out for the sort of enlightened foreign administration once provided by self-confident Englishmen in jodhpurs and pith helmets."[58]

This preoccupation with colonialism as the main measure of empire ignores the fact that the British themselves preferred when possible to exert political power over other peoples through less intrusive means than direct rule. Historians have long recognized that Britain extended its reach well beyond the territories colored red on maps, coercing many formally independent countries to submit to its will. China saw its political autonomy so severely eroded in the nineteenth century by "the triple assault" of gunboat diplomacy, predatory capitalism, and missionary zealotry that it became the poster child for what is commonly referred to as Britain's informal empire.[59] The Ottoman Empire, Persia, and various Latin American states also came under coercive pressure from Britain. In each of these cases, there is some ambiguity about when and where to draw the line between influence and imperialism. Elsewhere, however, the line was clear, and clearly crossed. A few examples should suffice. Although the Persian Gulf protectorates of Kuwait, Qatar, and the United Arab Emirates (Trucial States) were purportedly autonomous polities, their affairs were actually overseen by British imperial agents. A more significant case was Egypt, where the British maintained the pretense for decades after their 1882 invasion that they administered the country on behalf of the khedive, whose state remained nominally part of the Ottoman Empire. Across the globe the British imposed various forms of indirect rule over putatively independent states.

The United States has adopted similar strategies in many of its dealings with other countries. Caribbean and Central American neighbors have been the frequent targets of American gunboat diplomacy and other instruments of informal imperialism. On various occasions over the past century the United States has invaded Cuba, Haiti, the Dominican Republic, Panama, Nicaragua, Honduras, Grenada, and other countries in the region, impeding revolutions, overthrowing governments, and installing rulers amenable to its interests.[60] The subservient regimes that resulted have been dismissively characterized as banana republics. Since the Second World War, the United States' efforts to surround itself with client states have extended across the globe, resulting in strategies that ranged from financial assistance and military advisors for friendly governments to economic sanctions and CIA-sponsored coups against unfriendly ones. Whether the largesse that the United States lavishes on a country like Egypt (currently the second largest beneficiary of American foreign aid) amounts to informal imperialism is open to debate, but surely the coups carried out at America's behest in Iran in 1953 and Guatemala in 1954 are proof of this phenomenon. The "status of force" agreements that exempt US personnel stationed in other countries from their laws, passport and immigration controls, and other powers of national sovereignty have been compared to the extraterritorial agreements that Britain imposed on China, the Ottoman Empire, and other states whose political autonomy it had eroded.[61]

Bernard Porter argues that America prefers informal to formal empire because its ruling class is capitalist to its core, whereas Britain forged a formal empire because it remained under the thrall of an atavistic aristocratic elite that liked to lord it over other peoples. But the contrast in elites' intentions should not be exaggerated: John Gallagher and Ronald Robinson reminded us long ago that the British only turned to colonial conquest in the nineteenth century when informal empire broke down.[62] A more compelling explanation for the divergent courses taken by the two empires has to do with the very different global environments within which they operated. The British faced far less congenial conditions for the advance of their capitalist interests in various parts of the world than does the United States, which enjoys the benefits of communication infrastructures, market systems, and cooperative regimes that often came into being as a result of colonial rule by Britain and others. And the growing array of competitors that confronted Britain in the late nineteenth century set off an unprecedented scramble for colonial possessions. The United States, by contrast, ascended to global predominance in the context of the European empires' decay and dissolution as a result of the Second World War, giving it and its rival, the Soviet Union, an incentive to condemn colonialism and promote the nation-state as the only political unit worthy of recognition in international relations.

America's interventions in Afghanistan and Iraq have generated talk of empire at least in part because they so eerily echo the British imperial experience in these countries. Paul Bremer, the US administrator of Iraq until limited sovereignty was restored in 2004, may not have worn a plumed helmet, but he certainly adopted the demeanor and wielded the power of a British proconsul.[63] And Hamid Karzai may have been president of a putatively free and independent Afghanistan, but he struggled mightily to overcome the widely held view that he was the puppet of an administration that "effectively remains an extension of the U.S. government."[64] What makes the likeness to an earlier empire's involvement in these countries all the more striking is that the British themselves disavowed any desire to claim them as colonies. Although the British invaded Afghanistan on three separate occasions (1838, 1878, and 1919), the outcome they sought was not direct rule, but the installation of an emir who would be amenable to their geopolitical concerns.[65] And although the British occupied Iraq during the First World War and governed it afterward, they operated under the international sanction of a League of Nations mandate from 1920 and served a state whose official ruler from 1921 was King Feisal, the Hashemite wartime ally whose accession to the throne they had engineered.[66] No one now questions that these were acts of imperialism, but they were conducted by means that maintained the pretense that Afghans and Iraqis enjoyed political autonomy. Is it any wonder then that the American occupations of these countries gave rise to similar charges?

* * *

The military might that the United States recently brought to bear on Afghanistan and Iraq also has occupied a central place in the debate about American imperialism. Force is an integral feature of all empires, as Charles Maier observes in an apt aphorism: "The life-blood of empires is blood."[67] The stunning speed with which US forces overthrew the Taliban in Afghanistan and the Baathist regime in Iraq set off a scramble among commentators to coin a new term to describe its military supremacy: "hyperpower," "überpower," and "superempire" jockeyed to succeed the now passé "superpower."[68] Much of this slack-jawed awe dissipated as the United States became bogged down in bloody counterinsurgency campaigns in both countries, and it has diminished even further with the Syrian civil war and the rise of ISIS. Even so, the Pentagon's dream of "full spectrum dominance," its phrase for unchallenged military superiority, has come as close to being realized as such chimeras can be. Over the past few decades, the United States has devoted more of its budget to military expenditures than all other major powers combined. Its forces "garrison the globe" with at least 725 military bases in at least 38 countries (some bases and their hosts are kept secret), serving as the logistical launching pads for surveillance activities, covert operations, constabulary missions, and military measures of other sorts.[69] These efforts are overseen by an oligarchy of commanders in chief (Andrew Bacevich calls them "uniformed proconsuls"), each of whom has jurisdiction over a major region of the world—the Pacific and East Asia, Europe, Africa, the Middle East, and Latin America.[70] Their commands, in effect, encompass the entire globe.

This colossal military enterprise is foremost in the minds of most of those commentators who refer to the United States as an empire. For many of them, it is "a new form of empire," one whose power so far surpasses that of any empire in the past that it stands in a class all its own.[71] If power is measured in terms of sheer destructive force, this is no doubt true, but it is a truth that simply speaks to the cumulative advances in military technology. By this measure, it could be claimed that contemporary Britain, with its nuclear arsenal and other sophisticated weaponry, is more powerful than its imperial forebear, a proposition that is all but meaningless. Military power, like any kind of power, must be measured in relative terms, set against the countervailing forces it confronts. Understood as such, the question that needs to be asked is how the power the United States has wielded relative to its rivals compares with the power the British Empire wielded relative to the rivals it once faced. There is no readily available calculus for answering this question.[72] Historians are deeply divided, for example, in their views of when and why the Britain Empire began to decline, an issue made more challenging still by the fact that military power is inextricably bound up with political and economic power.[73] This should not prevent us, however, from making some general comparative observations about the military resources available to the two empires and how they have been used to project power.

As the iconic lyrics to "Rule Britannia" proclaimed, it was above all because the Royal Navy "ruled the waves" that the British were both free and free to exert their will on other peoples around the globe.[74] The navy's ability to patrol the seas and to project power along coasts and navigable rivers made it an intimidating instrument of imperial might in the nineteenth century, able at its peak to safeguard the global system of trade that Britain depended upon, as well as to coerce those recalcitrant or belligerent states that interfered with its interests and ambitions. In the United States' modern arsenal, airpower (understood to include satellites and land- and sea-based missiles) can be viewed as the equivalent to the Royal Navy. It carries greater destructive punch, but only in the aftermath of the Soviet Union's disintegration has it attained the unquestioned superiority over its rivals that the British navy enjoyed through much of the nineteenth century. The United States' airpower does not face the same constraints that British sea power did in its dealings with land powers like Germany and Russia.[75] Still, it has serious limitations of its own, as the insurgencies in Iraq and Afghanistan amply demonstrated, and it requires a similar network of bases around the world to supply its forces and stage their strikes. America's "empire of bases," which stretches from Guam to Guantanamo, would have been instantly intelligible to Victorian lords of the Admiralty, whose own strategically important Indian Ocean base of Diego Garcia has become a key air base for American forces.[76]

If we turn to land power, the American military seems far more formidable relative to its rivals than the British military ever was. Its forces are unmatched by any other army today in terms of training, armaments, and logistics, if not sheer numbers. The British Army, by contrast, was puny compared to the armies of the great continental European states, and it was indifferently armed and equipped. It was, however, well suited to the colonial warfare it conducted with such numbing frequency against Asian and African forces, enabling Col. C. E. Caldwell to distill the military lessons his countrymen had learned in these campaigns in his classic *Small Wars*.[77] Britain's technological superiority over its non-Western foes resulted on occasion in outcomes like the Sudan campaign of 1898, where its forces wreaked a late-Victorian version of "shock and awe." Furthermore, it was able to overcome many of its domestic manpower limitations by drawing on overseas resources, the most important of which was its "English barracks in an Oriental sea"—the Indian army, one of the largest armies in the world.[78] When mercenary auxiliaries like the Gurkhas and a host of other colonial forces are added to the list (nearly twenty locally enlisted overseas forces were commanded by seconded British officers), the British had a huge reservoir of manpower to carry out constabulary duties across the globe.[79]

The United States military doctrine appears in the aftermath of the collapse of the Soviet Union to be shifting toward a strikingly similar conception of its forces' future role. The influential military theorist Thomas Barnett argues that the United States can expect to fight a lot of wars in the near future, small wars in "failed" states in which security has broken down and "subversive" elements have gained a foothold.[80] One study has counted nearly fifty military interventions by the United States in the decade between 1989 and 1999, compared to just sixteen during the Cold War.[81] Anticipating many more, the Bush administration's secretary of defense, Donald Rumsfeld, pushed the Pentagon to restructure its forces into smaller, more mobile units better prepared to meet these multiple low-level threats.[82] More recently, the increasing use of drone aircraft to strike at terrorist targets in remote locations is another indication of this shifting strategy. The Pentagon also has turned increasingly to private firms like Dycorp, run by retired military men, to carry out logistical and security tasks as "subcontractors," which is little more than a euphemism for mercenaries.[83] In 2003–04, it spent $750 million on private contractor services in Iraq alone.[84] In addition, troops from countries like Mongolia were well rewarded by the United States for their participation in the "coalition of the willing" that occupied Iraq (where the Mongols made their last memorable appearance in 1258).[85] While these American military initiatives are driven by their own particular dynamics and circumstances, they share at least some of the strategic and structural characteristics of a British military that was designed to maintain an empire.

* * *

Military force is usually regarded as the measure of last resort in international relations, undertaken when states fail to achieve their objectives by other means. Among the most important of these objectives for imperial Britain was the advancement of its global economic interests. The first country to experience an industrial revolution, Britain became "the workshop of the world" in the nineteenth century, producing the preponderance of the cotton textiles, iron and steel products, and other manufactured goods that entered the global marketplace. It also built the ships that moved these goods from domestic producers to overseas consumers and it controlled the shipping lanes along which they traveled. The profits it accumulated turned the City of London into the world's financial center and made British sterling the standard measure for international currency exchange. Although Britain's manufacturing sector began to retreat from its position of predominance under the growing competition from the United States, Germany, and other newly industrialized nations in the late nineteenth century, its financial, services, and commercial sectors remained strong until the international economy collapsed with the onset of the Great Depression. British power waxed and waned with its international economic standing.

The classic theories of imperialism advanced by John Hobson and Vladimir Lenin arose in large measure out of their desire to explain the workings of this relationship.[86] While particulars of their interpretations have been discredited, their insistence that capitalism often acted in tandem with imperialism has not. Peter Cain and A. G. Hopkins argued that British imperialism was intimately associated with the needs of metropolitan capitalist interests, particularly from the financial and services sectors.[87] While the precise causal relationship between the various elements of the British economy and various manifestations of imperial power remains a matter of debate, most historians agree that the correspondence between the two was no accident: the forces that made Britain a capitalist powerhouse are inexorably entangled with those that made it an imperial titan.

The United States became the engine that drove the global economy after the Second World War. American capital fueled the postwar revival of international trade and American factories met the pent-up demand for consumer goods. Wall Street replaced the City of London as the world's main money market and the dollar replaced sterling as its default currency. This economic ascendancy supplied the United States with a surplus of what has been called "soft power," the ability to exert its will in indirect and informal ways. Charles Maier, who refers to the United States as a "post-territorial empire," attributes its power to the unrivaled capacity it exhibited after the Second World War for mass production—and, more recently, for mass consumption, which it has financed through a feedback loop of credit from countries whose own economic growth is dependent on American consumers' continued demand for their goods.[88] Whether this system can be sustained is uncertain, especially in light of the international financial crisis of 2008 and the growing economic power of China. Yet the United States remains for the time being "the indispensable nation," though not exactly in the self-satisfied sense Madeleine Albright intended when she coined the phrase as secretary of state in the Clinton administration. For commentators like Deepak Lal and Niall Ferguson, the United States is indeed indispensable to the world economy, providing the imperial oversight that makes globalization possible. Others, while agreeing with the imperial designation, argue that the United States has "gamed" the rules of international trade to give itself an unfair advantage. It has done so, they suggest, both by engaging in direct coercion of other states through trade and credit sanctions and by relying on organizations like the World Bank and the International Monetary Fund to police their economic behavior.[89]

(Donald Trump recently won the presidency by turning this critique upside down, improbably arguing that the United States itself is the victim of international trade agreements and advocating protectionist policies to restore its industrial sector.)

Although the international economic environment over which the United States exerts so much influence is in many respects very different from the one the British dealt with in the nineteenth and early twentieth centuries, both states have espoused much the same set of liberal economic doctrines, stressing the benefits of free trade, safeguards for private property, and so forth.[90] (By the same token, the critique of trade agreements by Trump bears some similarity to Joseph Chamberlain's assault on free trade in Britain in the early twentieth century.) So long as they have been the dominant states in their respective systems of trade, both Britain and the United States have stood to gain from the expansion of trade and the liberalization of other countries' economic policies, giving them an incentive to pressure weaker states and societies that have resisted such practices. On some occasions, the leverage has taken the form of gunboat diplomacy, on others the subtler manipulations of the British sterling zone and American dollar diplomacy, but invariably it has advanced the economic interests of the two empires.

For all its importance, the economics of imperialism has played a subordinate role in the current debate about the United States as an empire. The only notable neo-Marxist analysis has come from David Harvey, whose dark warning that the Bush administration's belligerent actions were evidence of a structural crisis in capitalism looks prescient in light of the 2008 financial collapse.[91] Other commentators have noted the importance of oil to US policy in Iraq, though rarely have they followed up this observation with a full-fledged analysis of the political economy of modern capitalism's most critical resource.[92]

A second aspect of the economics of empire that deserves closer attention is the "military-industrial complex" that President Dwight Eisenhower famously warned against in his farewell address.[93] Though this phrase is inextricably associated with the nexus of forces that arose in the United States after the Second World War, an earlier configuration of the phenomenon reared its head in imperial Britain. One reason John Hobson's *Imperialism: A Study* remains worth reading today is its analysis of the arms merchants, mining magnates, military officers, and other interest groups that gained professional benefits from the imperial wars Britain waged and the colonial territories it conquered.[94] A similar study begs to be done about the many private firms that profited from the wars in Afghanistan and Iraq. The press gave intermittent attention to the government contracts awarded to Halliburton, the conglomerate previously piloted by the Bush administration's vice president, Dick Cheney, but there are plenty of other consultants and contractors who won bids to restart oil fields, rebuild bridges and buildings, and provide private security and prison guards (including some of those involved in the Abu Ghraib prison scandal). An analysis of this huge and expanding "military-industrial complex" is one way to connect the economic dimension of American policy to its military imperatives. It also points to intriguing parallels with the British imperial experience.

* * *

Lastly, Michael Mann notes the importance of ideological power, to which I would add cultural power. Here too the British experience offers some useful points of comparison to the American one. All empires offer an ideological rationale for their rule over other peoples, invariably condensed in the claim that they are carrying out a civilizing mission.[95] The British saw their mission as a liberal one, freeing their colonial subjects from the shackles of tradition and tyranny through the introduction of good government and legal rights, commerce and Christianity, medicine and modern education, and other emblems of Western modernity. This determination to lead the "poor benighted heathen" to the promised land of civilization was famously expressed by Rudyard Kipling in his poem "The White Man's Burden"— written for his American cousins as they set out to acquire an overseas empire at the end of the nineteenth century. While the British themselves often failed to heed Kipling's call to "fill the mouth of Famine and bid the sickness cease," we cannot dismiss this rhetoric as merely empty or hypocritical.[96] Its moral injunctions had a powerful hold on the political imaginations of the empire's expatriate agents and it influenced the attitudes of local Westernized elites as well. This liberal ideology, with its promise of progress, gave the British imperial project a hegemonic strength that it would never have achieved had it relied entirely on brute force.

The United States crafted its own technocratic version of this civilizing mission.[97] It honed a rhetoric of development and modernization that held great appeal, especially after the Second World War, when the American economy dominated the international scene. According to Harry Harootunian, the belief of President Bush and his advisors that they could remake the Middle East harkened back to this postwar confidence in America's modernizing mission.[98] Its lineage, however, can be traced to the same liberal roots that informed the British rationale for reforming other societies. Juan Cole has noted the parallels between the United States' insistence that its purpose is to bring political and economic liberty to Iraq and the liberal rhetoric the British used to justify their invasion and occupation of Egypt in 1882 (which itself echoed Napoleon's pronouncements when his army occupied Egypt in 1798). The theme trumpeted in Bush's 2004 inaugural address was that the United States had an obligation to advance the cause of liberty around the world (the words freedom and liberty appear 25 times and 13 times respectively in the speech). Although it seems counterintuitive to associate liberty with empire, Edward Rhodes demonstrates in his penetrating analysis of Bush's "grand strategy" that its crusading ambitions were profoundly imperial in nature.[99]

Some political theorists aver that imperialism is integral to liberal doctrine, coded into its core universalist principles. They argue that liberalism inherited from John Locke a legacy of excluding certain classes of peoples from political participation on the basis of their presumed incapacity for reason.[100] Like women at home, non-Western colonial subjects were often characterized by their British masters as the equivalent of children, incapable in their current condition of governing themselves. Because Americans have had less incentive to impose colonial rule over other peoples, they have had less recourse to such rhetoric, though it did inform their commentary on Filipinos and Haitians, among others, in the early part of the twentieth century. Its echo could be heard in May 2004 in the patronizing remarks President Bush made to Republican senators: it was time "to take the training wheels off" the Iraqi government.[101] This statement also affirmed, however, liberalism's promise that those who met its universalist standards would be welcomed as free and autonomous individuals.

No such promise is offered by the most extreme variant of exclusionism, racism, which insists instead on the irreducible otherness of its objects. Most empires face conflicting pressures to incorporate and differentiate subject populations, but these tensions have been particularly pronounced in liberal empires.[102] Thomas Metcalf has observed that British India experienced an "enduring tension between two ideals, one of similarity and the other of difference."[103] Even though Queen Victoria's 1858 proclamation establishing crown rule over India famously promised to treat Indians in an "equal and impartial" manner, many of her countrymen in India signally failed to keep that promise.[104] Racism was most pronounced in those colonies where white settlers competed with indigenous peoples and nonwhite immigrants for land, labor, and other resources. Here arose what Patrick Wolfe termed the "logic of elimination," which did so much to determine the fate of American Indians.[105] At the same time, American settlers' demand for African slave labor gave rise to an enduring system of institutionalized racism in the United States. Does this heritage make the American empire more racist than its British predecessor? Porter thinks so.[106] I was skeptical in the original version of this chapter, which appeared in 2007, and I took comfort in the election of the biracial Barack Obama as president of the United States a year later. But more recent events—the spate of police shootings of unarmed black men, the overtly racist campaign for president by Donald Trump, and more—have caused me to revise my views and acknowledge the merits of Porter's argument. This domestic heritage of racism has been reproduced in Americans' imperial adventures overseas, as manifested, for example, in the use of derogatory terms like "gooks" during the Vietnam War and "rag-heads" during the Gulf Wars. Such racial attitudes and actions have undermined America's claims for itself as the leading international agent of liberal principles.

One of the most striking features of the ideological and cultural forces that have shaped America's stance toward the world in recent years is the informal alliance of secular neoconservatives and evangelical Christians. Porter is one of the few commentators to note this curious convergence of interests. He sees the neoconservatives, among whom he detects the "resonances of fascism," and the evangelical right, whose views he considers to be marked by "madness," joining together to give US foreign policy a newly messianic character.[107] Porter treats this development as confirmation that America's imperial ambitions are at odds with the pragmatism of Britons. In fact, the ideological alliance resembles the one that formed in the early nineteenth century between the Utilitarians, rational secularists driven by the desire for radical social and political change, and Evangelicals, religious proponents of moral reform. Despite their differences, they found common ground in the determination to transform Indian society, introducing Western educational and legal institutions, abolishing sati (the burning of widows), and transforming other traditional practices deemed backward or morally reprehensible.[108] Were the neoconservatives' and Christian fundamentalists' designs on the Middle East all that different? In both cases, the ambitions of these improbable partners were both deeply idealistic and profoundly ethnocentric.

One further thread of continuity joins the British ideological rationale for empire with the arguments many Americans have made to justify the occupation of Afghanistan (though not Iraq). The British believed that the status of women in a society was one of the key indicators of where it stood on the ladder of civilization. Primitive societies oppressed women; civilized ones privileged them.[109] One of the most compelling moral arguments that the Bush administration made for the invasion of Afghanistan was that it would free Afghani women from the oppressive Taliban regime. (The argument gained far less purchase in Iraq, where the Baathist regime had been one of the most progressive in the region regarding women's rights.) But even if the US occupation has brought Afghani females greater opportunities for schooling, obstetric care, and other services, these achievements cannot be divorced from the brute force of empire. The connection was made chillingly clear in comments by Marine Corps General James "Mad Dog" Mattis (now secretary of defense for the Trump administration): "You go to Afghanistan, you got guys who slap women around for five years because they didn't wear a veil. You know, guys like that ain't got no manhood left anyway. So it's a hell of a lot of fun to shoot them."[110] Is there a better illustration of the bargains and tensions that underlie the imperial project?

* * *

The American empire was not the immaculate conception of those neoconservatives and their allies who controlled the country's foreign policy after the 2000 presidential election. The United States has exerted its awesome powers around the world in various ways for a very long time. In some respects, it has done so differently from empires in the past, but there has never been a universally recognized template for how empires should act. By comparing the American empire to the British Empire we can at least differentiate between the aspects of its experience that resemble its most important predecessor on the world stage and those that make it stand apart.

The United States has been a different kind of empire at different periods in its history, reflecting how its place in the world changed and collided with countervailing forces. What precipitated the debate over the past decade about America as an empire was the Bush administration's adoption of a posture and policies that differed significantly from those of its immediate predecessors. The differences can be characterized in terms of the distinction between "empire" and "imperialism."[111] The 9/11 attacks gave the Bush administration's neoconservatives the opportunity to unleash an ideological agenda that embraced the aggressive form of empire we call imperialism. War has always tended to encourage imperial ambitions: the "war against terrorism" is no different. The US government took a more unilateral stance in international relations, made more aggressive use of military power, and showed greater disregard for international law. The culmination of these developments was the 2003 invasion of Iraq, an unprovoked war against a sovereign state. If this is not imperialism of the sort the British practiced in their heyday, it is hard to know what is. The United States has been an empire for some time, but during the first decade of the twentieth century it became an empire that not only dared to speak its name, contra Ferguson, but pursued an imperial agenda with unabashed gusto.

8

The Means and Ends of Empires

I expand on some of the central issues raised in the previous chapter in this review essay on Julian Go's Patterns of Empire: The British and American Empires (2011), *the most rigorous analysis of the subject to date. It appeared as part of a roundtable on the book in* Comparative Studies of South Asia, Africa, and the Middle East *in 2014. While I endorse Go's argument that American claims of historical exceptionalism crumble in the face of comparison to the British experience, I question his insistence that the United States is following the same irreversible path of imperial decline that he purports to detect in the British case. The jury is still out, I believe, on America's future as an empire.*

In the summer of 2000 I moved to my present position at George Washington University, located in the heart of Washington, D.C. As a newcomer to the city, I was immediately struck by its imperial grandeur. The massive government buildings, museums, and monuments that lined its stately avenues in their colonnaded splendor proclaimed it to be a place of pageantry and power. What is more, certain influential voices were actively praising and promoting imperial ideas and policies at this time. Neoconservatives in particular were proclaiming that the United States was an empire and should act like one. When George W. Bush won the presidency in November, he staffed his foreign policy team with leading proponents of this view. The invasions of Afghanistan and Iraq soon followed, accompanied by boasts that the "shock and awe" of American power would cow the enemy and transform these countries—and, indeed, the regions they occupied—in our image.

The repercussions of these events on our perceptions of the United States' role in the world have been profound. We have been deluged over the past decade by books and articles about America as an empire.[1] Some have sought to cast the American empire in a positive light, though most have not. This is hardly the first time that overseas interventions by the United States have led to charges that it is an empire. As Paul Kramer has observed, commentaries on American imperialism have "crested during controversial wars, invasions, and occupations, and ebbed when projections of American power have receded from public view."[2] I came of age during the previous high-water mark for such commentaries, the Vietnam War. Like many of my generation, I considered the war an incontrovertible case of American imperialist aggression. In retrospect, I can see that my efforts to make sense of that war informed, if only obliquely, my decision to study British imperial history. Similarly, the recent resurgence of academic interest in the history of empires in general and the American empire in particular surely cannot be understood apart from the intellectual and emotional impact of the wars in Afghanistan and Iraq. Julian Go's stimulating comparative study of the American and British empires, *Patterns of Empire: The British and American Empires, 1688 to the Present*, openly acknowledges these associations, making clear that his purpose is to examine the past in order to illuminate the present. This is both the book's strength and its weakness.

* * *

Go states in the preface to *Patterns of Empire* that one of his main objectives is to overturn "a way of thinking called 'exceptionalism'," which considers the historical experience of the United States to be unique and informed by superior standards of governance and character.[3] Go's objections to this way of thinking are certainly not unprecedented: various historians have sought to challenge American exceptionalism in recent years.[4] Yet claims of exceptionalism remain a staple of public discourse, especially in the political arena, so we can be grateful to Go for contributing such a vigorous critique of this vainglorious myth. Moreover, Go's strategy for discrediting American exceptionalism—that is, by comparing the American pattern of global expansion to the British experience—allows him to show that even the influential body of work that William Appleman Williams and his fellow New Left historians produced on America's imperial past is unduly exceptionalist in its approach.[5]

By using the British Empire as the point of reference for America's imperial past and present, Go adopts an approach that, it should be acknowledged, has its own problematic heritage. British imperialists themselves were among the first to draw comparisons between their own empire and the one being forged by the United States, suggesting that the two peoples' common origins as Anglo-Saxons gave them a shared talent for ruling over others. With British power on the wane after the Second World War, its leaders became fond of comparing themselves to latter-day Greeks mentoring their Roman-like successors, the Americans.[6] This view has endured in the work of Niall Ferguson, Walter Russell Mead, and other conservative scholars, who have argued that the British–American imperial nexus has laid the foundations for globalization and the spread of democratic institutions.[7] Go rightly rejects that perspective. The most important contribution he makes to the debate about American imperialism is his examination of the means by which the United States expanded its territorial reach and became a global power, pointing to the ways it resembled Britain's imperial experience and diverged from it.

What is an empire and how does it work? As a historical sociologist, Go brings a definitional clarity and analytical rigor to these questions that is uncommon among historians. He declares at the start that he considers empires to be "sociopolitical formations that are constructed and maintained through the exercise of political power" over "a subordinate society, peoples, or space."[8] Colonialism, he stresses, is only one of the ways empires exercise this power, a point important to his argument that the United States has been and remains an empire. Yet he draws a distinction between empires and hegemons: the former exert political domination, the latter economic domination. It is possible, then, for an empire to lack economic hegemony and a hegemon to lack imperial power. For both Britain and the United States, hegemony and empire overlapped in certain periods, but not others. These shifts are central to Go's explanation of the trajectories taken by the British and American empires, accounting especially for fluctuations between periods of informal influence and periods of military conquest.

While the sociological orientation that Go brings to this study is advantageous in some respects, it is less so in others. It uses the terms "empire" and "hegemon" as heuristic categories that stand apart in certain respects from the distinctively modern historical processes within which the British and American experiences are so deeply embedded. The economic hegemony exercised by both countries at important points in their histories has to be understood as a function of the global capitalist system that came into being in recent centuries, not as a perennial phenomenon. This point, which is integral to the argument of Niall Ferguson, Go's bête noire, is largely overlooked in his own analysis. Go does a better job of historicizing the term "empire," though here too he suggests that the patterns he traces for the British and American cases comprise a "natural history" that is applicable to empires in general.[9] In this regard, the effort to undermine exceptionalist thinking is taken too far.

Yet when Go shifts his attention from transhistorical categories and patterns to the specific modalities of the two empires being compared, his work acquires great analytical force. It is easily the best comparative study of the British and American cases to date.[10] His examination of the successive stages of American territorial expansion is especially illuminating, compelling us to think anew about a subject we thought we already understood. "America's continental colonialism," he declares in one provocative passage, "was more imperial and authoritarian than

Britain's settler empire in theory, and it was even more so in practice."[11] He backs up this claim by pointing out that new territories acquired by the United States between 1784 and 1912 were under military or other modes of authoritarian rule for a cumulative 544 years prior to their incorporation as states, and even after statehood most nonwhite residents were long denied citizenship rights. As the United States expanded overseas at the turn of the century, it extended a system of authoritarian governance to some 2.5 million peoples in territories that were little more than colonies by another name. Given Go's previous work on the Philippines, it should not be surprising that his discussion of American rule over those islands convincingly challenges the conventional claim that it was more enlightened than British rule in India. Indeed, he shows that Americans employed much the same "logic of legitimation" as did the British in their respective strategies of colonial governance,[12] arguing that the particular social and economic circumstances they confronted on the ground had far more to do with those strategies than did the national character or ideological principles of the governing empire.

Finally, Go advances an interpretation of America's international role after the Second World War that stresses its parallels to Britain's position in the world through much of the nineteenth century. While acknowledging that the postwar political environment made it unrealistic for the United States to acquire formal colonies, Go simultaneously rejects both the conventional view that it renounced imperialism in favor of a new international order of nation-states *and* the revisionist view that it forged its own uniquely American brand of empire through an informal system of client states. Against the first view, he observes that the United States acquired Strategic Trust Territories in the Pacific after the war, "outsourced [some of] its aims to European allies" whose colonies it helped to restore and maintain, and retained control of Puerto Rico, Guam, Samoa, and the Virgin Islands, making it "probably the *only* colonial empire that has *not* decolonized."[13] And against the second view, he argues that the power America exerted over client states in the decades after the Second World War bears more than a passing resemblance to the informal empire the British established in the mid-Victorian era. In both cases, economic coercion, gunboat diplomacy, and other forms of imperial pressure were placed on states that remained ostensibly independent. In both cases, these exercises in informal imperialism were made possible by the hegemonic position that Britain and the United States attained in the global economy in the mid-nineteenth century and the post–Second World War era respectively. By turning to the British Empire for points of comparison, Go provides a bracing challenge to various versions of American exceptionalism.

It should be noted, however, that Go gives a fairly conventional account of the British Empire, one that relies mainly on old classics like the work of John Gallagher and Ronald Robinson. While I would have wished he had given greater attention to recent scholarship in the field, I think I understand why he does not do so. First, much of the new imperial history has taken a cultural turn that bears little relationship to the concerns of *Patterns of Empire*. Second, the strength of Go's analysis of the American case derives from the confidence that can be placed in the example against which it is compared. The traditional historiography of the British Empire serves this purpose far better than more recent, overtly revisionist scholarship. For Go, then, the history of the British Empire is merely the means by which he can reevaluate and reinterpret the American experience, not a subject that is itself scrutinized in a fresh way.

* * *

While *Patterns of Empire* excels in its analysis of the means by which empires exert their will on other places and peoples, it disappoints in its argument that empires follow similar trajectories to a common end. The decline of empires is addressed most directly in Chapter 5 of Go's book, but the issue looms over the entire book: it provides the moral of the story, the proof that America is currently in the throes of inexorable imperial decline. While some might wish this to be true, the case Go makes for it falls short both on evidentiary and interpretive grounds.

The evidentiary problems are clear in Go's discussions of both empires. In the British case, the curiously contradictory attention he gives to the relatively obscure invasion of Abyssinia in 1868 sharply exposes the strains in his larger argument about imperial decline. He initially introduces the Abyssinian war to illustrate his point that Britain at its hegemonic height avoided colonial commitments: it withdrew from that East African country after achieving military victory instead of claiming it as a colony.[14] But the Abyssinian case comes up again later in the book, and this time it is offered as evidence of "a radical turn" away from the informal imperialism it had exemplified earlier. Here Go focuses on Britain's initial decision to invade Abyssinia instead of its subsequent withdrawal. He attributes this decision to "the new imperialism," which was precipitated, he suggests, by the financial crisis of 1866, an event that he improbably credits for setting in motion "British economic decline."[15] His argument here is that Abyssinia is evidence of the reckless imperial adventurism that Britain pursued as it lost its hegemonic position in the world economy. The same event is thus employed in the service of contradictory claims.

It is the latter claim that seems the most strained. Go declares the invasion of Abyssinia to be "a critical turning point" for Britain's fortunes. A few pages later, the invasion of Egypt in 1882 is pronounced "a critical turning point" as well.[16] While his larger point is that both of these events are symptomatic of a deeper economic malaise, Go never satisfactorily explains when or why this malaise set in, nor does he make a convincing case that it resulted in irreversible decline. Britain had overcome major economic setbacks in the past—consider the "Hungry Forties"—and its financial fortunes would fluctuate a great deal from 1866 onward. Go's argument that economic troubles precipitated outbursts of imperial aggression certainly did not apply to the Hungry Forties nor would it do so during the greatest economic crisis Britain faced in the twentieth century, the Depression of the 1930s. Although Go earlier drew a sharp distinction between imperialism and hegemony, here he suggests that they are causally connected, with the empire enjoying economic hegemony at its height, but responding to its loss with acts of imperial aggression that signal a downward spiral.

Go's discussion of the decline of America's fortunes suffers from similar problems. Inconsistent claims and selective use of evidence mar his analysis of its apparent loss of hegemony. The 1973 oil crisis is presented as the key turning point, with America's subsequent standing in the global economy deteriorating inexorably. But does the evidence support his argument? Go points out that US labor productivity declined from 2.8 percent in the period 1948–73 to 1.2 percent in the period 1981–86, a precipitous drop that seems to portend dire economic problems. Yet the same Bureau of Labor Statistics data show that labor productivity increased to 2.2 percent in the 1990s and to 2.7 percent in 2000–07—a rate virtually identical to the productivity during America's presumed heyday as a hegemon.[17] (Even after the economic collapse of 2008, productivity only dropped to 1.9 percent, which is far better than the rate for the 1980s.) In other words, Go's selective use of labor productivity data leaves the misleading impression that the 1970s set in motion an inexorable decline in the economy, when in fact the figures for subsequent decades reveal quite a different story. A similar complaint can be lodged against Go's interpretation of data that show the United States' contribution to the world's gross production slid from about 50 percent in 1950 to 21 percent in 2002 and its contribution to manufacturing production fell from 60 percent in 1950 to 25 percent in 1999. He offers these figures as evidence that the country experienced a precipitous slide in its global position, but fails to note that in 1950 the great industrial centers of Europe and Asia were still reeling from the destruction of the Second World War. American statesmen and business leaders knew that their long-term economic interests rested in reducing these disparities by strengthening their trading partners through the Marshall Plan and other measures. Thus, the proportional decline in production over the last half of the twentieth century probably tells us less about America's standing in the global economy than the many other measures that indicate production and prosperity increased significantly in absolute terms.

Go also argues that economic decline led the United States to lash out in acts of military adventurism. He sees the invasion of Grenada in 1983 as "the beginning of America's new imperialism," similar to the significance he attaches to Britain's invasion of Abyssinia.[18] Yet the United States has been invading countries in the Caribbean (and other parts of the Americas) for well over a century, making it difficult to understand what makes the case of Grenada so different. To be sure, Go provides a chart showing that

US military interventions have spiked in the years since Grenada, but his argument that this increase can be attributed to economic decline ignores the fact that the American economy did not steadily deteriorate from the 1970s onward.[19] On the contrary, it improved markedly in the late 1980s and 1990s; yet his chart shows no decline in military interventions in those years. His interpretation allows for few other causal explanations, though the sudden collapse of the Soviet Union and its satellite states, the subsequent increase in political instability across Eastern Europe, Central Asia, and other regions, and the heightened sense of power on the part of American leaders, who proclaimed victory in the Cold War and asserted a New World Order, surely cannot be ignored. The neoconservatives most certainly didn't believe that the United States was a declining empire: they were convinced that the collapse of the Soviet Union had created a unipolar world, ripe for remaking by a resurgent America. Nor were they alone in holding such views: commentators of various stripes became convinced that America had become an unrivaled superpower or "hyperpower" with geopolitical interests and moral obligations around the globe. Far from having harbored forebodings of imperial decline, recent American administrations appear instead to have been inspired in their military adventurism by a sense of imperial hubris.

In making his case that the United States has entered the same phase of imperial decline that Britain reached, by his reckoning, in the late nineteenth century, Go skirts awfully close to a determinist teleology. He is overly preoccupied with "turning points" that lead inexorably from one stage to another. He too readily equates an empire to an organic entity that passes through life cycles: it initially exhibits "youthful imperial aggression," then a confident hegemonic maturity, followed by decline and desperation, becoming "an aging empire watching dreadfully as rivals threaten to take their slice of the pie."[20] I think Go would have benefited from reading more widely in recent scholarship on the British Empire, which has shown that its decline from the late nineteenth century onward was hardly as uninterrupted and ineluctable as he suggests. Even John Gallagher rejected such determinism in his Ford lectures, posthumously published as the aptly titled *The Decline, Revival, and Fall of the British Empire*.[21] A broad consensus now exists among historians of the British Empire that Joseph Chamberlain's "weary titan" revived and reasserted itself as a global power at several points in the first half of the twentieth century. If Britain's decline was so circuitous, how much confidence can be placed in the claim that America has entered its twilight years?

* * *

The preoccupation with imperial decline has a long intellectual lineage. Edward Gibbon wrote his immensely influential *Decline and Fall of the Roman Empire* in the shadow of the American Revolution, with its seemingly dire consequences for the British Empire. Rome's fate became a cautionary tale for generations of British leaders. As David Cannadine has pointed out, Joseph Chamberlain, Winston Churchill, and Margaret Thatcher all spoke the same "doom-laden language" about the future of Britain, though each of them believed the key moment of crisis was contemporary with their own political careers.[22] Nor have Americans been immune to anxieties about decline. Nearly thirty years ago Paul Kennedy warned in his bestselling tome, *The Rise and Fall of the Great Powers*, that America's days as a great power (the term *empire* not being in vogue when he wrote) were numbered.[23] The book sparked an anguished national debate about the country's future. At the time, the Soviet Union was still the United States' greatest geopolitical rival, while Japan had become a seemingly unstoppable economic juggernaut. Today, of course, Islamic terrorists and China have assumed the roles that the Soviet Union and Japan once played in the fevered dreams of America's doom-mongers.

I do not mean to suggest that those who insist that the American empire is in the throes of inexorable decline are demonstrably wrong. I simply offer a note of caution about the difficulty of differentiating temporary setbacks from lasting losses, especially without the benefit of hindsight. Empires can recover and remake themselves, as did the British Empire after 1776. When I walk through Washington these days, I see a city that in certain respects has become fearful and defensive, with public buildings ringed by barriers of bollards, secret agencies forging a national security state of unprecedented scale and penetrative capacity, and a new president promising to build walls, expel illegal immigrants, and keep out Muslims. But I also see a thriving and confident city, its skyline dotted with construction cranes, its lobbyists and think tanks and NGOs abuzz with ambitions and ideas, and its government as determined as ever to exert its will on the lives of peoples around the world.

9

The Imperial History Wars

As its title suggests, this chapter draws together some of the central themes that run through the book. It asks how British imperial history made the transition from an increasingly marginalized, shrinking field of study in the 1970s to the vibrant, vigorously contested subject of inquiry it has become in recent years. It argues that this historiographical revival needs to be placed in the context of the broader social, political, and ideological forces that were at work during these decades, especially in Britain and the United States, the two academic centers of imperial history. The chapter originated as a presidential address to the North American Conference of British Studies in 2013, which was published in 2015 in The Journal of Imperial History.

It has become all but impossible for historians who study modern Britain to ignore its empire. The field has been swamped in recent years by a seemingly endless stream of books, articles, conferences, and other scholarly expressions of this preoccupation with Britain's imperial past. Although plenty of British historians still steadfastly resist the siren song of empire, they have seen countless others succumb to its appeal. Consider, for example, how many well-known historians who made their reputations with work on British domestic history have subsequently taken the "imperial turn."[1] Their change of direction is indicative of the way the boundaries of British historiography, and, indeed, British studies more generally, have broadened over the past two decades to incorporate Britain's engagement in empire. This is a striking, even surprising, development, yet the reasons for it have rarely been examined. Why should an empire that for all practical purposes disappeared some fifty years ago retain such a powerful hold over our imaginations? Or, to put it more precisely, why should our collective interest in that empire have increased rather than decreased even though it has receded ever further into the past?

In order to answer these questions we need to direct our attention to the circumstances that have given rise to this growing body of scholarship: in other words, its conditions of production. These conditions operate at several distinct levels of effect. The first and most familiar level consists of the analytical, methodological, and theoretical considerations that inform our practices as historians. A great deal of attention has been devoted to this dimension of the imperial turn. One need only examine the review essays that so frequently assess the latest scholarship in the field to gain an appreciation of its ever-widening range of concerns.[2] Far less attention has been paid to a second level of effect: the role that social and ideological forces play in shaping the questions we pose and the answers we offer about imperial Britain. This requires greater reflexivity about our own subject positions than we are inclined as professional historians to address. The same can be said for the third level of effect, which concerns the geopolitical locations from which we work and write.[3] While the renewed interest in the imperial dimensions of British history occurred on both sides of the Atlantic, it took a discernibly different trajectory among US-based historians than it did among their UK-based counterparts. The aim of this chapter is to offer a preliminary and decidedly personal assessment of the circumstances—especially those at the second and third level of effect—that have brought the empire to such prominence in modern British historiography.

At the heart of this assessment lies the argument that the renewed attention historians have given to empire is inextricably entwined with contemporary public debates about certain highly contentious social and political issues that have arisen both in Britain and in the United States. Contending interpretations of Britain's imperial past and the meanings it carries for our current condition have figured prominently in these debates. By characterizing them as "the imperial history wars," I am evoking a phrase that has been widely used in recent years with respect to controversies about the memories and meanings we attach to our collective pasts.[4] All of these wars highlight the polemical power of history and the complex array of politically and morally freighted meanings that inform its practice. When academic historians venture into such contested terrain, we have an obligation to reflect on our own subjectivities and their role in shaping our understandings of the past.

* * *

In 1984 the Cambridge historian David Fieldhouse published an influential article that decried what he saw as the disintegration of British imperial history as a distinct and coherent field of study. It had shattered, he argued, into a series of separate nationalist histories, each intended to promote the interests of the new nation-states that had arisen out of the process of decolonization. He wondered, "Can Humpty-Dumpty be put together again?" That same year, the Yale historian Robin Winks reached a similar conclusion about imperial history's health in a historiographical essay that characterized it as the "Problem Child of British History." Nearly a decade later, Phillip Buckner lamented its passing in his presidential address to the Canadian Historical Association, which he titled, "Whatever Happened to the British Empire?" Each of these authorities regarded British imperial history as a field that was dying, if not dead.[5]

My own experience upon entering academia as a newly minted PhD in 1981 seemed to confirm these gloomy assessments. In American universities, at least, history departments had ceased hiring specialists in British imperial history. The job situation in Britain was obviously far less dire, both because British imperial history was, after all, an integral part of Britain's own history, though a largely marginalized one, and because it had become institutionally embedded in some of the country's leading universities as a result of the founding many decades earlier of endowed professorships in the field.[6] From an American perspective, then, conditions seemed much healthier across the Atlantic. Yet that was clearly not the view of Fieldhouse, who raised the alarm from the privileged precincts of Cambridge, where he was the Vere Harmsworth Professor of Naval and Imperial History.

The crisis that confronted imperial history in the 1970s and 1980s had several distinct sources. One was the growing appreciation that African, Asian, and other ex-colonial peoples had histories of their own that simply could not be subsumed within British imperial history. As Fieldhouse pointed out, this was due in part to pressure from postcolonial countries to claim their own national histories. But it was also driven by developments in the West, especially in the United States, where the geopolitical imperatives of the Cold War had generated an unprecedented demand for experts in the languages, cultures, and traditions of these ex-colonial territories. The area studies programs that arose to meet this demand provided much of the impetus for those newly developed fields of history (African, Indian, etc.) that began to crowd out the old imperial history. A second factor was the enormous sway that domestic social history of the sort practiced by the great E. P. Thompson exerted among British historians. For history departments seeking specialists whose work was considered cutting-edge, it was those individuals who did British—or more precisely English—"history from below," especially as it pertained to class, who most often fit the bill. Imperial historians, by contrast, seemed to be stuck in an intellectual and methodological time warp. Most of them continued to draw their main intellectual inspiration from John Gallagher and Ronald Robinson, the Oxbridge historians whose key coauthored works had appeared as the British Empire was disintegrating in the late 1950s and early 1960s. For Gallagher and Robinson, the crucial factors that informed how the imperial system worked were the strategic considerations of the British governing elite ("the official mind"), the use of economic coercion and gunboat diplomacy to maintain a vast "informal empire," the collapse of cooperative non-Western regimes ("breakdowns on the periphery") that provoked military intervention and direct imperial rule, and the cultivation of indigenous "collaborators" to assist in the governance of colonial territories. The impact of their ideas resembled the black holes posited by physicists: they created such an overpowering gravitational field that a generation or more of imperial historians were sucked into their vortex. Dissertation after dissertation, article after article, book after book entered the void, emitting ever weakening signals that echoed snatches of Gallagher and Robinson's golden oldies—"informal empire," "the official mind," and the like.[7]

A few imperial historians did, to be sure, manage to make productive use of Gallagher and Robinson's work even while advancing new lines of inquiry. Peter Cain and A. G. Hopkins embraced the notion of informal empire in *British Imperialism 1688-2000*, but it was their thesis that the financial concerns of "gentlemanly capitalists" comprised the real engine of empire—an interpretation that shifted the focus from the colonial periphery to the imperial metropolis and from political and strategic factors to financial and social ones—that garnered the greatest interest.[8] An occasional imperial historian succeeded in escaping Gallagher and Robinson's gravitational pull altogether. Perhaps the most notable example was John MacKenzie, whose graduate training in Canada and early fieldwork in southern Africa launched him into a distinctly different orbit, one that resulted in a series of important books on British imperial history as well as the influential and still-vibrant Studies in Imperialism series, which he founded at Manchester University Press in 1984—the very same year, it should be noted, that Fieldhouse and Winks were lamenting the field's sorry state of affairs.[9]

What is most striking, however, is how much of the freshest, most innovative work on the British imperial past at this time came from scholars trained in other fields and disciplines. It turned out that the Africanists, South Asianists, Caribbeanists, and other area studies specialists whose divergent pursuits seemed so destructive to imperial history, at least as its metropolitan-based practitioners understood it, were actually forging new frameworks for thinking about empire as a whole, as the work of C. A. Bayly, Timothy Parsons, and others amply demonstrate.[10] So too were literary scholars like Edward Said and Homi Bhabha, historical anthropologists like Bernard Cohn and Ann Laura Stoler, feminist historians like Antoinette Burton and Catherine Hall, and others whose unconventional vantage points gave them new insights into British imperial history. They soon began to overrun the field as it was defined and defended by the likes of Fieldhouse and Winks. They brought to the study of imperialism a theoretical perspective inflected by poststructuralist and postcolonial thought, a cultural preoccupation with issues such as race and gender, and a political determination to demonstrate that modern Britain itself had been shaped in profoundly important ways by its empire.[11]

These invaders of imperial history's domains marched under two main banners—postcolonial studies and the new imperial history. Edward Said led the former contingent with *Orientalism*, his strikingly original mélange of literature, history, and polemic, which appeared in 1978.[12] Like many of my fellow historians of empire, I was slow to recognize the significance of this book. But it became impossible to ignore as the school of postcolonial studies it did so much to spawn produced a steady stream of scholarly provocations regarding imperial culture from its breeding grounds in literature departments and cultural studies programs. Most mainstream historians of the British Empire responded to the work of Said and his allies with hostility, finding their terminology and theory baffling and their historical claims simplistic, if not simply erroneous. Yet postcolonial studies offered a perspective on the imperial past that attracted a growing number of proponents, not least because of the explicit associations it drew between the past and the present. By arguing that the discursive dimensions of imperial power—its ability to impose its own conceptual categories and systems of meaning on other societies—had not disappeared with decolonization, but had endured in contemporary attitudes and actions, it attached a relevance to the study of empire that had largely disappeared from the work of imperial historians. This was an important reason why Said's *Orientalism* enjoyed such success: it insisted that the ideologies that had informed European empires' projections of power over the peoples of the Middle East remained alive in contemporary American and European attitudes toward Palestinians and other Arabs.

Current preoccupations informed the new imperial history as well. Although no single individual looms as large in its genesis as Said does for postcolonial studies, its early advocates shared the conviction that conventional narratives of British history as a self-contained "island story" failed to acknowledge the manifold ways empire had shaped its course and character. If "Europe was made by its imperial projects," as Ann Laura Stoler and Frederick Cooper asserted in a widely cited essay, then surely no European country was more fully and profoundly made by these projects than Britain.[13] It seems clear in retrospect that this newfound conviction that Britain's relationship with its empire was mutually constitutive drew much of its inspiration from contemporaneous political and social developments. The Thatcher government's skillful appeal to British nationalist pride and imperial nostalgia during the 1982 Falklands War, for example, provided the essential backdrop to John MacKenzie's *Propaganda and Empire: The Manipulation of British Public Opinion, 1880-1960*, which was published two years after the war.[14] This book was an important landmark in the effort to understand the empire's impact on Britain itself, a theme that would become integral to the new imperial history. Yet most of the new imperial historians were less interested in the manipulation of the British electorate by governmental elites than they were in the infiltration of colonial peoples, products, and customs into British society and popular culture. They were responding in part to the social and cultural changes they observed around them. In Britain itself, one of the most striking developments was the growing number of residents who hailed from the West Indies, South Asia, East Africa, and other ex-colonial territories. Their highly visible markers of difference stirred ethnic anxieties within the majority white population and led to increasingly tight restrictions on further immigration from the same regions. Making sense of these developments demanded a deeper understanding of the imperial origins of this pool of immigrants *and* the imperial attitudes that informed white Britons' reactions. If class had been the master category of modern British history through the 1970s, thereafter it increasingly turned to issues of race and ethnicity.

Since the problem of race in particular had long loomed larger in American society—and hence in American social theory—than it had in Britain, it is hardly surprising that American scholars were quicker than their British counterparts to take up the new imperial history, with its insistence that racial difference lay at the heart of the relationship between metropole and colony. A related impetus for the revival of academic interest in British imperial history in the United States was the growing conviction that students needed to know more about the growing ethnic diversity within American society (coded as multiculturalism) and about America's growing engagement with the wider world (coded as globalization). In response, the Western Civilization survey was gradually supplanted by world history as a gateway course in the curricula of American high schools and colleges, a trend that has placed world history second only to US history as a core history requirement today.[15] While this development eroded the standing of domestic British historians, whose bread-and-butter course had been Western Civilization, it became a boon for specialists in British imperial history, who could claim that their transnational or global perspective made them particularly well qualified to teach world history.[16] That was certainly my experience: I was the first member of my department to teach world history both at the University of Nebraska-Lincoln, where I was a faculty member till 2000, and subsequently at my present institution, George Washington University. I also was a member of the committee that drafted the NACBS Report on the State and Future of British Studies (1999), chaired by Peter Stansky, which argued that one way to limit the loss of British history positions in American colleges and universities was to promote British imperial history as useful preparation for teaching world history.[17]

The publication in 1998–99 of the five-volume *Oxford History of the British Empire* seemed to confirm the revival of interest in Britain's imperial past. The series bore the canonical banner of "The Oxford History" and included a multitude of contributors. It was clearly meant to be the authoritative word on the subject, designed to define the boundaries of imperial history as a field of study and set the terms of its research agenda for decades to come. This was evident in the revealing pronouncement made by editor in chief Wm. Roger Louis in his preface to the series. He declared that "the passions aroused by British imperialism have so lessened that we are now better placed than ever before to see the course of the Empire steadily and to see it whole."[18]

This suggestion that historians of the empire had reached some sort of consensus about their subject was, at best, wishful thinking. Reactions to the *Oxford History of the British Empire* exposed the fissures within the field that it had sought to transcend, or at least paper over. Reviewers sympathetic to the new imperial history, such as myself, noted with dismay that most of the contributors came from a common Oxbridge-trained cohort that still looked to Gallagher and Robinson as their intellectual lodestar.[19] Louis's own lengthy survey of British imperial historiography, written as an introduction to the volume devoted to that subject, concluded with an encomium to the accomplishments of Gallagher and Robinson.[20] It was not unreasonable for readers to infer that Louis viewed the scholarship that had followed in their wake as little more than embellishments to the grand edifice they had built. Key contributors to the *Oxford History* found time to snipe at postcolonial theorists and other interlopers, but the series as a whole was largely silent on issues such as race, gender, and culture, which had been central to some of the most innovative work on the British imperial experience in recent years. Not all of the series' many contributors, it should be said, toed the party line. And Louis, to his credit, responded to the complaints of his critics by launching the Companion Series to the Oxford History, which published volumes on *Gender and Empire*, *The Black Experience and the Empire*, and other subjects that had received little attention in the original series.[21]

Far from imposing a stultifying orthodoxy on the field, then, the *Oxford History* had the opposite effect, generating a productive, if often contentious, debate about the aims and ends of imperial history. That debate would soon take historians down a number of different paths, sparking productive inquiries into imperial networks, settler colonialism, liberal imperialism, "the British world," and other topics too rich and varied to consider here. Some imperial historians, it should be noted, continued to preach the gospel of Gallagher and Robinson. Only recently a leading disciple proclaimed that their "brilliant historical insights remain the point of departure for most *serious* work on the history of empire."[22] But for those of us who identified with one or another variant of the new imperial history, it seemed increasingly evident that the intellectual logjam left by Gallagher and Robinson had begun to break up and the flow of ideas had turned in our favor. We were heartened by the reorientation of imperial studies from politics to cultures, from institutions to identities, from the intentions of imperial elites ("the official mind") to the experiences of colonial subjects ("subalterns" in all their variety). We were emboldened by a sense of intellectual purpose, though it no doubt seemed smugly self-righteous to others. We believed we were grappling with issues integral to the making of the British Empire and the British nation alike, issues such as race, gender, sexuality, religion, and other categories of difference. And we were confident that our work had relevance, contributing to a keener appreciation of the enduring legacy of the imperial past.

* * *

Yet even as we were laying claim to our kingdom, the ground was shifting beneath our feet. We had barely begun to supplant old orthodoxies with our own when a new set of challenges arose. The cultural turn that gave rise to postcolonial studies and the new imperial history is often associated with the collapse of Marxist theory, which appeared discredited by the disintegration of the Soviet Union and China's turn to capitalism. These geopolitical developments had a complementary consequence, however. They left the United States as the world's sole superpower, seemingly unbound in its global sway. Secretary of State Madeleine Albright famously proclaimed America to be the "indispensable nation." France's foreign minister coined a new term to describe this unprecedented state of affairs: the United States, he declared, had become a "hyperpower."[23] Insofar as the past provided any parallel to this moment of unrivaled supremacy, mid-nineteenth-century Britain appeared to come closest to matching America's hegemonic sway. Various commentators began to argue that the time had come for the United States to acknowledge and embrace its imperial destiny, to accept its role as imperial Britain's heir, to complete its mission to promote liberal—or rather neoliberal—policies around the globe.[24]

Some of the most forceful proponents of this view were neoconservatives like William Kristol and Paul Wolfowitz, who—as we now know—used 9/11 as a pretext to aggressively assert American military power by invading Afghanistan and Iraq, where "shock and awe" were put on theatrical display. Although neoconservatives led the charge, plenty of liberals agreed that the United States had an obligation to fix "failed states" and build democratic institutions. Michael Ignatieff, then a Harvard professor, later the leader of the Liberal Party of Canada, advocated "empire lite," a view shared by the influential *New York Times* columnist Thomas Friedman and various other self-styled liberals.[25] Since both Afghanistan and Iraq had been under Britain's imperial sway in the past, and Britain was now America's key partner in these foreign wars, it is hardly surprising that the British imperial experience became a point of reference for current events. General David Petraeus and other military commanders turned to T. E. Lawrence, whose reflections on the desert campaign in Arabia during the First World War were mined for insights into what came to be known as asymmetric warfare. Commentators from across the political spectrum wrote op-eds and other instant assessments that drew widely divergent lessons from the British colonial presence in Afghanistan and Iraq. Academics quickly organized conferences to this end: the proceedings from one of them were published under the bluntly didactic title *Lessons of Empire*.[26]

Niall Ferguson, celebrity historian and celebrant of empire, became the most visible and self-confident diviner of such lessons. Gifted, hard-working, and pugnacious, Ferguson forcefully advanced a historical argument in support of those who advocated more aggressive use of American power around the world. In his book *Empire: The Rise and Demise of the British World Order and the Lessons for Global Power*, he made the case that the British Empire had been a "good thing" because it had established the institutional order necessary for international trade to thrive and prosperity to spread, resulting in what he cleverly called "anglobalization."[27] Ferguson's book became a bestseller, and the TV series it was written to accompany ensured its message reached an even larger audience when it was broadcast in Britain.[28] It did not much matter that specialists in British imperial history found his analysis seriously flawed: Ferguson was invited to contribute op-eds and articles to leading American newspapers and magazines and to consult with US government officials. And lest anyone had failed to grasp the contemporary implications of his historical lesson, a year later he followed up his book on the British Empire with one on its American successor: *Colossus: The Price of America's Empire*. Here he argued that the United States had always been an empire, albeit one that was reluctant to admit its nature.[29]

He had a point. Despite the neoconservatives' insistence that Americans should accept the fact that their country was an empire and embrace its obligations, the term retained negative connotations for most Americans. Patrick Buchanan, a leading spokesman for isolationist, xenophobic conservatives (disdainfully called "paleoconservatives" by their critics), believed that empire was inextricably associated with decadent European traditions of statecraft. In a book written in part as a riposte to the neoconservatives, he insisted that America was, as its title declared, *A Republic, Not an Empire*.[30] Liberal interventionists were uneasy about calling the United States an empire as well. Ignatieff's diffident endorsement of "empire lite" seemed as far as any of them were willing to go down that rhetorical road. While at odds with paleoconservatives in most other respects, liberal interventionists shared their belief in American exceptionalism, including its exception from the temptations of empire. Even the neoconservatives began to retreat from their previous praise of empire as America's destiny once the military campaigns in Afghanistan and Iraq turned into bloody quagmires.[31] In fact, the only group that never wavered from the view that the United States was an empire was a small, largely marginalized contingent of leftist critics like Noam Chomsky, and for them the term empire had always carried negative, accusatory associations.

Although Ferguson made only limited headway in his efforts to draw a direct association between the British Empire at its height and the modern American "colossus"—or even, for that matter, to establish their moral equivalency as "good things"—his provocation was soon followed by a plethora of comparative studies of empires that commented directly on the contemporary global reach of the United States. The British imperial historian Bernard Porter agreed with Ferguson that the United States was an empire, but argued that its power and ambition far surpassed that of the British Empire. In his estimation, this was decidedly not a good thing.[32] The historical sociologist Julian Go, by contrast, insisted that the American empire fit the mold of the British Empire and faced the same fate—inexorable decline.[33] The modern European historian Charles Maier was more wide-ranging in his comparisons and cautious in his conclusions. The United States, he stated, "reveals many, but not all—at least not yet—of the traits that have distinguished empires."[34] Timothy Parsons, a historian of modern Africa and British imperialism, was far less reticent, concluding in *The Rule of Empires*, a comparative study of Roman, Spanish, British, and other imperial regimes, that the United States cannot be classified as an empire.[35] A far cruder version of the same view came from Kimberly Kagan, a military historian who served as an advisor to General Petraeus in Afghanistan, who argued that the United States was not an empire for the simple—or dare one say simplistic—reason that its leaders did not declare it to be an empire.[36]

In addition to historians, polemicists with political axes to grind turned their attention to the British Empire, using its example to promote their views on America's role in the international arena. Consider *The Politically Incorrect Guide to the British Empire*, a mind-bending romp through British imperial history by the neoconservative journalist W. H. Crocker III. Like Ferguson, Crocker insisted that the British Empire "was incontestably a good thing." He assured his readers that American colonists did not break away from Britain because they objected to empire; on the contrary, they were "motivated by the British Empire not being imperialist enough," a deficiency that he argues the new republic did its best to rectify. Eager to live up to the promise of his title, Crocker offered an abundant array of outrageous claims, some of which deserve quotation. He stated that it was "easy to see why the English, when not regarding [the Irish] as comical, tended to see them as shiftless, ignorant, stubborn, contumacious, and cruel"; after all, they were "shockingly lacking in moral scruple." He praised Brig. Gen. Reginald Dyer, the man responsible for the massacre of hundreds of Indians at Amritsar in 1919, as "a hero of the old school . . . a man who stood by the British imperial principles of justice, fair play, and decency."[37] In a *Washington Times* article glossing the book, Crocker acknowledged that his aim was to persuade Americans, though presumably not those of Irish or Indian heritage, to emulate the British and take up the white man's burden.[38]

A curious postscript to this infatuation with empire and demonization of those critical of it came with the release of the film *2016: Obama's America* during the 2012 presidential campaign. Adapted by the conservative author Dinesh D'Souza from his book *The Roots of Obama's Rage*, the movie argued that Obama's career in politics has been motivated first and foremost by the "anti-colonial beliefs" of his Kenyan grandfather and father. D'Souza characterized them as active supporters of the Mau Mau rebellion against British rule (an unsubstantiated claim that ignores the fact that Obama's paternal forbearers were Luo from western Kenya, whereas the Mau Mau rebellion was instigated by and largely limited to the Kikuyu people in Kenya's central highlands.) The film starts with what many Conservatives considered a nearly sacrilegious act by Obama shortly after his inauguration—his decision to return to the British Embassy the bust of Winston Churchill that had graced his predecessor's desk in the Oval Office. D'Souza interpreted this action as a sign of Obama's desire to wreak revenge on the West for its exploitation of colonial peoples. The president, he asserted, secretly considers the United States "the most evil nation in the world," and is determined to undermine its power and prestige.[39] *2016: Obama's America* became the most successful documentary film released in 2012 and the paranoid suspicions it voiced were echoed by several prominent Republicans. Mike Huckabee, a conservative talk show host, past presidential candidate, and ex-governor of Arkansas, worried that Obama "probably grew up hearing that the British were a bunch of imperialists who persecuted his grandfather."[40] Newt Gingrich, a contender for the Republican presidential nomination in 2012 and a past Speaker of the House of Representatives, declared that the only way to understand Obama's agenda was to place it in the context of "Kenyan anti-colonial behavior."[41] As an ex-college history professor who had written his dissertation on the Belgian Congo, Gingrich was hardly ignorant of what had happened in colonial Kenya, which makes his remarks especially cynical and opportunistic. But they were indicative of broader efforts to mobilize the British imperial past to advance an agenda that had its impetus in modern American racial politics.

* * *

If the British Empire has been meaningful in the American context mainly by way of analogy to America's standing as the sole superpower in the aftermath of the Cold War and as a means of giving coded expression to the country's anxieties about race, it has assumed a very different valence in contemporary British discourse. Here it has taken on importance not only in terms of contending memories of the imperial past and divergent interpretations of its meaning, but also in terms of debates about the future of the British nation itself.[42]

American neoconservative and liberal interventionists found a kindred spirit at the beginning of the new century in Britain's prime minister, Tony Blair. He and his chief foreign policy advisor, Robert Cooper, had been keen to adopt an assertive foreign policy from the moment Blair took office. Cooper publicly advocated what he called the "new liberal imperialism."[43]

For Blair, it was a small step from pressing for NATO intervention in Kosovo in 1998 and sending troops to war-ravaged Sierra Leone in 2000 to committing his country to the campaigns in Afghanistan and Iraq.[44] And as was the case in the United States, these military missions soon generated an intense public debate about the nature and purposes of empire, though this debate had more to do with the empire Britain had lost than the one the United States had gained.

As Blair saw it, the problem with the British was that they had lost their sense of pride in their imperial past. The British Empire, he insisted, should cause "neither apology nor hand-wringing."[45] Gordon Brown voiced similar sentiments, telling a Tanzanian audience that "the days of Britain having to apologize for its colonial history are over. . . . We should celebrate . . . our past rather than apologize for it."[46] The subsequent Conservative-led coalition government was equally vocal in urging Britons to take pride in their imperial heritage. David Cameron stirred the faithful at the Conservative Party conference in 2011 when he proclaimed that "Britannia didn't rule the waves with her armbands on." He also announced his intention to restore the British Empire Medal, which had been abolished nearly twenty years earlier.[47] Foreign Minister William Hague declared: "We have to get out of this post-colonial guilt."[48] And Education Secretary Michael Gove insisted that schools need to teach their pupils to "take pride" in Britain's empire, "celebrating" its achievements.[49] To this end, he invited the ubiquitous Niall Ferguson to help revamp the British history curriculum.

Ferguson's grand idea was to use video war games and TV programs to teach history to students—with his own series on the British Empire presumably on the syllabus.[50] By 2012, a new documentary series about Britain's imperial past was being aired on British TV, this one a BBC production with "Newsnight" interviewer Jeremy Paxman, who guided his viewers through "amazing stories of adventure." "It's nothing short of a scandal," Paxman scolded, "that this history is not taught in schools." The purpose of the series, he explained, was to refute "the conventional view" that the British Empire "was A Thoroughly Bad Thing."[51] (The TV personality and naturalist Sir David Attenborough apparently did not get the memo: he complained that Paxman was "far too negative about the British Empire.")[52] Other prominent figures who felt that the public needed to be reeducated about the virtues of the British Empire and the achievements of its heroes were the popular historians Andrew Roberts, Lawrence James, and Max Hastings. The biographer Tim Jeal wrote a book about Henry Morton Stanley that declared him to be "Africa's greatest explorer" and dismissed charges that he had massacred Africans during his expeditions or that he bore any responsibility for the brutal regime King Leopold instituted in the Congo.[53] Jeal became one of the leading proponents of a controversial campaign to erect a statue honoring Stanley at his place of birth, the Welsh town of Denbigh. As Jeal saw it, the time had come to dispense with "post-imperial guilt."[54]

For Jeal and those who shared his views, this call to arms was fueled in part by resentment at what he dismissed as the "moral Brownie points" politicians and others sought to accrue by "well-publicised 'apologies' for 'crimes' committed by earlier generations."[55] He was no doubt alluding to Tony Blair's apologies for Britain's role in the African slave trade and the Irish potato famine, Gordon Brown's apology for the export of child migrants to Australia and other colonies, and David Cameron's apology for the Bloody Sunday massacre in Londonderry. During a visit to India, Cameron also conceded that the British bore some blame for the conflict over Kashmir and expressed regret—what the *Washington Post* called a "near-apology"—for the Amritsar massacre of 1919.[56] Thus, even as Blair and his successors were urging the British to take pride in their imperial past, they were also doing a lot of apologizing for it.

There were those, of course, who thought the British had a lot to apologize for. Paxman's complaint that the empire is often portrayed as "A Thoroughly Bad Thing" does contain a kernel of truth: some authors have been no less strident in their moral condemnation of the British Empire than others have been in praising its virtues. Take, for example, John Newsinger's *The Blood Never Dried: A People's History of the British Empire*—its title tells you pretty much all you need to know about the book's contents.[57] A more recent and widely reviewed condemnation of the violence perpetrated by the British against the peoples they conquered comes from Richard Gott, the veteran left-wing journalist and *Guardian* columnist, in his book *Britain's Empire*. Gott's stated aim was to counter the "tendency to view the imperial experience through the rose-tinted spectacles of heritage culture" by demonstrating that the empire was "the fruit of military conquest and of brutal wars."[58] What follows that declaration of intent are nearly 500 pages that describe in gory yet monotonous detail the awful violence the British inflicted on the peoples they conquered and whose rebellions they suppressed. And Gott only takes his story to 1858!

More nuanced assessments of the British imperial legacy have come from two historians who served in Parliament, where politician and intellectual seem less contradictory terms than they do in the US Congress. Tristram Hunt, until recently the Labour Party's shadow secretary of state for education and a senior lecturer at Queen Mary, University of London, published *Ten Cities That Made an Empire*. Stressing the culturally hybrid character of imperial cities, Hunt makes the case that this hybridity has been a key source of economic productivity and social achievement. The intended significance of his study for the challenges confronted by contemporary Britain, especially with regard to immigration, ethnicity, and cultural diversity, is not difficult to discern. Kwasi Kwarteng, an up-and-coming Conservative MP who is the son of African immigrants from Ghana and holds a PhD in history from Cambridge, has written the widely reviewed *Ghosts of Empire*, which attracted added attention because of its author's unusual background. Kwarteng advances an argument that places emphasis on the social origins of the colonial administrators, making a case that most of them came from old landed families whose hereditary elite status imbued them with autocratic, anti-modern sensibilities starkly at odds with the liberal principles that the British professed to be promoting among their colonial subjects. Their misguided policies, he argues, left a legacy of disorder in lands as varied as Burma, Iraq, Sudan, and Nigeria. Kwarteng takes direct aim at Niall Ferguson, arguing that the "British Empire is a bizarre model to follow for fostering stability in today's world" because it "openly repudiated ideas of human equality and put power and responsibility into the hands of a chosen elite . . . [that] was anti-democratic."[59] His critique spotlights a question that has attracted a great deal of attention from historians and other scholars in recent years: how was it possible for a country that took such pride in its liberal values and institutions to simultaneously impose a system of autocratic and oppressive rule over a quarter of the world's population in the nineteenth and early twentieth centuries?[60]

Nothing has brought these contradictions between liberal ideals and imperial practice to the attention of the British government and public with greater force in recent years than the outcome of the legal case that four elderly Kenyans filed against the British government. They sought damages for the torture that colonial authorities had inflicted on them as internees during the Mau Mau rebellion in the 1950s. A lawsuit that at first seemed doomed to failure took an unexpected turn when the London High Court ruled in 2012 that the plaintiffs had legal standing to sue the British government. This decision sent shockwaves through Whitehall and compelled authorities to negotiate an out-of-court settlement that promised £20 million in compensation to the four plaintiffs and 5,225 other surviving Kenyans whose abuse at the hands of colonial authorities could be documented.

What turned the case in the Kenyans' favor was the stunning revelation that a vast cache of politically explosive documents about the Mau Mau rebellion and other late-colonial crises had been deposited during the retreat from empire in Hanslope Park, the government's signals intelligence center, where they had remained hidden for the past fifty years. After repeated denials, authorities were forced to acknowledge the existence of the secret archive and grant the Kenyan plaintiffs' legal team access to relevant files, which provided incontrovertible evidence that torture and other crimes had been sanctioned at the highest levels of the British government. This disclosure destroyed the government's case. It also discomfited some celebrants of Britain's imperial heritage, though they did their best to minimize its significance. Lawrence James, for example, acknowledged that some "nasty expedients [had been] employed occasionally," but he scolded the BBC and the *Guardian* newspaper for their "predictable hand-wringing and breast-beating" and he maintained that "the faults of the Empire are more than outweighed by the benefits it extended to its millions of subjects."[61] There can be little doubt, however, that the discovery of the Hanslope Park archive, which includes nearly 9,000 files on morally and legally questionable activities in 37 former colonies, has opened the floodgate for further revelations and lawsuits.

It should be noted that several prominent historians of colonial Kenya played important roles in these proceedings. Much of the impetus for the court case came from the publication in 2005 of Caroline Elkins' *Imperial Reckoning: The Untold Story of Britain's Gulag in Kenya* and David Anderson's *Histories of the Hanged: The Dirty War in Kenya and the End of Empire*, which provided compelling documentation of widespread British abuses of Kenyans during the Mau Mau Emergency.[62] The two books appeared soon after the Abu Ghraib scandal had come to light in American-occupied Iraq and opened the door to further disclosures about the sanctioned use of torture by the CIA and other US government agencies. Because these revelations seemed so eerily similar to the historical crimes exposed by Elkins and Anderson, their books attracted unusually wide interest, with Elkins's work winning the Pulitzer Prize for history (the first work on an African subject to achieve that honor). When the lawsuit on behalf of the four Kenyans was filed in British courts, Elkins and Anderson became expert witnesses for the plaintiffs, as did Huw Bennett, an authority on the British counterinsurgency campaign against Mau Mau.[63] It was their relentless search for missing historical records that uncovered the secret Hanslope Park archive. When the government conceded defeat, the *Guardian* and the *New York Times* turned to Elkins and Anderson to reflect on the implications of the case. Both of them anticipated that it would lay the groundwork for further lawsuits by other victims of British abuse in Malaya, Cyprus, Aden, and elsewhere. In his *Times* op-ed, Anderson also brought its implications full circle by wondering when the United States would face similar lawsuits from detainees incarcerated in Guantanamo.[64] It is an important question, one that the aftermath of the British imperial experience has made all but impossible to ignore.

* * *

If the preceding pages seem to have taken a trajectory that accentuates recent political debates and controversies, this has been unavoidable. The question I posed at the beginning of this chapter was why Britain's imperial past has continued to attract so much attention among historians of Britain. The obvious answer is because it speaks to moral concerns and political issues that remain very much with us. These concerns and issues are not—and should not be—confined to professional historians. Political leaders and foreign policy elites, members of the media, and the public at large have had compelling reasons of their own to contemplate Britain's imperial past and consider its implications for the present. But their perspectives on the past and its relationship to the present have been shaped, I have argued, by their location, as have the perspectives of professional historians. In the

United States, British imperial history has served as a useful analogy that various parties have brought into play to advance their agendas regarding America's domestic racial politics and its international role as a superpower. By way of example, the recent Russian aggression against Ukraine has given new life to the neoconservatives who believe that the United States must be more assertive in projecting its power and fulfilling its destiny as an empire.[65]

In Britain, the echoes of its imperial past have reverberated in the public consciousness in various ways, but most clearly as a consequence of the country's recent role in the military occupations of Iraq and Afghanistan. The empire remains an integral element of the collective memory of the nation and its citizens, and it elicits a wide range of emotions, including pride, nostalgia, guilt, resentment, anger, and wishful thinking. One of the more plaintively amusing examples comes from a recent *Telegraph* headline: "Britain may have invaded 90 percent of the world, but we're not hated everywhere."[66] A far more serious indication of this ongoing process of coming to terms with Britain's imperial past and its postimperial present has been the question posed most acutely by the Scottish referendum: does a British identity—and a British state—remain viable? As Norman Davies has observed, "the United Kingdom was established to serve the interests of Empire and… the loss of Empire has destroyed its raison d'etre."[67]

When Roger Louis proclaimed in his preface to the *Oxford History of the British Empire* that the passions aroused by British imperialism had lessened, permitting historians to achieve some measure of consensus about its nature and significance, he could hardly have foreseen how the events of the past decade and a half would revive those passions. At the same time, it was perhaps unrealistic of Louis to suppose that any historiographical assessment of the British Empire could avoid debate, dissent, and even moral outrage, especially in light of the profoundly problematic impact that empire has had on our world. There are those historians, to be sure, who maintain that "the idea of a powerful and constraining colonial legacy is seriously flawed," especially as an explanation for the failures of those states that arose from the collapse of empires in Africa and elsewhere, because it neglects both precolonial and postcolonial contributions to contemporary problems while overemphasizing colonialism's continued effects.[68] In other words, it is time to get over it. There are other historians who maintain the closely related position that the British Empire was never as powerful and transformative as it is often made out to be; it was an "improvised and provisional" empire, "always ramshackle and quite often chaotic."[69] In other words, it was not that big a deal anyway. I would suggest that both of these positions are as deeply embedded in contemporary perspectives and concerns as are those of the historians whose interpretations they reject. An Olympian aloofness from the moral and political passions that surround us is neither fully possible nor, I believe, entirely desirable. It is the power of these passions that has sustained such an intense and immensely productive engagement in the history of British imperialism in recent decades. But this engagement carries a twofold obligation for professional historians. The first is to be as self-aware of our own subject positions as possible, recognizing that our time and place inform our efforts to make meaningful sense of the past.[70] This should not prevent us, however, from insisting on scholarly standards of evidence and integrity. Our second obligation, then, is to holding those to account who make fatuous, tendentious, or deceptive claims about the past. But we should seek not simply to expose the problems with such claims, but to understand *why* they are made, asking ourselves what agendas they are meant to serve. Only then will we gain a meaningful grasp of the forces that have helped to ensure that British imperial history retains its relevance today.

Epilogue: Does British History Matter Anymore? Reflections on the Age of Brexit and Trump

Does British history matter anymore? I raise this question in the aftermath of the two political earthquakes that shook Britain and the United States—along with much of the rest of the world—in 2016. One was the British referendum on "Brexit," which resulted in the shocking decision to leave the European Union. The other was the American presidential election, which produced the even more shocking victory by Donald Trump. If continuity and change are the yin and yang of history, then the latter has become ascendant. Do these events on either side of the Atlantic have implications for how the historiographical issues addressed in this book are likely to be addressed in the future? How could they not? Each in its own way simultaneously reminds us that the British imperial past remains a powerful imaginative presence in contemporary politics and forces us to ask what the future holds for serious scrutiny of that past.

* * *

Various commentators on the Brexit referendum have noted that the "Leave" campaigners actively promoted their cause in historical terms. Leading Brexiteers issued nostalgic appeals to the past, promising to restore Britain to its former glory, a glory they associated with the British Empire and the triumph over Nazi tyranny. One leader of the "Leave" campaign, Michael Gove, had made his reputation as the government's education minister by introducing a controversial history curriculum that a prominent critic, the historian Richard J. Evans, characterized as an attempt to "impart a patriotic sense of national identity through the uncritical hero-worship of great men and women from the British past."[1] The other prominent Tory Brexiteer, Boris Johnson, shared Gove's view of history, publishing a hagiographic account of the life of Winston Churchill. (Johnson's immodest subsidiary aim was to promote himself as Churchill's political heir: judge for yourself.) An historical perspective was also integral to the ultra-nationalistic United Kingdom Independence Party (UKIP): its founder was the historian Alan Sked, and its campaign to exit the EU was led by Nigel Farage, whose pub-crawling persona evoked a nostalgic, ethnically homogenous sense of Britain's past.

Brexit, however, may well make *British* history obsolete. Election returns revealed that different regions of Britain responded to the referendum in strikingly different ways. "Leave" supporters carried the day in England and Wales, where they racked up large majorities in suburbs, small towns, and rural areas, but "Remain" voters won handily in Scotland and by a smaller margin in Northern Ireland. This split decision has led the Scottish government to announce plans for a new referendum on Scottish independence from the UK. It has also widened the gulf between Unionists and Republicans in Northern Ireland over the future of its relations with neighboring Eire. An increasingly dis-United Kingdom also means an increasingly disunited view of its past. Scottish-, Irish-, and Welsh-centered histories have already gained significant sway over public sentiment in their respective regions, and there is every reason to believe these separatist histories will become even more prevalent in the aftermath of Brexit. So too for an English-centered historical consciousness, which was central to the pro-Brexit campaign. UKIP in particular draped itself in St. George's Cross, the increasingly pervasive English flag. An already frayed sense of the past as a shared British story now appears at real risk of coming apart altogether.

For Brexit's proponents, however, leaving the EU is seen as an opportunity to bring about an imperial reunion. Boris Johnson and Nigel Farage, among others, are said to favor the establishment of "imperial networks in a postimperial era, based on ideas of Anglo-Saxon fraternity."[2] Since the election, the historian Andrew Roberts and other conservative voices have called for the creation of CANZUK, an economic alliance with Canada, Australia, New Zealand, and the UK.[3] While the idea of a renewed relationship with the former "white dominions" (excluding, it should be noted, now black-ruled South Africa) holds special appeal among xenophobic racists, the British government is also looking to reestablish ties with other countries that had once been part of the empire. The first overseas trip made by Prime Minister Theresa May was to India in the seemingly forlorn hope of forging a new economic relationship with a land that had enriched Britain's coffers in the heyday of the Raj. And Liam Fox, the Tory government's international trade secretary, has proposed a new trade association with the African members of the Commonwealth, an idea that one Whitehall official wryly referred to as "Empire 2.0."[4] What makes these schemes so stupefying is that their advocates seem to suppose that the countries they seek to woo will welcome a restoration of some sort of imperial relationship with open arms. It speaks to the poverty of their historical imaginations that they cannot comprehend the resentments and suspicions that ex-colonial peoples might retain regarding those who had once subjugated them.

What does Brexit mean for British history's appeal on the American side of the Atlantic? The reign of King Canute may stir a flicker of interest among English school kids and the schism in the Presbyterian Church may merit attention in Scottish classrooms, but neither these nor other parochial aspects of their histories hold much interest outside their borders. Nor does a nostalgic, roseate remembrance of the British imperial past. During the referendum campaign, more than 300 British historians signed a letter warning that a vote for Brexit would condemn Britain to "irrelevance." While their purpose was to affirm that "Britain has had in the past, and will have in the future, an irreplaceable role to play in Europe," the risk of irrelevance applies not merely to Britain's future, but to its past.[5] And nowhere is this more likely to be true than in the United States, where Brexit may well bring a sharp and decisive end to the privileged place that British history once enjoyed in the history curriculum.

There was a time when most large history departments at American universities had three British historians on staff—a modernist, an early modernist, and a medievalist. You could usually find British historians in smaller departments as well. Their prevalence was, of course, a consequence of the Eurocentric orientation of the historical profession itself. British historians were often mainstays of the Western civilization survey, a bread-and-butter course for almost all US history departments.

This began to change in the 1970s and 1980s as departments hired more Africanists, Asianists, and other non-Western historians and transitioned from the Western civilization to the world history survey. In the zero-sum game that characterized academic hiring in these financially straitened times, the number of British history positions declined. By the late 1990s, the rate of attrition was so pronounced that the North American Conference of British Studies established a special committee to study the problem. Its most notable recommendation was that new PhDs in British history make themselves more marketable by acquiring an expertise in imperial history, thereby enlarging their knowledge of the non-Western world and enhancing their ability to teach the world history survey.[6] Whether this recommendation did anything to stop the slide in the number of British history positions is debatable, but it did offer new British history PhDs seeking employment a strategy for responding to the changing job market and improving their competitiveness for positions requiring some sort of transnational expertise. The British history jobs that did open up increasingly advertised for candidates who had some sort of imperial or global expertise.

The point, then, is that insofar as British history has maintained a foothold in the American history profession in the era of globalization, it has done so largely because it has come to be seen as a meaningful point of entry to an examination of the wider world. What makes Brexit potentially so detrimental to British history's survival as a field of study in the United States is that it marks Britain's retreat from the world stage. Not only does Brexit divorce Britain from the rest of Europe, which has been its main avenue of engagement with the international community since it lost its empire; it also sets it on an increasingly insular, parochial path that favors the fissiparous forces of nativism, placing the UK itself at risk.

The Brexiteers' belief that they can beat back these forces by establishing an updated version of the empire is nothing more than a fantasy. While Britain's post-Brexit future may not change the facts about its history, it will change how we view that history and what significance we draw from it. We will find it more difficult in the aftermath of Brexit to make the case that British history provides special insight into how we got to where we are today. Sure, the British had a disproportionate influence on global affairs when they were at the height of their power. So did plenty of other peoples at other times. The Mongols, for example, were no slackers when it came to making their mark on history, yet where is the demand for historians of Mongolia?

The fallback position for British history's defenders in the American academy is that it holds a special place in American history because of its influence on our political institutions, legal codes, cultural values, and so forth. There's something to be said for this argument, though not as much as there used to be. American historians have become increasingly attentive to the wide range of peoples, cultures, and traditions that comprise the American historical experience. There's an inverse side of this story, however, and here Brexit does make British history more relevant to the American experience. The deeply rooted nativism and racism that Brexit brought to the surface of British life have their obvious counterparts in the United States. One need look no further than the dark forces channeled by Donald Trump during his presidential campaign and instantiated by his administration after the election. The United States, however, arguably has a much longer, deeper, darker history of such sentiments, so it is not clear how much we can learn from British history. But let's look at the bright side: British history may matter less in the United States after Brexit, but US history may matter a lot more in Britain.

* * *

But US history is itself contested, as our recent election has made abundantly clear. Like the Brexiteers in their message to British voters, Donald Trump offered the American electorate a nostalgic appeal to the past, promising to "Make America Great Again." No wonder he and Nigel Farage became best mates. After all, they share much the same political vision, one premised on racially exclusionary, hyper-nationalist policies that equate greatness with imperial power.

Still, what relevance does the British past have to America's dramatic lurch to the right? One answer to that question can be found in the reverence for Winston Churchill within the Republican Party and among American conservatives more generally. I noted in Chapter 9 that there were howls of outrage among right-wing commentators when Barack Obama returned to the British Embassy the bust of Churchill that had been placed in the Oval Office during George W. Bush's presidency, replacing it with a bust of Martin

Luther King Jr. Soon after Donald Trump succeeded Obama as president, his son-in-law Jared Kushner and chief advisor Steven Bannon requested the return of Churchill during a meeting with Foreign Minister Boris Johnson. When Prime Minister Theresa May visited Trump in the White House, she brought the bronze icon as an offering of friendship.

This is not the only Churchill bust that Republicans have placed in the halls of power in Washington, D.C. When John Boehner was Speaker of the House, he installed a larger than life head of Churchill in the Capitol, where it has resided ever since. His successor, Paul Ryan, has said he has *three* busts of Churchill in his office. Nor are such sculptures the only signs of enthusiasm for Churchill among Republicans. Senator Marco Rubio told a reporter during his campaign for president that he was reading a biography of Churchill because he was "so fascinated by the leadership he provided."[7] But the man who won the Republicans' "Winston Churchill of our time" sweepstakes was Donald Trump. The conservative radio host Michael Savage used those words to praise Trump during the primaries. And after he won the nomination, the prominent Christian conservative Jerry Falwell Jr. trumpeted: "Trump is the Churchillian leader we need."[8]

Why are Republicans so infatuated with Churchill? What is it about this man they aspire to emulate? We can assume it is not the important social welfare legislation he helped to craft early in his career. Nor his willingness during his final stint as prime minister to maintain the National Health Service and other welfare programs put in place by the previous Labour government. And Churchill's unshakable faith in free trade, strong support for NATO, and stern warnings about Russian aggression clearly do not mesh well with Donald Trump's stance on these issues. The larger point is that Churchill had a long, eventful, highly varied political career, and it produced a number of positions and policies that stand starkly at odds with those held by Trump and other Republicans who seek to claim his mantle.

The Churchill that most appeals to most Republicans is, of course, the Churchill that most appeals to most everyone else—the man of indomitable courage who opposed appeasement and resisted Hitler. The leadership Churchill displayed in that period of profound crisis is the essential source of his enduring attraction. If Republicans seem more inclined than their Democratic rivals to hold the quaint conviction that a totemic display of Churchill's brooding bust will inspire them to attain the same ineffable qualities of leadership he so demonstrably possessed, this seems a harmless affectation.

But there is more to the right's adoration of Churchill than its desire to emulate the leadership he showed in overcoming the German threat. Consider, for example, the assessment of Churchill in Larry Arnn's *Churchill's Trial: Winston Churchill and the Salvation of Free Government*. Arnn is president of Hillsdale College, an influential private institution in Michigan that advertises itself as a bastion of conservative thought and training ground for its future leaders. A statue of Churchill graces the Hillsdale campus and a portrait of Churchill hangs in Arnn's office.[9] For Arnn, Churchill's greatness lies not merely in his prewar warnings against appeasement and his wartime resistance to Hitler, nor even in his postwar opposition to the Soviet Union. Churchill is characterized by Arnn as the great critic of "the leftward turn in Western democracies." The notorious "Gestapo" charge that Churchill leveled against the Labour Party during the 1945 election is portrayed as a prescient warning of the dangers that its welfare state program would pose to "freedom." Most revealing, however, is Arnn's unabashed embrace of Churchill's views on empire. "The empire made Britain . . . noble," Arnn declares: "The empire gave the British a service to do for the world." Churchill was right, according to Arnn, to insist that Indians and other peoples were incapable of self-government and that the British had a "moral duty" to govern them. In a conclusion of breathtaking sophistry, Arnn proclaims: "One does not have to be an imperialist . . . to believe that all people have a right to live under laws that protect their freedom. One does not have to be a racist to believe that some people cannot achieve that on their own at any given time."[10] In other words, Arnn holds that it is neither racist nor imperialist to rule other peoples against their will so long as it is done for what the rulers deem to be their subjects' benefit. To use the name of freedom to deny freedom, as Arnn does in this passage, is perverse beyond measure. While such a claim would no doubt have resonated with Churchill, he would rarely have engaged in such deliberate obfuscation. Nor, for that matter, does the so-called "Winston Churchill of our time," Donald Trump. Like Churchill, he is open and unabashed in his racist sentiments, and his repeated musings about taking Iraq's oil is as crude and explicit a declaration of imperial intent as any American president has proclaimed in recent years.

* * *

This brings us back to the question that opened this epilogue: does British history matter anymore? It obviously matters to those Americans on the political right who see themselves as Churchill's heirs. And it matters to those Britons on the political right who believe that exiting the EU will bring about "Empire 2.0." This means it matters to the ongoing struggle over both countries' futures. It matters, then, that we get that history right. It matters that those of us who are specialists in the history of Britain and its empire make our voices heard. It matters that we guard against the tendentious, deceptive, and nostalgic uses of the British past. While we will never return to that era when Britain's disproportionate influence on the world gave the study of its history a disproportionate influence as well, this does not mean that it no longer matters. In some ways it matters more than ever. So long as fantasists and neofascists seek to distort that past to serve their present political purposes, the British imperial history wars are sure to go on.

Notes

Introduction

1. Nor a more contentious time, as is evident from the roundtable on Darwin's work, which includes the "Reply" from which this statement is drawn. See Burton et al. (2015), 997. Also see Schwarz (2015) and MacKenzie (2015).
2. Burton and Kennedy (2016).
3. See https://yougov.co.uk/news/2014/07/26/britain–proud–its–empire/

Chapter 1

1. To maintain some consistency of terminology in this book, I have removed the hyphen from "post-colonial," which I used when this essay was originally published. I have done the same for "post-structuralist." In both cases, the absence of the hyphen reflects contemporary usage.
2. Madden and Fieldhouse (1986), especially the essay by Ronald Robinson; Symonds (1986).
3. Robinson and Gallagher with Denny (1981).
4. Cain and Hopkins (1993).
5. Williams and Chrisman (1994); Barker, Hulme, and Iversen (1994); Ashcroft, Griffiths, and Tiffin (1995).
6. McMillen (1993); Jacoby (1995); Hughes (1993).
7. MacKenzie (1994), 9, refers to some of the attention surrounding Said: the Reith lectures he gave on BBC radio, the "Arena" television documentary about his career, and the controversy sparked by Ernest Gellner's review of his book *Culture and Imperialism* in the *Times Literary Supplement* in 1993.
8. The most notable exception is John M. MacKenzie (1994 and 1995), who has made an important intervention in the debate with Said and his followers.
9. McClintock (1995), intro. See also note 1.
10. For an appreciation of Said, see Sprinker (1992), especially the essays by Benita Parry, Richard Fox, and Partha Chatterjee.
11. The implications of this position are developed in Breckenridge and Van Der Veer (1993).
12. Ahmad (1992).
13. Porter (1983).
14. Clifford (1980), 209.
15. Collini (1993), 458.

16 Young (1990).
17 It is striking how little attention has been paid by postcolonial theorists to this troubling fact. Stoler (1995) has the forthrightness to frame her Foucauldian analysis of European colonialism around the issue of Foucault's neglect of colonialism and racism.
18 Young (1995). This endorsement comes even though Young acknowledges that Deleuze and Guattari's analysis is obscure and their conception of culture "too simplistic" (173).
19 Bhabha (1994).
20 Young (1990), 156, 158.
21 Showalter (1994), 12.
22 Cotton (1993), 463.
23 Thiong'o (1986).
24 Buell (1994), 221.
25 Bhabha (1994), 62.
26 Significantly, I think, questions similar to these are posed in an interview with Gayatri Spivak conducted by three Delhi-based Indians in Spivak (1990), 69.
27 See the pointed remarks by Ahmad (1992), *passim*; Sarkar (1994); Parry (1987); Barkan (1994).
28 MacKenzie (1995), xvii, *passim*.
29 Spivak (1985), 332.
30 Nandy (1995), 65.
31 Nandy (1983), xv.
32 Young (1990). For a more subtle reading of these antihistorical tendencies in postcolonial theory, see Buell (1994), ch. 9.
33 Chakrabarty (1992), 2. See also Prakash (1990, 1994).
34 Ashcroft, Griffiths, and Tiffin (1989), 11.
35 Donaldson (1992), 9, *passim*.
36 Spurr (1993).
37 Spurr (1993), 10.
38 Spurr (1993), 93.
39 Pratt (1992).
40 Viswanathan (1989).
41 Youngs (1994).
42 Sharpe (1993). For a more simplistic approach to this subject, see Paxton (1992).
43 Brantlinger (1998).
44 This is one of the principal criticisms made by MacKenzie (1995), ch. 1.
45 Thomas (1994), x. Thomas's book is a critique of postcolonial theory's representations of colonialism as "a unitary totality" (ix).
46 Sarkar (1994), 217. See also Ahmad (1992), 172, *passim*; Cooper (1994), 1531.
47 Majeed (1992).

48 Buzard (1993).
49 Sharpe (1993), 9.
50 Bhabha (1994).
51 Spivak (1988). For an influential application of Spivak's argument, see Mani in Sangari and Vaid (1990), who presents the widows who committed sati in early-nineteenth-century India as silent victims of a struggle between British colonial officials and Indian high-caste males.
52 Prakash (1994), 1482, 1483.
53 Ahmad (1992); Mallon (1994); Cooper (1994).
54 Youngs (1995), 164, 165.
55 Suleri (1992), 12–13.
56 Said (1993), ch. 3.
57 This is one of the main themes of Ahmad's *In Theory*.
58 In addition to Pratt (1992) and Youngs (1994), see Porter (1991); Mills (1991); Behdad (1994).
59 See Mitchell (1988) and Chatterjee (1993).
60 MacKenzie (1995); MacKenzie (1994).
61 MacKenzie (1995), chs. 1 and 2; Sarkar (1994), *passim*.
62 Cohn (1990); Dirks (1992a,b); and essays by Arjun Appadurai, David Lelyveld, and David Ludden in Breckenridge and van der Veer (1993).
63 Pandey (1990); Freitag (1990); Chatterjee (1993); Vail (1989); Berman and Lonsdale (1992); Cohen and Odhiambo (1989); Comaroff and Comaroff (1991); Crais (1992).
64 Guha (1983), and, more generally, the work of the Guha-led subaltern studies collective.
65 See Stoler (1989, 1995); Sinha (1995).
66 Arnold (1993); Vaughan (1991); White (1995).
67 Metcalf (1994).
68 Fieldhouse (1984).
69 Said (1993).
70 Majeed (1992); Viswanathan (1989).
71 Ferguson (1993), ch. 2.
72 Young (1995), chs. 2 and 3.
73 Youngs (1994), 6. See also McClintock (1995).
74 Burton (1994a); Zastoupil (1994).
75 It should be said that P. J. Cain and A. G. Hopkins have sought the same ends through more traditional means in their two-volume *British Imperialism*, but their efforts have simply swung the pendulum back from the peripheral perspective encouraged by Robinson and Gallagher to the Anglocentric one that had previously dominated imperial historiography. What distinguishes postcolonial theory in its more successful manifestations is its determination to trace the points of the mutual exchange between metropole and periphery.

76 See, for example, Burton (1994b).
77 MacKenzie (1995); Hildreth (1995).

Chapter 2

1 Louis (2000), 9.
2 *Sunday Times* (January 21, 1996), sect. 1, 8. Wm. Roger Louis and Judith Brown responded in letters to the *Sunday Times* (January 28, 1996), sect. 3, 8.
3 Beloff (1996), 14.
4 Louis subsequently received a knighthood for his work on the *Oxford History of the British Empire*. His scholarly accomplishments are detailed in an appreciation by the doyen of imperial historians, Ronald Robinson, in King and Kilson (1999).
5 Volumes 3 and 4 are especially weighted with Oxbridge- and London-trained historians. As editor of volume 5, Yale historian Robin W. Winks has drawn on a wider range of scholars, including eight who got their degrees from his own institution. It is also worth noting that one of the principal financial sponsors of the *Oxford History* was the Rhodes Trust—the other being the National Endowment for the Humanities.
6 The irony of this preemptive strike by the right is that it may have helped to mute criticisms from the left, which I will suggest has reasons of its own to object to the direction taken by the project.
7 For an early examination of "imperial nostalgia," see Resaldo (1989). For a "coffee table" book that exemplifies this phenomenon, see Foley (1993). Regarding the political uses of the colonial legacy, see Robert Mugabe's efforts to shift the blame for Zimbabwe's economic troubles to white farmers.
8 The works of synthesis and reference include James (1994); Judd (1996); Kitchen (1996); Marshall (1996); Olson (1996); Palmer (1996); McIntyre (1998); Smith (1998); Boyce (1999); Parsons (1999); Thompson (1999); and White (1999); plus new editions of Hyam (1993); Lloyd (1996); and Porter (1996).
9 See Robinson (1982), 30–48.
10 This was one of the principal objections raised by Buckner in his comments at a roundtable panel on the *Oxford History of the British Empire*, held at the American Historical Association's annual meeting in January 2000. Also see the compelling case he makes for renewed attention to the colonies of settlement in his presidential address to the Canadian Historical Association, published as Buckner (1993).
11 The *Oxford History*'s inclusion of Ireland within its parameters is part of a broader scholarly effort to reframe the Irish experience within the empire. See, e.g., Bayly (2000); Jeffrey (1996); and Howe (2000).
12 Louis (2000), 8.
13 Louis (1976).
14 Winks (1984), 462.

15 Lloyd (2000), 253. I am grateful to Professor Lloyd for sharing his review prior to publication.
16 Wolfe (1997).
17 Cain and Hopkins (1993). Also see Dumett (1999).
18 Once again, it is worth noting that Cain and Hopkins (1993) work within Robinson and Gallagher's frame of reference with the emphasis they give to "informal empire" in their magnum opus. For another effort by a prominent imperial historian to grapple with this issue, see Darwin (1997).
19 See, e.g., Beloff (1970); Barnett (1972); and, more recently, Orde (1996). P. Kennedy (1987) set this interpretation of the British experience in the twentieth century in a much broader context.
20 Gallagher (1982).
21 Louis and Robinson (1994).
22 Given the claims made for the originality of their interpretation, Cain and Hopkins (1993) follow the lead of Robinson and Gallagher in this regard as well.
23 Robinson and Gallagher (1961). The fullest theoretical exposition of this explanation of expansion is Robinson (1972). On this issue, at least, Cain and Hopkins differ, arguing that imperial expansion was driven mainly by metropolitan forces.
24 Fieldhouse (1984).
25 This point is made by Adas (1993).
26 See, e.g., Palat (1996); Lambert (1996).
27 A cogent and balanced introduction to the subject is provided by Moore-Gilbert (1997). See also Young (1990), an early and influential assessment. One of the most powerful assaults on the theoretical underpinnings of postcolonial theory has come from Ahmad (1992).
28 The most notable example is MacKenzie (1995). Also see my 1996 essay, reprinted here as chapter one, and Darby (1998).
29 Robinson (1972).
30 Stoler and Cooper (1997), 1.
31 Colley (1992a) has been especially influential in this regard. See also Colley (1992b). Several works that explore the connections between national identity and empire from a postcolonial stance are Schwarz (1996); Gikandi (1996); and Baucom (1999). For a contrasting perspective on the origins of English and British national identity, see the review essay by Clark (2000).
32 See the forum on this subject in the *American Historical Review*, especially the introductory essay by Armitage (1999). Buckner has argued along these lines as well. There is a certain irony in the fact that this interest in Greater Britain as a category of identity brings us back full circle to the concerns of Seeley and other late-nineteenth-century commentators on the British Empire: cf. J. A. Froude (1885) and Dilke (1868).
33 Majeed (1992); Said (1993); Zastoupil (1994); Mehta (1999); Codell and Macleod (1998).

34 On cities and empire, Schneer (1999) and Driver and Gilbert (1999). On colonial subjects in the metropolis, Visram (1986); Fischer (1997); Tabili (1994); Lahiri (2000); Green (1998); Burton (1998).
35 Burton (1997). For an illuminating critique of the way empire has been written out of modern British social history, see Gregg and Kale (1997).
36 Most relevant are MacKenzie (1984) and MacKenzie (1986). For a fuller treatment of the influence of empire on post–Second World War British culture, see Ward (2001).
37 Guha (1983); Chakrabarty (1989); Amin (1995).
38 Burton (1994); Midgley (1992); Ferguson (1993); Fletcher, Mayhall, and Levine (2000); Sangari and Vaid (1990); Jayawardena (1995); Hunt, Lin, and Quataert (1997); Chowdhury (1998).
39 Sinha (1995); Rutherford (1997); Hall (1992); Dawson (1994).
40 On efforts to integrate the analysis of different dimensions of identity within the imperial context, see McClintock (1995); Stoler (1995); Pierson and Chaudhuri (1998); Levine (1998). On race and racism, see West (1996); Bush (1999). On sexuality and gender, see Midgley (1998); Peers (1998); Burton (1999). On religious identities, see J. and J. Comaroff (1990, 1997); Landau (1995); Viswanathan (1998). On caste and communalism, Freitag (1990); Pandey (1990); Dirks (1992a).
41 Dunlop (1999); Griffiths and Robbin (1997); Tyrrell (1999). Much of the intellectual inspiration for this work comes from Crosby (1986).
42 See Grove (1996); Grove, Damodaran, and Sangwan (1998); and, more generally, MacKenzie (1990).
43 Arnold (1993), 23. See also Vaughan (1991) and Harrison (1999).
44 For geography, Godlewska and Smith (1994); Bell, Butlin, and Hefferan (1995); Edney (1997); Driver (2001). For anthropology, Kuklick (1991); Stocking (1991); Wolfe (1999); Pels and Salemink (1999).
45 The foundational text that laid the groundwork for these claims is, of course, Said (1978). Two of the more interesting and provocative works to pursue the implications are Chakrabarty (2000) and Prakash (1999).
46 Hopkins (1999), 199 and 203. See also Hopkins (1997).
47 Among the many notable works of world history that speak directly to the concerns of imperial historians, see Pomeranz (2000); Wolf (1997); Wallerstein (1976); Adas (1986); Landes (1998); and, of course, Crosby (1986).

Chapter 3

1 Bush (2006).
2 Guha (1983).
3 See Chaturvedi (2000); also Chakrabarty (2002), esp. ch. 1.
4 Scott (1986), Butler (1990). See the historiographical survey by Ghosh (2004).
5 Cohn (1990, 1996); Asad (1973); Comaroff (1991); Harley (2001); Harvey (1989).

6 See, for example, MacKenzie (1995); Irwin (2006).
7 Graham (2013).
8 See Ahmad (1992), ch. 2; also Cannadine (2005).
9 Kennedy (2001).
10 On this cultural turn, see Hunt (1989) and Ortner (1999).
11 Cohn (1990, 1996); Dirks (2001).
12 Freitag (1990); Pandey (1990).
13 Cohen and Odhiambo (1989, 1992); Vail (1991).
14 Mani (1987); see also Sangari and Vaid (1990).
15 Sinha (1995).
16 Foucault (1980); Stoler (1989, 1995, 2002).
17 Levine (2003).
18 See, for example, McCulloch (2000).
19 Arnold (1993); Anderson (2006); Vaughan (1991). See also Ballantyne and Burton (2005).
20 Collingham (2001); Burke (1996).
21 Stoler and Cooper (1997), 4.
22 See esp. MacKenzie (1984).
23 Colley (1992); Pocock (1975). See also Samuel (1989).
24 Burton (1994).
25 Hall (2002).
26 Wilson (2003), 17. Other relevant works include Wilson (2004); Hall (2000); and Hall and Rose (2006).
27 Bridge and Fedorowich (2003). See also Ward (2008).
28 See, for example, Perry (2001).
29 Wolfe (2001, 2016).
30 Lake and Reynolds (2008).
31 Porter (2006). A more balanced assessment is offered by Thompson (2005).
32 Cannadine (2001).
33 Cooper (2005), ch. 3.
34 Hall (2002); Burton (2007); Kennedy (2005); Lambert and Lester (2006).
35 Bayly (2004), 106.
36 Said (1978), ch. 1.
37 Chakrabarty (2000), 41.
38 Bishop (1989).
39 Arnold (2006).
40 Mitchell (1988), x.
41 Burnett (2000); Edney (1997); Etherington (2007); Richardson (2005).
42 Burton (1997; also 2003b).

43 Chatterjee (1993).
44 Banivanua Mar (2016), 17, 20.
45 Hopkins (1999, 2002), but also see Ferguson (2003).
46 Gilroy (1993); Ballantyne (2002, 2006); Lester (2001).
47 See, for example, Bell (2007); Potter (2007).
48 Ghosh and Kennedy (2006).
49 Harland-Jacobs (2007); Metcalf (2007); Troutt Powell (2003).
50 See, for example, Bose (2006); Ho (2006); Sinha (2006).
51 Curthoys (2003).
52 Metcalf (1994); Armitage (2000).
53 Mehta (1999).
54 Dirks (2006).
55 See Pitts (2005); Mantena (2010).
56 Semmel (1970) and Zastoupil (1994).
57 Hodge (2007).
58 Chakrabarty (2000); McClintock (1994).
59 See, for example, Prakash (1999); Tsin (1999); Duara (2003); Alu and Perdue (2009).
60 Mamdani (1996); Satia (2008).
61 Dirks (2001), ch. 6.
62 Burton (2003a; also 2005).
63 Chakrabarty (2000), 7.
64 Guha (2002).
65 Muthu (2003). See also Pitts (2005), intro.
66 Bell (2007).
67 Cooper (2005).
68 Roque and Wagner (2012).
69 Ghosh (2006).
70 Hardt and Negri (2001).
71 See, for example, Prestholdt (2008); Belich (2009); Thompson and Magee (2011); Beckert (2014).
72 Travers (2007); Heath (2010); Stern (2011).
73 Anderson (2005); Elkins (2005); Wilson (2016); Hoock (2017).

Chapter 4

1 Fernández-Armesto (2006).
2 Kennedy (2014), 1–2.
3 Stafford (1999b).

4 Among the best examples of this genre are Brodie (1967) and Jeal (1973, 2007). For some thoughtful reflections on the biographical approach to exploration, see Driver (2007).
5 Curtin (1964).
6 Rotberg (1970).
7 Among the more successful accounts of African exploration, for example, were Moorehead (1960 and 1963) and Hibbert (1982).
8 Asad (1973); Fabian (1983); Stocking, Jr (1987); Marcus and Fisher (1986).
9 Livingstone (1993); Lewis and Wigen (1997).
10 Miller and Reill (1996); Bourguet, Licoppe, and Siburn (2002).
11 Said (1978).
12 Carter (1987), xvi.
13 Pratt (1992), 2, 9.
14 See, for example, Bishop (1989); Greenblatt (1991); Youngs (1994); Leask (2002).
15 Smith (1985 [1960]).
16 See, for example, Johns et al. (1998).
17 The attention to visual evidence is apparent in a number of the essays in Driver and Martins (2005). Also see McAleer (2010).
18 See Dening (1988); Salmond (2003); Thomas (2003); Comaroff and Comaroff (1991).
19 Scott (1999); Thomas (1994). Also see the debate between Obeyesekere (1992) and Sahlins (1995).
20 Richardson (2005), 6.
21 Thomas (1985), ch. 2; Mackay (1985).
22 Ritchie (1967).
23 Wulf (2015).
24 Bravo (1999), 169, 172.
25 Waller (1990).
26 Edney (1997), 36.
27 Kennedy (2013), ch. 4.
28 Gascoigne (1994).
29 Miller and Reill (1996).
30 Drayton (2000).
31 Stern (2004).
32 Driver (2001), ch. 2.
33 Stoddart (1980).
34 Stafford (1989) 21, *passim*.
35 Withers (2010).
36 Brockway (1979); Drayton (2000), chs. 6 and 7; Arnold (2006).

37 MacKenzie (2009); Ritvo (1989); Sheets-Pyenson (1987).
38 See Strafford (1999a) for an excellent introduction to this issue.
39 Bourguet, Licoppe, and Siburn (2002), 3, 8.
40 Maitland (1971), frontispiece photograph.
41 Driver (2004); Driver (2001), ch. 3.
42 Jackson (1845).
43 See Ryan (1997), esp. ch. 1. For a fascinating glimpse of the photographs taken by Henry Morton Stanley during his expeditions, see the exhibit catalog published by the King Baudouin Foundation (2007).
44 Bravo (1999), 176.
45 Gillham (2001).
46 Burton (1995 [1860]), vii. On the clash between armchair geographers and explorers, see Ryan (1996), 35–39, 42; Driver (2001), 12, 127–30; Stoddart (1980), 195.
47 Keighren, Withers, and Bell (2015).
48 Koivunen (2009).
49 Pettitt (2007); Pettitt (2014).
50 Jeal (1973); Ross (2002); Helly (1987); MacKenzie (1996).
51 Pettitt (2007); Newman (2004); Driver (1991).
52 Frank (1986); Winstone (1978).
53 Coombes (1994).
54 Driver (2001), 149.
55 Newman (2004).
56 Driver and Martins (2005).
57 Arnold (2006). It should be noted, however, that India came to be represented as tropical *after* it had come under British imperial control, when the traveler had replaced the explorer.
58 See the essays by Claudio Greppi and Michael Dettelbach in Driver and Martins (2005).
59 Ryan (1996), 208.
60 Edney (1997).
61 Burnett, (2000), 15, 255.
62 Kennedy (2013), 115.
63 Rockel (2006). The first historical study to focus on the Africans who assisted the explorers was Simpson (1976).
64 Driver and Jones (2009); Konishi, Nugent, and Shellam (2015).
65 Murgatroyd (2002).
66 Kennedy (2013), ch. 6.
67 Lamb (2001).
68 Leask (1987); Cumming (1987).

69 Kennedy (2005).
70 Fabian (2000).
71 Carroll (2015).
72 Hansen (2001).
73 See, for example, Kennedy (2013); Thomas (2015).

Chapter 5

1 Dilke (1868).
2 Bell (2009).
3 Roberts (2016), www.telegraph.co.uk/news/2016/09/13/canzuk-after-brexit-canada-australia-new-zealand-and-britain-can/
4 Belich (2009), 4, 9.
5 Brantlinger (2003). If you search for "dying races" on Google these days, you will find racist sites warning that the "white race" is dying, confirming that what goes around, comes around.
6 Robinson (2016).
7 Pearson (1893); Lake and Reynolds (2008), ch. 3. Also see note 4.
8 It should also be noted that calls came from early modern British historians at this time to reclaim the idea of Greater Britain as a way to reconnect Britain's domestic and imperial histories during the Stuart and Georgian eras. See Armitage (1999).
9 Pocock (1975, reprinted 2005); Colley (1992).
10 Bridge and Fedorowich (2003); Buckner and Francis (2005); Buckner and Francis (2006); Darian-Smith, Grimshaw, and Macintyre (2007).
11 Bridge and Fedorowich (2003), 11.
12 Buckner and Francis (2005), 13.
13 See especially Crosbie and Hampton (2016).
14 The settlers of Kenya and Southern Rhodesia are placed in the company of British expatriate communities in Argentina, Egypt, India, Ceylon, Malaya, and Shanghai by Bickers (2010), though he also insists that they created "mini-Britains" (2) that corresponded in many respects to the larger settler societies that are more commonly understood to comprise the British world.
15 An excellent survey of these issues is Ward (2008).
16 Buckner and Francis (2005), 16; Bickford-Smith (2003); MacKenzie (2007); Aled Jones and Bill Jones (2003); Crosbie (2016).
17 See especially Lowry (2003). Reed (2016) is a fine study of a range of colonial subjects who made such civic claims.
18 Gordon (1928), 74.
19 Schwarz (2007), 23.
20 Lake and Reynolds (2008); Schwarz (2011). For the intellectual foundations of this racial project, see also Bell (2009); Koditschek (2011); and Behm (2015).

21 Denoon (1983).
22 Magee and Thompson (2010), 20.
23 Magee and Thompson (2010), 234.
24 Belich (2009), 181.
25 Wolfe (1999), 2.
26 Veracini (2010), 99, 33–52.
27 Veracini (2010), 12, 69.
28 Edmonds and Carey (2013), 2; Bateman and Pilkington (2011), 2. Veracini's first book was a study of Israel as a settler colony. His latest is tellingly titled *The Settler Colonial Present* (2015).
29 Moses (2004). Patrick Wolfe influentially addressed the issue of settler colonialism and genocide in Wolfe (2006).
30 Coombes (2006), 2.
31 Wolfe (2001).
32 Sadly, Patrick Wolfe recently passed away, but with the view that his publications provide a kind of afterlife, I will refer to him in the present tense.
33 Wolfe (2016), 7.
34 Ignatiev (1995).
35 Hopkins (2008); Ward (2005, 2007).
36 Veracini (2010), 95.
37 Weaver (2003), 30.
38 Belmessous (2012; 2013; 2015).
39 Elkins and Pedersen (2005).
40 Crosby (1986). Also see Diamond (1997); McNeill (2010).

Chapter 6

1 Barnett (1972); Woodcock (1974). Even the arch-imperialist Winston Churchill was judged a guilty man by Charmley (1993), who suggests he would have been better advised to negotiate with Nazi Germany than accept the United States' smothering embrace.
2 Darwin (1991).
3 The collection is available online at http://bdeep.org/. An important predecessor was the documentary collection of volumes on the British withdrawal from India: Mansergh and Moon (1970–83).
4 Darwin (1984, 1988); Louis (1978, 1984); Louis and Robinson (1994); Holland (1985, 1991).
5 Heinlein (2002); Butler (2002); Hyam (2006); Darwin (2009); Husain (2014).
6 Boyce (1997), 270. Note too that he identifies the British Empire with "England."

7 McIntyre (1998) 103.
8 White (1999), 98.
9 Hyam (2006), 404.
10 Anderson (2005); Elkins (2005).
11 Branch (2009); Bennett (2013).
12 Bayly and Harper (2007). Also see Spector (2007).
13 Grob-Fitzgibbon (2011).
14 Sinclair (2006); Thomas (2008); Walton (2013).
15 See Elkins and Pedersen (2005); Murphy (2015).
16 Edgerton (2006).
17 Scott (1993).
18 French (2012), 1–2. Also see French (2011, 2015); Newsinger (2002); Dixon (2012).
19 Bennett (2013), 268.
20 Thomas (2014).
21 Klose (2013).
22 Reis (2015), 131.
23 Darwin (2009), 654.
24 Porter (2004). Focusing specifically on the era of decolonization, Howe (2006) makes a similar argument. For a more balanced assessment, see Thompson (2005).
25 Thompson (2012).
26 Douglas (2002), 161–62.
27 Kahler (1984).
28 Whiting (2012).
29 Schwarz (2011).
30 Schofield (2013).
31 Murphy (2013).
32 Nairn (1977).
33 See Glass (2014); Colley (2014); Kumar (2015); Nielsen and Ward (2015).
34 Grob-Fitzgibbon (2016).
35 Kenny and Pearce (2015).
36 See, most recently, Darwin (2015).
37 Buettner (2016).
38 Bailkin (2012), 12. Also see Bailkin (2015).
39 House and Thompson (2013).
40 Matera (2015); Paul (1997).
41 Webster (2012).
42 Boucher (2014). The case for the decolonization of the white dominions is made by Hopkins (2008).

43 Buettner (2016), 223–28; Buettner (2010).
44 The interviews collected in Walker (1993) give some hint of this impact.
45 Consider by way of example Philip Mason, a member of the Indian Civil Service from 1928 to 1947, who subsequently became the founding director of the Institute of Race Relations.
46 Collingham (2007); Buettner (2008, 2009). French food historians have begun to follow a similar line of inquiry. See, for example, James (2016).
47 A helpful introduction to these issues is offered in the essay by Andrew Thompson with Meaghan Kowalsky in Thompson (2012).
48 Webster (2005), 8, *passim*. Also see Ward (2001) and, for a comparative perspective, Craggs and Wintle (2016).
49 Winder (2006), 144–45.
50 Ward (2001), 10.
51 See, for example, Shepard (2006); Hargreaves (2005).

Chapter 7

1 It also gave rise to the important work of William Appleman Williams and his students, who reshaped the history of American foreign policy with their studies of American imperialism. See, e. g., Williams (1969).
2 Louis (2006), 6.
3 Both Britain in the nineteenth century and the United States since 1945 are characterized as hegemonic states, not empires, by Wallerstein (2005) and O'Brien and Clesse (2002).
4 For a vigorous critique of American exceptionalism, see Bender (2001).
5 Robin (2004), B1. This remark echoes the one that President Clinton's secretary of state, Madeleine Albright, put to Colin Powell, then chairman of the Joint Chiefs of Staff: "What's the point of having this superb military you are always talking about if we can't use it?" For a fascinating analysis of one of the intellectual sources of neoconservatism and its endorsement of empire, see Norton (2004).
6 Project for the New American Century (2000), "Rebuilding America's Defenses: Strategy, Forces, and Resources for a New Century" (September), iv, i. Available online at www.newamericancentury.org.
7 Ricks, (2001), A1, A13.
8 Buchanan (1999).
9 Remnick (2003), 21, 23. In Britain, the prime minister, Tony Blair, and his advisers shared the Bush administration's belief in the need for an assertive foreign policy, and were equally unabashed in embracing the label "imperial." See Cooper (2002).
10 Ferguson (2003a,b).
11 Ferguson (2004), 29, 2.
12 Boot (2001), 7, 5; Boot (2002).

13 Among the conservative commentators who have endorsed the notion of American empire are Krauthammer (2002/2003), and D'Souza (2002).
14 Ignatieff (2003). The *New York Times* columnist Thomas Friedman and the *Washington Post* columnist Sebastian Mallaby took similar positions. For an early endorsement of empire as a vehicle of humanitarian intervention, see Rieff (1999).
15 Lal (2004); Ferguson (2003).
16 Barnett (2004); Tyson (2005).
17 Kaplan (2002); Kaplan (2005).
18 Cohen (2004), 61.
19 See http://www.nationalwarcollege.org/EMPIRES/
20 Suskind (2004), 51.
21 The following list of books includes only those that refer to "empire" or "imperialism" in their titles: Barber (2003); Landau, (2003); Mann, (2003); Newhouse (2003); Burbach and Tarbell (2004); Dorrien (2004); Eland (2003); Garrison (2004); Harootunian (2004); Judis (2004); Khalidi (2004); Scheuer (2004); Boggs (2005); Gardner and Young (2005); Foster (2006).
22 Chomsky (2004, 2005, 2006). It is worth noting that Venezuelan president Hugo Chavez recommended the first of these books in his fiery September 2006 speech to the United Nations.
23 Harvey (2003).
24 Johnson (2000, 2004); Bacevich (2002, 2003, 2005).
25 The argument that America is not an empire has been made by Nye (2002); Hanson (2003); Pagden (2005).
26 The most prescient spokesman for this position is Wallerstein (2003). For a recent reiteration of this view, see Schell (2006).
27 Preble (2004). Fukuyama (2006) breaks with his colleagues over Iraq.
28 Ferguson (2006).
29 Newhouse (2003).
30 Fukuyama (1992); Boggs (2005).
31 Garrison (2004); Walker (2002).
32 Barfield (2001).
33 Lieven (2002), xiii.
34 Calhoun et. al. (2006); *Daedalus*, 84/2 (2005). Also see the forum on "An American Empire?" in *The Wilson Quarterly*, 26/3 (Summer 2002).
35 Khalidi (2004).
36 Maier (2006); Burbank and Cooper (2011); Parsons (2010).
37 Maier (2006), 3, 9, 41.
38 Jasanoff (2005), 1–2.
39 Louis and Robinson (1994).
40 Goldberg (2005), 36.
41 See Cowell (2004), 4; Colley (2002); Pryce-Jones (2002).

42 Ferguson (2004, 2005). For a penetrating critique of the first book, see Cooper (2004).
43 Elkins (2005a); Dalrymple (2005).
44 Cole (2006); Khalidi (2004); Meyer (2004); Ingram (2005).
45 Colley (2005).
46 Hopkins (2007), 107. A long-awaited book by Hopkins on the American empire is forthcoming.
47 Porter (2006), 71.
48 Porter (2006), 34, 37, 38, 39.
49 Porter (2006), 44.
50 Porter (2006), 88, 92.
51 Mann (2003), 13.
52 The emphasis on the formal empire was enshrined in Benians (1929–59) and persists in works such as Lloyd (1996).
53 Anderson and Cayton (2005).
54 Adas (2001); Lamar and Thompson (1981).
55 The experiences of American Indians may be more directly comparable to the incorporation of Britain's Celtic fringe, as detailed by Hechter (1975).
56 See Go (2006).
57 Louis (1978).
58 Boot (2001).
59 Osterhammel (1999). The term "triple assault" comes from Abernethy (2000).
60 Kinzer (2006).
61 Steinmetz (2006), 155.
62 Gallagher and Robinson (1963).
63 Though a remarkably incompetent one according to Chandrasekaran (2006).
64 Anderson (2005), 73.
65 Siegel (2002) refers to Afghanistan as a "semi-protectorate."
66 Dodge (2003).
67 Maier (2006), 20.
68 Cohen (2006); Porter (2006); Joffe (2006).
69 Johnson (2004), 1, 154.
70 Bacevich (2002), 167.
71 Johnson (2004), 1.
72 Some political scientists may disagree: see the table that quantifies the decline of British naval power in Thompson (2001), 287.
73 For the standard interpretation of the rise and fall of British power, see Kennedy (1987). For forceful rebuttals, see the special issue of *The International History Review*, 13/4 (November 1991) on "The Decline of Great Britain," with essays by G. Martel, K. Neilson, J. R. Ferris, and B. J. C. McKercher; and Ingram (2003).

74 Kennedy (1976); Gough (1999).
75 Martel (1991), 680–683; Ingram (2003), 25, *passim*.
76 Johnson (2004), 23.
77 Callwell (1996 [1909]).
78 Heathcote (1974).
79 See Lunt (1981).
80 Barnet (2004).
81 Eland (2003), 13.
82 Ricks (2004); Graham (2003).
83 See Avant (2005).
84 This included a company of Gurkhas. Ricks (2006), 176, 371.
85 Young (2005), 44.
86 Hobson (1972 [1902]); Lenin, V. I. (1970 [1916]) Also see Fieldhouse (1967).
87 Cain and Hopkins (2002).
88 Maier (2006), 107.
89 Finnegan (2003).
90 O'Brien (2002).
91 Harvey (2003).
92 A notable exception is Klare (2004).
93 See Carroll (2006).
94 Hobson (1997 [1902]), part 2, ch. 1.
95 Pomeranz (2005).
96 Davis (2001).
97 Adas (2006).
98 Harootunian (2004).
99 Rhodes (2005).
100 Mehta (1999).
101 Milbank and Babington (2004), A4.
102 Cooper (2005), 201; Burbank and Cooper (2011).
103 Metcalf (1994), x.
104 "Proclamation by the Queen in Council to the Princes, Chiefs, and People of India," November 1, 1858, MSS Eur D620, British Library.
105 Wolfe (2001).
106 Porter (2006), 120.
107 Porter (2006), 109, 112.
108 Metcalf (1994), ch. 2.
109 See Levine (2004).
110 Tyson (2005b), A5.
111 I am grateful to Marilyn Young for helping me to sharpen this distinction.

Chapter 8

1. Kennedy (2007), revised here as Chapter 8.
2. Kramer (2011), 1348.
3. Go (2011), ix.
4. Adas (2001); Bender (2002).
5. Williams (1969).
6. Kumar (2012), 101; Hitchens (1990).
7. Ferguson (2003, 2004); Mead (2008).
8. Go (2011), 6, 7.
9. Go (2011), 24.
10. Porter (2006); O'Brien and Clesse (2002).
11. Go (2011), 47.
12. Go (2011), 97.
13. Go (2011), 138, 118.
14. Go (2011), 108–10.
15. Go (2011), 185–87.
16. Go (2011), 184, 187.
17. See United States Department of Labor, Bureau of Labor Statistics, chart of productivity changes in the nonfarm business sector, 1947–2012, at http://www.bls.gov/lpc/prodybar.htm.
18. Go (2011), 191.
19. Go (2011), 178.
20. Go (2011), 207, 167.
21. Gallagher (1982).
22. Cannadine, (2003), 43.
23. Kennedy (1987).

Chapter 9

1. The list includes Linda Colley, James Epstein, Catherine Hall, Philippa Levine, Richard Price, and Martin Wiener. On the imperial turn, see Burton (2003).
2. Recent examples include Howe (2012); Ghosh (2012); and Ballantyne (2010).
3. For a model on how to address these interconnected issues with sensitivity and insight, see Eley (2005).
4. See Linenthal and Engelhardt (1996); Macintyre and Clark (2003); MacMillan (2009).
5. Fieldhouse (1984), Winks (1984); Buckner (1993).

6 These included the Beit Professor at Oxford, the Smuts Professor and Vere Harmsworth Professor at Cambridge, and the Rhodes Professor at Kings College London.
7 Gallagher and Robinson (1953); Robinson and Gallagher with Denny (1961).
8 Cain and Hopkins (1993).
9 For a recent assessment of MacKenzie and the "Studies in Imperialism" series, see Thompson (2013).
10 A point made about Africanists by Zimmerman (2013).
11 The latter point had already been made from a political economy perspective, especially by Eric Hobsbawm (1968), and in his great trilogy on nineteenth-century Europe, Hobsbawm (1962, 1975, 1987) but this approach gained remarkably little purchase in British imperial historiography. I am grateful to Richard Price for reminding me of this tradition.
12 Said (1978).
13 Stoler and Cooper (1997), 1.
14 Mackenzie (1984).
15 Pomeranz (2014), 13.
16 An example of a prominent new imperial historian who embraced world history is Antoinette Burton (2012).
17 The report can be found on the NACBS website at http://www.nacbs.org/archive/nacbs-report-on-the-state-and-future-of-british-studies.
18 Louis, "Foreword" to each volume of the *Oxford History*, vii.
19 For my own critique, see Chapter 2.
20 Wm. Roger Louis (1999).
21 Levine (2004); Morgan and Hawkins (2004); Beinart and Hughes (2007).
22 Darwin (2012), 12. Italics added.
23 Albright on the NBC *Today* show on February 5, 1998; Foreign Minister Hubert Verdrine in "To Paris, U.S. Looks Like a 'Hyperpower'," *New York Times*, February 19, 1999.
24 For an early warning of the neocon agenda, see Ricks (2001). The intellectual roots of neoconservatism's embrace of empire are traced in Norton (2004).
25 Ignatieff (2003). The liberal case for an American empire is dissected in Bacevich (2002).
26 Calhoun, Cooper, and Moore (2006).
27 Ferguson (2004).
28 Fleming (2010), 9.
29 Ferguson (2005).
30 Buchanan (1999).
31 Preble (2004).
32 Porter (2006a).
33 Go (2011). For my critique of Go, see Chapter 8.

34 Maier (2006), 43.
35 Parsons (2010).
36 Kagan (2010). On Kagan's role in Afghanistan, see Chandrasekaran (2012).
37 Crocker III (2011a), 3, 4, 78, 146.
38 Crocker III (2011b).
39 Quotes come from the film "2016: Obama's America" (2012). Also see D'Souza (2011).
40 Quoted in Walsh (2011).
41 Quoted in Reeves (2010).
42 For a valuable overview, see de Groot (2013).
43 R. Cooper (2002).
44 See Naughtie (2004).
45 Quoted in Gott (2011b).
46 Brogan (2005). Brown went on to say: "We should talk, and rightly so, about British values that are enduring . . . . Our strong traditions of fair play, of openness, of internationalism, these are great British values."
47 Gimson (2011); "British Empire Medal to Return says David Cameron," *BBC News* (October 28, 2011), www.bbc.com/news/.
48 "William Hague Says UK Must Shed 'Guilt' Over Empire," *BBC News* (August 31, 2012), www.bbc.com/news/.
49 Baxter (2013); Penny (2010).
50 Ferguson credited his sons with the inspiration for this idea, though he also acknowledged that his daughter showed less enthusiasm for video war games. See Vasagar (2010).
51 Paxman (2012).
52 Eden (2012). In a rich irony, David Attenborough defended the 1973 BBC series "The British Empire" against critics who complained that it cast the empire in too negative a light: he was then the BBC's director of programming. See Fleming (2010).
53 Jeal (2007).
54 Jeal (2011).
55 Jeal (2011).
56 Lakshmi (2013), A10.
57 Newsinger (2006).
58 Gott (2011a), 3.
59 Hunt (2014); Kwarteng (2011), 2, 8. The journalist and historian Pankaj Mishra also recently launched a high-profile salvo against Ferguson, calling him an "evangelist-cum-historian of empire" and comparing him to the early-twentieth-century American racial theorist Lothrop Stoddard in an incendiary review in the *London Review of Books*, 33/21 (2011), 11–12. Ferguson threatened to sue Mishra for defamation. See Beaumont (2011). Mishra (2012) has written a study of Asian critics of empire.

60 See, for example, Mehta (1999); Pitts (2005); Mantena (2010); and Koditschek (2011).
61 James (2012). Also see Warren (2012) and Allen (2012).
62 Elkins (2005); Anderson (2005).
63 For commentaries on the case from each of the three historical experts, see Anderson (2011), Elkins (2011), and Bennett (2011).
64 Anderson (2013), Elkins (2013).
65 Kaplan (2014).
66 Freeman (2012). The article was a commentary on Laycock (2012).
67 Davies (2001), 1053.
68 Wiener (2013), 32. For someone who once famously argued that British industrial decline in the late twentieth century was attributable to the embrace of gentlemanly values by the middle class a century earlier, Wiener's insistence that the adverse effects of British imperial rule had passed its sell-by date for the Indians, Africans, and other ex-colonial peoples who gained their independence some fifty years ago seems inconsistent with his earlier views on the past's power to shape the present. See Wiener (1982).
69 Darwin (2012), xii, xiii. Also see Darwin (2009). Taking these two books together, Darwin devotes nearly 1,300 pages to this ramshackle empire.
70 This is the subject of Burton and Kennedy (2016), with contributions from a wide array of British imperial historians.

Epilogue

1 Evans (2013).
2 Smith and Gray (2016).
3 Roberts (2016).
4 Abidi (2017).
5 "Lessons from History for the Brexiters," *The Guardian* (May 24, 2016), accessed online. The number of self-identified pro-Brexit historians was far smaller, though nine of them pronounced themselves Historians for Britain and published a glossy booklet, *'Peace-Makers or Credit Takers?' The EU and Peace in Europe*, edited by David Abulafia, which can be found at http://historiansforbritain.org/wp-content/uploads/sites/12/2016/02/WzW-Historians-for-Britain-essays-web2.pdf.
6 See Peter Stansky, chair, *NACBS Report on the State and Future of British Studies* (1999), at http://www.nacbs.org/archive/nacbs-report-on-the-state-and-future-of-british-studies. I was a member of the committee.
7 Osnos (2015), 55. Rubio was reading William Manchester's three volume biography of Churchill.
8 Burke (2015); Falwell Jr. (2016).
9 Eckholm (2017).
10 Arnn (2015), xx, 101, 109, 115–16.

WORKS CITED

Abernethy, David B. (2000), *The Dynamics of Global Dominance: European Overseas Empires 1415-1980*, New Haven: Yale University Press.
Abidi, Adnan (2017), "Ministers Aim to Build 'Empire 2.0' with African Commonwealth," *The Times* (March 6), accessed online.
Adas, Michael (1989), *Machines as the Measure of Men: Science, Technology, and Ideologies of Western Dominance*, Ithaca: Cornell University Press.
Adas, Michael (1993), "'High' Imperialism and the 'New' History," in Michael Adas (ed.), *Islamic and European Expansion: The Forging of a Global Order*, 311–44. Philadelphia: Temple University Press.
Adas, Michael (2001), "From Settler Colony to Global Hegemon: Integrating the Exceptionalist Narrative of the American Experience into World History," *The American Historical Review*, 106/5 (December): 1692–1720.
Adas, Michael (2006), *Dominance by Design: Technological Imperatives and America's Civilizing Mission*, Cambridge, MA: Harvard University Press.
Ahmad, Aijaz (1992), *In Theory: Classes, Nations, Literatures*, London: Verso.
Allen, John (2012), "To talk about British atrocities in Kenya during the Mau Mau era is nonsense," *The Guardian.Co.UK* (May 9).
Amin, Shahid (1995). *Event, Metaphor, Memory: Chauri Chaura, 1922-92*, Berkeley: University of California Press.
Anderson, David (2005), *Histories of the Hanged: The Dirty War in Kenya and the End of Empire*, New York: W. W. Norton.
Anderson, David (2011), "Mau Mau in the High Court and the 'Lost' British Empire Archives: Colonial Conspiracy or Bureaucratic Bungle?" *Journal of Imperial and Commonwealth History*, 39/5: 699–716.
Anderson, David (2013), "Atoning for the Sins of Empire," *The New York Times* (June 13).
Anderson, Fred, and Andrew Cayton (2005), *The Dominion of War: Empire and Liberty in North America 1500-2000*, New York: Viking.
Anderson, Jon Lee (2005), "The Man in the Palace," *The New Yorker* (6 June).
Anderson, Warwick (2006), *The Cultivation of Whiteness: Science, Health, and Racial Destiny in Australia*, Durham: Duke University Press.
Armitage, David (1999), "Greater Britain: A Useful Category of Historical Analysis?," *The American Historical Review*, 104/2 (April): 427–45.
Armitage, David (2000), *The Ideological Origins of the British Empire*, Cambridge: Cambridge University Press.
Arnn, Larry P. (2015), *Churchill's Trial: Winston Churchill and the Salvation of Free Government*, Nashville: Nelson Books.
Arnold, David (1993), *Colonizing the Body: State Medicine and Epidemic Disease in Nineteenth-Century India*, Berkeley: University of California Press.

Arnold, David (2006), *The Tropics and the Traveling Gaze: India, Landscape, and Science, 1800-1856*, Seattle: University of Washington Press.
Asad, Talal, ed. (1973), *Anthropology and the Colonial Encounter*, London: Ithaca Press.
Ashcroft, Bill, Gareth Griffiths, and Helen Tiffin, eds. (1989), *The Empire Writes Back: Theory and Practice in Post-Colonial Literatures*, London: Routledge.
Ashcroft, Bill, Gareth Griffiths, and Helen Tiffin, eds. (1995), *The Post-Colonial Studies Reader*, London: Routledge.
Avant, Deborah D. (2005). *The Market for Force: The Consequences of Privatizing Security*, Cambridge: Cambridge University Pres.
Bacevich, Andrew J. (2002), *American Empire: The Realities and Consequences of U.S. Diplomacy*, Cambridge, MA: Harvard University Press.
Bacevich, Andrew J, ed. (2003), *The Imperial Tense: Prospects and Problems of American Empire*, Chicago: Ivan R. Dee.
Bacevich, Andrew J. (2005), *The New American Militarism: How Americans are Seduced by War*, New York: Oxford University Press.
Bailkin, Jordanna (2012), *The Aftermath of Empire*, Berkeley: University of California Press.
Bailkin, Jordanna (2015), "Where Did the Empire Go? Archives and Decolonization in Britain," *American Historical Review*, 120/3: 884–99.
Ballantyne, Tony (2002), *Orientalism and Race: Aryanism in the British Empire*, New York: Palgrave.
Ballantyne, Tony (2006), *Between Colonialism and Diaspora: Sikh Cultural Formations in an Imperial World*, Durham: Duke University Press.
Ballantyne, Tony (2010), "The Changing Shape of the Modern British Empire and Its Historiography," *The Historical Journal*, 53/2: 429–52.
Ballantyne, Tony, and Antoinette Burton, eds. (2005), *Bodies in Contact: Rethinking Colonial Encounters in World History*, Durham: Duke University Press.
Banivanua Mar, Tracey (2015), *Decolonisation and the Pacific: Indigenous Globalisation and the Ends of Empire*, Cambridge: Cambridge University Press.
Barber, Benjamin R. (2003), *Fear's Empire: War, Terrorism, and Democracy*, New York: W. W. Norton.
Barfield, Thomas J. (2001), "The Shadow Empires: Imperial State Formation along the Chinese-Nomad Frontier," in Susan E. Alcock, Terence N. D'Altroy, Kathleen D. Morrison, and Carla N. Sinopoli (eds.), *Empires: Perspectives from Archaeology and History*, 10–41. Cambridge: Cambridge University Press.
Barkan, Elazar (1994), "Post-Anti-Colonial Histories: Representing the Other in Imperial Britain", *Journal of British Studies*, 33/2: 190–203.
Barker, Francis, Peter Hulme, and Margaret Iversen, eds. (1994), *Colonial Discourse and Post-Colonial Theory: A Reader*, Manchester: Manchester University Press.
Barnett, Correlli (1972), *The Collapse of British Power*, New York: William Morrow.
Barnett, Thomas P. M. (2004), *The Pentagon's New Map: War and Peace in the Twenty-First Century*, New York: Berkley.
Bateman, Fiona, and Lionel Pilkington, eds. (2011), *Studies in Settler Colonialism: Politics, Identity and Culture*, Basingstoke: Palgrave Macmillan.

Baucom, Ian (1999), *Out of Place: Englishness, Empire, and the Locations of Identity*, Princeton: Princeton University Press.
Baxter, Rory (2013), "Pupils Should Be Proud of British Heroism," *PS Public Service.Co.UK* (April 23), accessed online.
Bayly, Christopher (2000), "Ireland, India, and the Empire: 1780-1914," *Transactions of the Royal Historical Society*, 6th series, 10: 377–97.
Bayly, Christopher (2004), *The Birth of the Modern World 1789-1914: Global Connections and Comparisons*, Oxford: Blackwell.
Bayly, Christopher, and Tim Harper (2004), *Forgotten Wars: Freedom and Revolution in Southeast Asia*, Cambridge, MA: Belknap Press.
Beaumont, Peter (2011), "Niall Ferguson Threatens to Sue over Accusation of Racism," *The Guardian* (November 26), accessed online.
Beckert, Sven (2014), *Empire of Cotton: A Global History*, New York: Random House.
Behdad, Ali (1994). *Belated Travellers: Orientalism in the Age of Colonial Dissolution*, Durham: Duke University Press.
Behm, Amanda (2015), "Settler Historicism and Anticolonial Rebuttal in the British World, 1880-1920," *Journal of World History*, 26/4: 785–813.
Beinart, William, and Lotte Hughes (2007), *Environment and Empire*, Oxford: Oxford University Press.
Belich, James (2009), *Replenishing the Earth: The Settler Revolution and the Rise of the Anglo-World, 1783-1939*, Oxford: Oxford University Press.
Bell, Duncan, ed. (2007), *Victorian Visions of Global Order: Empire and International Relations in Nineteenth-Century Political Thought*, Cambridge: Cambridge University Press.
Bell, Duncan (2009), *The Idea of Greater Britain: Empire and the Future of World Order, 1860-1900*, Princeton: Princeton University Press.
Bell, Morag, Robin Butlin, and Michael Heffernan, eds. (1995), *Geography and Imperialism, 1820-1940*, Manchester: Manchester University Press.
Belmessous, Saliha, ed. (2012), *Native Claims: Indigenous Law Against Empire, 1500-1920*, New York: Oxford University Press.
Belmessous, Saliha, (2013), *Assimilation and Empire: Uniformity in British and French Colonies, 1541-1954*, New York: Oxford University Press.
Belmessous, Saliha, ed. (2015), *Empire by Treaty: Negotiating European Expansion*, New York: Oxford University Press.
Beloff, Max (1996), "The British Empire," *History Today*, 46/2: 13–20.
Beloff, Max (1970), *Imperial Sunset, Vol. 1: Britain's Liberal Empire, 1897-1921*, New York: Knopf.
Bender, Thomas, ed. (2001), *Rethinking American History in a Global Age*, Berkeley: University of California Press.
Benians, E. A., J. Holland Rose, Arthur P. Newton, and Henry Dodwell, eds. (1929–59), *The Cambridge History of the British Empire*, 9 vols., Cambridge: Cambridge University Press.
Bennett, Huw (2011), "Soldiers in the Court Room: The British Army's Part in the Kenya Emergency under the Legal Spotlight," *Journal of Imperial and Commonwealth History*, 39/5: 717–30.
Bennett, Huw (2013), *Fighting the Mau Mau: The British Army and Counter-Insurgency in the Kenya Emergency*, Cambridge: Cambridge University Press.

Berman, Bruce, and John Lonsdale (1992), *Unhappy Valley: Conflict in Kenya and Africa*, Athens: Ohio University Press.
Bickford-Smith, Vivian (2003), "Revisiting Anglicisation in the Nineteenth-Century Cape Colony," in Carl Bridge and Kent Fedorowich (eds.), *The British World*, 82–95. London: Frank Cass.
Bickers, Robert, ed. (2010), *Settlers and Expatriates*, New York: Oxford University Press.
Bishop, Peter (1989), *The Myth of Shangri-La: Tibet, Travel Writing and the Western Creation of Sacred Landscape*, Berkeley: University of California Press.
Bhabha, Homi (1994), *The Location of Culture*, London: Routledge.
Boggs, Carl (2005), *Imperial Delusions: American Militarism and Endless War*, Lanham: Rowman and Littlefield.
Boot, Max (2001), "The Case for American Empire," *The Weekly Standard*, 7/5 (15 October).
Boot, Max (2002), *The Savage Wars of Peace: Small Wars and the Rise of American Power*, New York: Basic Books.
Bose, Sugata (2006), *A Hundred Horizons: The Indian Ocean in the Age of Global Empire*, Cambridge, MA: Harvard University Press.
Boyce, David G. (1999), *Decolonization and the British Empire, 1775-1997*, London: Palgrave.
Boucher, Ellen (2014), *Empire's Children: Child Emigration, Welfare, and the Decline of the British World, 1869-1967*, Cambridge: Cambridge University Press.
Bourguet, Marie-Noëlle, Christian Licoppe, and H. Otto Siburn, eds. (2002), *Instruments, Travel and Science: Itineraries of Precision from the Seventeenth to the Twentieth Century*, London: Routledge.
Brantlinger, Patrick (1998), *Rule of Darkness: British Literature and Imperialism 1830-1914*, Ithaca: Cornell University Press.
Brantlinger, Patrick (2003), *Dark Vanishings: Discourse on the Extinction of Primitive Races, 1800-1930*, Ithaca: Cornell University Press.
Branch, Daniel (2009), *Defeating Mau Mau, Creating Kenya: Counterinsurgency, Civil War, and Decolonization*, Cambridge: Cambridge University Press.
Bravo, Michael T. (1999), "Precision and Curiosity in Scientific Travel: James Rennell and the Orientalist Geography of the New Imperial Age (1760–1830)," in Jas Elsner and Joan-Pau Rubiés (eds.), *Voyages and Visions: Towards a Cultural History of Travel*, 162–83. London: Reaktion.
Bridge, Carl, and Kent Fedorowich (2003), "Introduction: Mapping the British World," in Carl Bridge and Kent Fedorowich (eds.), *The British World: Diaspora, Culture and Identity*, 1–15. London: Frank Cass.
Breckenridge, Carol, and Peter Van Der Veer, eds. (1993), *Orientalism and the Postcolonial Predicament*, Philadelphia: University of Pennsylvania Press.
Brockway, Lucile H. (1979), *Science and Colonial Expansion: The Role of the British Royal Botanical Gardens*, New York: Academic Press.
Brodie, Fawn M. (1967), *The Devil Drives: A Life of Sir Richard Burton*, New York: W. W. Norton.
Brogan, Benedict (2005), "It's Time to Celebrate the Empire, Says Brown," *The Daily Mail* (January 15), accessed online.
Brown, Judith M., and Wm. Roger Louis, eds. (1999), *The Oxford History of the British Empire, Vol. 4: The Twentieth Century*, Oxford: Oxford University Press.

Buchanan, Patrick J. (1999), *A Republic, Not an Empire*, Washington, DC: Regnery.
Buckner, Philip (1993), "Whatever Happened to the British Empire?" *Journal of the Canadian Historical Association*, 4: 3–32.
Buckner, Philip, and R. Douglas Francis, eds. (2005), *Rediscovering the British World*, Calgary: Calgary University Press.
Buckner, Philip, and R. Douglas Francis, eds. (2006), *Canada and the British World: Culture, Migration, and Identity*, Vancouver: University of British Columbia Press.
Buell, Frederick (1994), *National Culture and the New Global System*, Baltimore: Johns Hopkins University Press.
Buettner, Elizabeth (2008), "'Going for an Indian': South Asian Restaurants and the Limits of Multiculturalism in Britain," *The Journal of Modern History*, 80: 865–901.
Buettner, Elizabeth (2009), "Chicken Tikka Masala, Flock Wallpaper, and 'Real' Home Cooking: Assessing Britain's 'Indian' Restaurant Traditions," *Food and History*, 7: 203–29.
Buettner, Elizabeth (2010), "'We Don't Grow Coffee and Bananas in Clapham Junction You Know!': Imperial Britons Back Home," in Robert Bickers (ed.), *Settlers and Expatriates*, 302–28. New York: Oxford University Press.
Buettner, Elizabeth (2016), *Europe After Empire: Decolonization, Society, and Culture*, Cambridge: Cambridge University Press.
Burbach, Roger, and Jim Tarbell (2004), *Imperial Overstretch: George W. Bush and the Hubris of Empire*, London: Zed Books.
Burbank, Jane, and Frederick Cooper (2011), *Empires in World History: Power and the Politics of Difference*, Princeton: Princeton University Press.
Burke, Cathy (2015), "Michael Savage: Trump is the 'Winston Churchill of our Time," *Newsmax* (November 27), accessed online.
Burke, Timothy (1996), *Lifebuoy Men, Lux Women: Commodification, Consumption, and Cleanliness in Modern Zimbabwe*, Durham: Duke University Press.
Burnett, D. Graham (2000), *Masters of All They Surveyed: Exploration, Geography, and a British El Dorado*, Chicago: University of Chicago Press.
Burton, Antoinette (1994a), *Burdens of History: British Feminists, Indian Women, and Imperial Culture, 1865-1915*, Chapel Hill: University of North Carolina Press.
Burton, Antoinette (1994b), "Rules of Thumb: British History and 'Imperial Culture' in Nineteenth- and Twentieth-Century Britain," *Women's History Review*, 3/4: 483–500.
Burton, Antoinette (1997), "Who Needs the Nation? Interrogating 'British' History," *Journal of Historical Sociology*, 10: 227–48.
Burton, Antoinette, ed. (1999), *Gender, Sexuality, and Colonial Modernities*, London, Routledge.
Burton, Antoinette (2003a), *Dwelling in the Archive: Women Writing House, Home, and History in Late Colonial India*, New York: Oxford University Press.
Burton, Antoinette, ed. (2003b), *After the Imperial Turn: Thinking with and through the Nation*, Durham: Duke University Press.
Burton, Antoinette, ed. (2005), *Archive Stories: Facts, Fictions, and the Writing of History*, Durham: Duke University Press.
Burton, Antoinette (2007), *The Postcolonial Careers of Santha Rama Rao*, Durham: Duke University Press.

Burton, Antoinette (2012), *A Primer for Teaching World History: Ten Design Principles*, Durham: Duke University Press.
Burton, Antoinette (2015), "Introduction: Empire of the Book," *Journal of British Studies*, 15/4: 971–97.
Burton, Antoinette, and Dane Kennedy, eds. (2016), *How Empire Shaped Us*, London: Bloomsbury.
Burton, Richard F. (1995 [1860]), *The Lake Regions of Central Africa*, New York: Dover Books.
Bush, Barbara (1999), *Imperialism, Race, and Resistance: Africa and Britain, 1919-45*, London: Routledge.
Bush, Barbara (2006), *Imperialism and Postcolonialism*, Harlow: Pearson Longman.
Butler, Judith (1990), *Gender Trouble: Feminism and the Subversion of Identity*, New York: Routledge.
Butler, L. J. (2002), *Britain and Empire: Adjusting to a Post-Imperial World*, London: I. B. Tauris.
Buzard, James (1993), "Victorian Women and the Implications of Empire," *Victorian Studies*, 36/4: 443–53.
Cain, P. J., and Hopkins, A. G. (1993), *British Imperialism: Vol I, Innovation and Expansion; Vol II, Crisis and Deconstruction*, London: Longman.
Cain, P. J., and Hopkins, A. G. (2002), *British Imperialism, 1688-2000*, 2nd ed. (Harlow: Longman).
Calhoun, Craig, Frederick Cooper, and Kevin W. Moore, eds. (2006), *Lessons of Empire: Imperial Histories and American Power*, New York: New Press.
Callwell, C. E. (1996 [1909]), *Small Wars: Their Principles and Practice*, 3rd ed., Lincoln: University of Nebraska Press.
Cannadine, David (2001), *Ornamentalism: How the British Saw their Empire*, New York: Oxford University Press.
Cannadine, David (2003), "Statecraft: The Haunting Fear of National Decline," in *Churchill's Shadow: Confronting the Past in Modern Britain*, 26–44, Oxford: Oxford University Press.
Cannadine, David (2005), "'Big Tent' Historiography: Transatlantic Obstacles and Opportunities in Writing the History of Empire," *Common Knowledge*, 11/3: 375–92.
Carroll, James (2006), *House of War: The Pentagon and the Disastrous Rise of American Power*, Boston: Houghton, Mifflin, Harcourt.
Carroll, Siobhan (2015), *An Empire of Air and Water: Uncolonizable Space in the British Imagination, 1750-1850*, Philadelphia: University of Pennsylvania Press.
Carter, Paul (1987), *The Road to Botany Bay: An Essay in Spatial History*, London: Faber and Faber.
Chakrabarty, Dipesh (1989), *Rethinking Working-Class History: Bengal, 1890-1940*, Princeton: Princeton University Press.
Chakrabarty, Dipesh (1992), "Postcoloniality and the Artifice of History: Who Speaks for 'Indian' Pasts?" *Representations*, 37: 1–26.
Chakrabarty, Dipesh (2000), *Provincializing Europe: Postcolonial Thought and Historical Difference*, Princeton: Princeton University Press.
Chakrabarty, Dipesh (2002), *Habitations of Modernity: Essays in the Wake of Subaltern Studies*, Chicago: University of Chicago Press.
Chandrasekaran, Rajiv (2006), *Imperial Life in the Emerald City: Inside Iraq's Green Zone*, New York: Vintage.

Chandrasekaran, Rajiv (2012), "Civilian analysts gained Petraeus's ear while he was commander in Afghanistan," *The Washington Post* (December 18), accessed online.
Charmley, John (1993), *Churchill: The End of Glory*, New York: Harcourt Brace.
Chatterjee, Partha (1993), *The Nation and Its Fragments: Colonial and Postcolonial Histories*, Princeton: Princeton University Press.
Chaturvedi, Vinayak, ed. (2000) *Mapping Subaltern Studies and the Postcolonial*, London: Verso.
Chomsky, Noam (2004), *Hegemony or Survival: America's Quest for Global Dominance*, New York: Holt.
Chomsky, Noam (2005), *Imperial Ambitions: Conversations on the Post-9/11 World*, New York: Metropolitan.
Chomsky, Noam (2006), *Failed States: The Abuse of Power and the Assault on Democracy*, New York: Holt.
Chowdhury, Indira (1998), *The Frail Hero and Virile History: Gender and the Politics of Culture in Colonial Bengal*, Delhi: Oxford University Press.
Clark, J. C. D (2000), "Protestantism, Nationalism, and National Identity, 1660-1832," *Historical Journal*, 43/1: 249–76.
Clifford, James (1980), "Orientalism," *History and Theory*, 19/2: 204–23.
Codell, Julia F., and Donald S. Macleod, eds. (1998), *Orientalism Transposed: The Impact on British Culture*, Aldershot: Ashgate.
Cohen, Eliot A. (2004), "History and the Hyperpower," *Foreign Affairs*, 83/4 (July/August): 49–63.
Cohen, William, and E. S. Atieno Odhiambo (1989), *Siaya: The Historical Anthropology of an African Landscape*, London: James Currey.
Cohen, William, and E. S. Atieno Odhiambo (1992), *Burying SM: The Politics of Knowledge and the Sociology of Power in Africa*, London: James Currey.
Cohn, Bernard (1990), *An Anthropologist among the Historians and Other Essays*, Delhi: Oxford University Press.
Cole, Juan (2006), "Empires of Liberty? Democracy and Conquest in French Egypt, British Egypt, and American Iraq," in Craig Calhoun, Frederick Cooper, and Kevin W. Moore (eds.), *Lessons of Empire: Imperial Histories and American Power*, 94–115. New York: New Press.
Colley, Linda (1992), *Britons: Forging the Nation, 1707-1837*, New Haven: Yale University Press.
Colley, Linda (1992), "Britishness and Otherness: An Argument," *Journal of British Studies*, 31/4: 309–29.
Colley, Linda (2002), "What Britannia Taught Bush," *The Guardian* (September 20), accessed online.
Colley, Linda (2005), "Imperial Trauma: The Powerlessness of the Power," *Common Knowledge*, 11/2: 198–214.
Colley, Linda (2014), *Acts of Union and Disunion*, London: BBC Books.
Collingham, E. M. (2001), *Imperial Bodies: The Physical Experience of the Raj, c. 1800-1947*, Cambridge: Polity Press.
Collingham, Lizzy (2007), *Curry: A Tale of Cooks and Conquerors*, New York: Oxford University Press.
Collini, Stefan (1993), "Badly Connected: The Passionate Intensity of Cultural Studies," *Victorian Studies* 36/4: 455–60.

Comaroff, Jean, and John Comaroff (1991), *Of Revelation and Revolution: Christianity, Colonialism, and Consciousness in South Africa*, vol. 1, Chicago: University of Chicago Press.
Coombes, Annie E. (1994), *Reinventing Africa: Museums, Material Culture and Popular Imagination in Late Victorian and Edwardian England*, New Haven: Yale University Press.
Coombes, Annie E, ed. (2006), *Rethinking Settler Colonialism: History and Memory in Australia, Canada, Aotearoa New Zealand and South Africa*, Manchester: Manchester University Press.
Cooper, Frederick (1994), "Conflict and Connection: Rethinking Colonial African History," *American Historical Review*, 99/5: 1516–45.
Cooper, Frederick (2004), "Empires Multiplied," *Comparative Studies of History and Society*, 46/2 (April): 247–72.
Cooper, Frederick (2005), *Colonialism in Question: Theory, Knowledge, History*, Berkeley: University of California Press.
Cooper, Robert (2002), "Why We Still Need Empires," *Sunday Observer* (April 7, 2002), accessed online.
Cotton, Daniel (1993), "Discipline and Punish," *Victorian Studies*, 36/4: 461–65.
Cowell, Alan (2004), "Britain's Imperial Lessons," *The New York Times Week in Review* (March 31), accessed online.
Craggs, Ruth, and Claire Wintle, eds. (2016), *Cultures of Decolonisation: Transnational Productions and Practices, 1945-70*, Manchester: Manchester University Press.
Crais, Clifton (1992), *White Supremacy and Black Resistance in Pre-Industrial South Africa*, Cambridge: Cambridge University Press.
Crocker III, H. W. (2011a), *The Politically Incorrect Guide to the British Empire*, Washington, DC: Regnery.
Crocker III, H. W. (2011b), "What America Could Learn From the British Empire: Frugality," *The Washington Times* (October 27), accessed online.
Crosbie, Barry (2016), "The Curious Case of the *Chabutra-Wallahs*: Britons and Irish Imperial Culture in Nineteenth-Century India," in Barry Crosbie and Mark Hampton (eds.), *The Cultural Construction of the British World*, 107–25. Manchester: Manchester University Press.
Crosbie, Barry, and Mark Hampton, eds. (2016), *The Cultural Construction of the British World*, Manchester: Manchester University Press.
Crosby, Alfred (1986), *Ecological Imperialism: The Biological Expansion of Europe, 900-1900*, Cambridge: Cambridge University Press.
Cumming, Duncan (1987), *The Gentleman Savage: The Life of Mansfield Parkyns 1823–1894*, London: Century.
Curthoys, Ann (2003), "We've Just Started Making National Histories, and You Want Us to Stop Already?" in Antoinette Burton (ed.), *After the Imperial Turn*, 70–89. Durham: Duke University Press.
Curtin, Philip D. (1964), *The Image of Africa: British Ideas and Action, 1780–1850*, Madison, WI: University of Wisconsin Press.
Dalrymple, William (2005), "An Essay in Imperial Villain-Making," *The Guardian* (May 24), accessed online.
Darby, Phillip (1998), "Taking Fieldhouse Further: Post- Colonizing Imperial History," *Journal of Imperial and Commonwealth History*, 26/2: 232–50.

Darian-Smith, Kate, Patricia Grimshaw, and Stuart Macintyre, eds. (2007), *Britishness Abroad: Transnational Movements and Imperial Culture*, Melbourne: Melbourne University Press.

Darwin, John (1997), "Imperialism and the Victorians: The Dynamics of Territorial Expansion", *English Historical Review*, 112/447: 614–42.

Darwin, John (1984), "British Decolonization since 1945: A Pattern or a Puzzle?" *Journal of Imperial and Commonwealth History*, 12/2: 187–209.

Darwin, John (1988), *Britain and Decolonisation: The Retreat from Empire in the Post-War World*, Houndmills: Macmillan.

Darwin, John (1991), *The End of the British Empire: The Historical Debate*, Oxford: Basil Blackwell.

Darwin, John (2009), *The Empire Project: The Rise and Fall of the British World-System 1830-1970*, Cambridge: Cambridge University Press.

Darwin, John (2012), *Unfinished Empire: The Global Expansion of Britain*, New York: Bloomsbury.

Darwin, John (2015), "Memory of Empire in Britain," in Dietmar Rothermund (ed.), *Memories of Post-imperial Nations: The Aftermath of Decolonization, 1945–2013*, 18–37. Delhi: Cambridge University Press.

Davies, Norman (2001), *The Isles*, New York: Oxford University Press.

Davis, Mike (2001), *Late Victorian Holocausts: El Nino Famines and the Making of the Third World*, London: Verso.

Dawson, Graham (1994), *Soldier Heroes: British Adventure, Empire, and the Imagining of Masculinities*, London: Routledge.

de Groot, Joanna (2013), *Empire and History Writing in Britain c. 1750-2012*, Manchester: Manchester University Press.

Dening, Greg (1988), *Islands and Beaches: Discourse on a Silent Land, Marquesas, 1994–1880*, Honolulu: University Press of Hawaii.

Denoon, Donald (1983), *Settler Capitalism: The Dynamics of Dependent Development in the Southern Hemisphere*, Oxford: Clarendon Press.

Diamond, Jared (1997), *Guns, Germs, and Steel: The Fates of Human Societies*, New York: W. W. Norton.

Dilke, Charles Wentworth (1868), *Greater Britain: A Record of Travel in English-Speaking Countries during 1866 and 1867*, London: Macmillan.

Dirks, Nicholas (1992), "From Little King to Landlord: Colonial Discourse and Colonial Rule," in Nicholas Dirks (ed.), *Colonialism and Culture*, 175–208, Ann Arbor: University of Michigan Press.

Dirks, Nicholas (1992a), "Castes of Mind," *Representations*, 37 (Winter): 56–78.

Dirks, Nicholas (2006), *The Scandal of Empire: India and the Creation of Imperial Britain*, Cambridge, MA: Belknap Press.

Dixon, Paul, ed. (2012), *The British Approach to Counterinsurgency: From Malaya and Northern Ireland to Iraq and Afghanistan*, Houndmills: Palgrave Macmillan.

Dodge, Toby (2003), *Inventing Iraq: The Failure of Nation-Building and a History Denied*, New York: Columbia University Press.

Donaldson, Laura (1992), *Decolonizing Feminisms: Race, Gender, and Empire-Building*, Chapel Hill: University of North Carolina Press.

Dorrien, Gary (2004), *Imperial Designs: Neoconservatism and the New Pax Americana*, New York: Routledge.

Douglas, Roy (2002), *Liquidation of Empire: The Decline of the British Empire*, Houndmills: Palgrave Macmillan.
Drayton, Richard (2000), *Nature's Government: Science, Imperial Britain, and the "Improvement" of the World*, New Haven: Yale University Press.
Driver, Felix (1991), "Henry Morton Stanley and His Critics: Geography, Exploration and Empire," *Past and Present*, 133: 134–66.
Driver, Felix (2001) *Geography Militant: Cultures of Exploration and Empire*, Oxford: Blackwell.
Driver, Felix (2004), "Distance and Disturbance: Travel, Exploration and Knowledge in the Nineteenth Century," *Transactions of the Royal Historical Society*, 6th series, 14, 79–86. Cambridge: Cambridge University Press.
Driver, Felix (2004–7), "The Active Life: The Explorer as Biographical Subject," *Oxford Dictionary of National Biography*, online ed. Oxford: Oxford University Press.
Driver, Felix, and David Gilbert, eds. (1999), *Imperial Cities: Landscape, Display, and Identity*, Manchester: Manchester University Press.
Driver, Felix, and Luciana Martins, eds. (2005), *Tropical Visions in an Age of Empire*, Chicago: University of Chicago Press.
Driver, Felix, and Lowri Jones (2009), *Hidden Histories of Exploration: Researching the RGS-IBG Collections*, London: Royal Holloway, University of London.
D'Souza, Dinesh (2002), "Two Cheers for Colonialism," *Chronicle of Higher Education* (10 May): B7–B9.
D'Souza, Dinesh (2011), *The Roots of Obama's Rage*, Washington, DC: Regnery.
Duara, Prasenjit (2003), *Sovereignty and Authenticity: Manchuko and the East Asian Modern*, Lanham: Rowman and Littlefield.
Dumett, Raymond E., ed. (1999), *Gentlemanly Capitalism and British Imperialism: The New Debate on Empire*, London: Routledge.
Dunlop, Thomas R. (1999), *Nature and the English Diaspora: Environment and History in the United States, Canada, Australia, and New Zealand*, Cambridge: Cambridge University Press.
Eckholm, Erik (2017), "Conservatism's Uncommon Core," *New York Times* (February 5), accessed online.
Eden, Richard (2012), "Sir David Attenborough battles Jeremy Paxman over the 'good' British Empire," *The Telegraph* (June 3), accessed online.
Edgerton, David (2006), *Warfare State: Britain, 1920-1970*, Cambridge: Cambridge University Press.
Edmonds, Penelope, and Jane Carey, "A New Beginning for *Settler Colonial Studies*," *Settler Colonial Studies*, 3/1 (2013): 2–5.
Edney, Matthew H. (1997), *Mapping an Empire: The Geographical Construction of British India, 1765-1843*, Chicago: University of Chicago Press.
Eland, Ivan (2003), *The Empire Has No Clothes: U.S. Foreign Policy Exposed*, Oakland: Independent Institute.
Eley, Geoff (2005), *A Crooked Line: From Cultural History to the History of Society*, Ann Arbor: University of Michigan Press.
Elkins, Caroline (2005), *Imperial Reckoning: The Untold Story of Britain's Gulag in Kenya*, New York: Henry Holt.
Elkins, Caroline (2005a), "Royal Screwup," *The New Republic* (19 December): 16–17.

Elkins, Caroline (2011), "Alchemy of Evidence: Mau Mau, the British Empire, and the High Court of Justice," *Journal of Imperial and Commonwealth History*, 39/5: 732–48.
Elkins, Caroline (2013), "Britain has said sorry to the Mau Mau. The rest of the Empire is still waiting," *The Guardian* (June 6), accessed online.
Elkins, Caroline, and Susan Pedersen, eds. (2005), *Settler Colonialism in the Twentieth Century*, New York: Routledge.
Etherington, Norman, ed. (2007), *Mapping Colonial Conquest: Australia and Southern Africa*, Crawley: University of Western Australia Press.
Evans, Richard J. (2013), "Michael Gove's History Wars," *The Guardian* (July 13), accessed online.
Fabian, Johannes (1983), *Time and the Other: How Anthropology Makes its Object*, New York: Columbia University Press.
Fabian, Johannes (2000), *Out of Our Minds: Reason and Madness in the Exploration of Central Africa*, Berkeley: University of California Press.
Falwell Jr., Jerry (2016), "Trump is the Churchillian leader we need," *The Washington Post* (August 21), accessed online.
Ferguson, Moira (1993), *Colonialism and Gender Relations from Mary Wollstonecraft to Jamaica Kincaid: East Caribbean Connections*, New York: Columbia University Press.
Ferguson, Niall (2003a), "The Empire Slinks Back," *New York Times Sunday Magazine* (April 27): 52–7.
Ferguson, Niall (2003b), "The 'E' Word," *The Wall Street Journal* (June 6), A10.
Ferguson, Niall (2004), *Empire: The Rise and Demise of the British World Order and the Lessons for Global Power*, New York: Basic Books.
Ferguson, Niall (2005), *Colossus: The Price of America's Empire*, New York: Penguin.
Ferguson, Niall (2006), "Empires with Expiration Dates," *Foreign Policy* (September/October): 46–52.
Fernández-Armesto, Felipe (2006), *Pathfinders: A Global History of Exploration*, New York: W. W. Norton.
Fieldhouse, David (1967), *The Theory of Capitalist Imperialism*, London: Longman.
Fieldhouse, David (1984), "Can Humpty-Dumpty Be Put Together Again? Imperial History in the 1980s," *Journal of Imperial and Commonwealth History*, 12/2: 9–23.
Finnegan, William (2003), "The Economics of Empire: Notes on the Washington Consensus," *Harper's Magazine* (May): 41–54.
Fischer, Michael H., ed. (1997), *The Travels of Dean Mahomet*, Berkeley: University of California Press.
Fletcher, Christopher, Laura Nym Mayhall, and Philippa Levine, eds. (2000), *Women's Suffrage in the British Empire*, London: Routledge.
Fleming, N. C. (2010), "Echoes of Britannia: Television History, Empire and the Critical Public Sphere," *Contemporary British History*, 24/1 (March): 1–22.
Foley, Tricia (1993), *The Romance of British Colonial Style*, New York: Clarkson Potter.
Foster, John Bellamy (2006), *Naked Imperialism: The U.S. Pursuit of Global Dominance*, New York: Monthly Review Press.
Foucault, Michel (1980), *The History of Sexuality, Vol. 1: An Introduction*, New York: Vintage.

Frank, Katherine (1986), *A Voyager Out: The Life of Mary Kingsley*, Boston: Houghton Mifflin.

Freeman, Colin (2012), "Britain may have invaded 90 per cent of the world, but we're not hated everywhere," *The Telegraph* (November 8), accessed online.

Freitag, Sandria (1990), *Collective Action and Community: Public Arenas and the Emergence of Communalism in North India*, Delhi: Oxford University Press.

French, David (2011), *The British Way of Counter-Insurgency, 1945-1967*, Oxford: Oxford University Press.

French, David (2012), *Army, Empire, and Cold War: The British Army and Military Policy, 1945-1971*, Oxford: Oxford University Press.

French, David (2015), *Fighting EOKA: The British Counter-Insurgency Campaign in Cyprus, 1955-1959*, Oxford: Oxford University Press.

Froude, James Anthony (1885), *Oceana, or, England and Her Colonies*, London: Longmans, Green.

Fukuyama, Francis (1992), *The End of History and the Last Man*, New York: Free Press.

Fukuyama, Francis (2006), *America at the Crossroads: Democracy, Power, and the Neoconservative Legacy*, New Haven: Yale University Press.

Gallagher, John (1982), *The Decline, Revival, and Fall of the British Empire*, Cambridge: Cambridge University Press.

Gallagher, John, and Ronald Robinson (1953), "The Imperialism of Free Trade," *Economic History Review*, 2nd ser., 6/2: 1–15.

Gardner, Lloyd C., and Marilyn B. Young, eds. (2005), *The New American Empire*, New York: New Press.

Garrison, Jim (2004). *America as Empire: Global Leader or Rogue Power?* San Francisco: Berrett-Koehler.

Gascoigne, John (1994), *Science in the Service of Empire: Joseph Banks, the British State and the Uses of Science in the Age of Revolution*, Cambridge: Cambridge University Press.

Ghosh, Durba (2004), "Gender and Colonialism: Expansion or Marginalization?" *The Historical Journal*, 47/3: 737–55.

Ghosh, Durba (2012), "Another Set of Imperial Turns?" *American Historical Review*, 117/3: 772–93.

Ghosh, Durba, and Dane Kennedy, eds. (2006), *Decentring Empire: Britain, India and the Transcolonial World*, Hyderabad: Orient Longman.

Gikandi, Simon (1996), *Maps of Englishness: Writing Identity in the Culture of Colonialism*, New York: Columbia University Press.

Gillham, Nicholas Wright (2001), *A Life of Sir Francis Galton: From African Exploration to the Birth of Eugenics*, New York: Oxford University Press.

Gilroy, Paul (1993), *The Black Atlantic: Modernity and Double Consciousness*, Cambridge, MA: Harvard University Press.

Gimson, Andrew (2011), "Conservative Party Conference 2011," *The Telegraph* (October 5), accessed online.

Glass, Bryan S. (2014), *The Scottish Nation at Empire's End*, Houndmills: Palgrave Macmillan.

Godlewska, Anne, and Neil Smith, eds. (1994), *Geography and Empire*, Oxford: Blackwell.

Go, Julian (2006), "Imperial Power and its Limits: America's Colonial Empire in the Early Twentieth Century," in Craig Calhoun, Frederick Cooper and Kevin W. Moore (eds.), *Lessons of Empire: Imperial Histories and American Power*, 201–14, New York: New Press.
Go, Julian (2011), *Patterns of Empire: The British and American Empires, 1688 to the Present*, Cambridge: Cambridge University Press.
Goldberg, Jeffrey (2005) "A Little Learning: What Douglas Feith Knew, and When He Knew It," *The New Yorker* (9 May), accessed online.
Gordon, Charlotte (1928), *Redgold*, Vancouver: McBeath-Campbell.
Gott, Richard (2011a), *Britain's Empire: Resistance, Repression and Revolt*, London: Verso.
Gott, Richard (2011b), "Let's End the Myths of Britain's Imperial Past," *The Guardian* (October 19), accessed online.
Gough, Barry M. (1999), "The Royal Navy and Empire," in Robin W. Winks (ed.), *The Oxford History of the British Empire, Vol. V: Historiography*, 327–41. Oxford: Oxford University Press.
Graham, Bradley (2003), "Pentagon Considers Creating Postwar Peacekeeping Forces," *Washington Post* (24 November): A16.
Gregg, Robert, and Madhavi Kale (1997), "The Empire and Mr Thompson: Making of Indian Princes and English Working Class," *Economic and Political Weekly*, 32/36 (September 6–12): 2237–88.
Green, Jeffrey (1998), *Black Edwardians: Black People in Britain, 1901-14*, London: Routledge.
Greenblatt, Stephen (1991), *Marvelous Possessions: The Wonder of the New World*, Chicago: University of Chicago Press.
Griffiths, Tom, and Libby Robbin, eds. (1997), *Ecology and Empire: Environmental History of Settler Societies*, Seattle: University of Washington Press.
Grob-Fitzgibbon, Benjamin (2011), *Imperial Endgame: Britain's Dirty Wars and the End of Empire*, Houndmills: Palgrave Macmillan.
Grob-Fitzgibbon, Benjamin (2016), *Continental Drift: Britain and Europe from the End of Empire to the Rise of Euroscepticism*, Cambridge: Cambridge University Press.
Grove, Richard H. (1996), *Green Imperialism: Colonial Expansion, Tropical Island Edens, and the Origins of Environmentalism*, Cambridge: Cambridge University Press.
Grove, Richard H, Vinita Damodaran, and Satpal Sangwan, eds. (1998), *Nature and the Orient: The Environmental History of South and Southeast Asia*, Delhi: Oxford University Press.
Guha, Ranajit (1983), *Elementary Aspects of Peasant Insurgency in Colonial India*, Delhi: Oxford University Press.
Guha, Ranajit (2002), *History at the Limit of World-History*, New York: Columbia University Press.
Guha, Ranajit, and Gayatri Chakravorty Spivak, eds. (1988), *Selected Subaltern Studies*, New York: Oxford University Press.
Hall, Catherine (1992), *White, Male, and Middle Class: Explorations in Feminism and History*, Cambridge: Polity.
Hall, Catherine (2000), "Introduction: Thinking the Postcolonial, Thinking the Empire," in Catherine Hall (ed.), *Cultures of Empire: A Reader*, 1–33. New York: Routledge.

Hall, Catherine (2002), *Civilizing Subjects: Metropole and Colony in the English Imagination, 1830-1867*, Chicago: University of Chicago Press.
Hall, Catherine, and Sonya Rose (2006), "Introduction: Being at Home with the Empire," in Catherine Hall and Sonya O. Rose (eds.), *At Home with the Empire: Metropolitan Culture and the Imperial World*, 1–31. Cambridge: Cambridge University Press.
Hanson, Peter H. (2001), "Coronation Everest: The Empire and Commonwealth in the 'Second Elizabeth Age'," in Stuart Ward (ed.), *British Culture and the End of Empire*, 57–72. Manchester: Manchester University Press.
Hanson, Victor D. (2003), "What Empire?" in Andrew Bacevich (ed.), *The Imperial Tense: Prospects and Problems of American Empire*, 146–55. Chicago: Ivan R. Dee.
Hardt, Michael, and Antonio Negri (2001), *Empire*, Cambridge, MA: Harvard University Press.
Hargreaves, Alec G., ed. (2005), *Memory, Empire, and Postcolonialism: Legacies of French Colonialism*, Lanham: Lexington Books.
Harland-Jacobs, Jessica (2007), *Builders of Empire: Freemasons and British Imperialism, 1717-1927*, Chapel Hill: University of North Carolina Press.
Harley, J. B. (2001), *The New Nature of Maps: Essays in the History of Cartography*, ed. Paul Laxton, Baltimore: Johns Hopkins University Press.
Harootunian, Harry (2004) *The Empire's New Clothes*, Chicago: Prickly Paradigm Press.
Harrison, Mark (1999), *Climates and Constitutions: Health, Race, Environment, and British Imperialism in India, 1600-1850*, Delhi: Oxford University Press.
Harvey, David (1989), *The Condition of Postmodernity: An Enquiry into the Origins of Cultural Change*, Oxford: Blackwell.
Harvey, David (2003), *The New Imperialism*, Oxford: Oxford University Press.
Heath, Deana (2010), *Purifying Empire: Obscenity and the Politics of Moral Regulation in Britain, India and Australia*, Cambridge: Cambridge University Press.
Heathcote, T. A. (1974), *The Indian Army: Garrison of British Imperial India, 1822-1922*, London: David and Charles.
Hechter, Michael (1975), *Internal Colonialism: The Celtic Fringe in British National Development*, Berkeley: University of California Press.
Heinlein, Frank (2002) *British Government Policy and Decolonisation, 1945-1963: Scrutinizing the Official Mind*, London: Frank Cass.
Helly, Dorothy (1987), *Livingstone's Legacy: Horace Waller and Victorian Mythmaking*, Athens: Ohio University Press.
Hibbert, Christopher (1982), *Africa Explored: Europeans in the Dark Continent 1769–1889*, London: Penguin.
Hildreth, Martha L. (1995), "Lamentations on Reality: A Response to John M. Mackenzie's 'Edward Said and the Historians'," *Nineteenth-Century Contexts*, 19/1: 65–73.
Hitchens, Christopher (1990), *Blood, Class, and Nostalgia: Anglo-American Ironies*, New York: Farrar, Straus, and Giroux.
Ho, Engseng (2006), *The Graves of Tarim: Genealogy and Mobility across the Indian Ocean*, Berkeley: University of California Press.
Hobsbawm, Eric (1962), *The Age of Revolution*, New York: Vintage.
Hobsbawm, Eric (1968), *Industry and Empire*, New York: Penguin.

Hobsbawm, Eric (1975), *The Age of Capital*, New York: Vintage.
Hobsbawm, Eric (1987), *The Age of Empire*, New York: Vintage.
Hobson, J. A. (1972 [1902]), *Imperialism: A Study*, Ann Arbor: University of Michigan Press.
Hodge, Joseph (2007), *Triumph of the Expert: Agrarian Doctrines of Development and the Legacies of British Colonialism*, Athens: Ohio University Press.
Holland, Robert F. (1985), *European Decolonisation 1918-1981: An Introductory Survey*, New York: St. Martin's Press.
Holland, Robert F. (1991), *The Pursuit of Greatness: Britain and the World Role, 1900-1970*, London: Fontana.
Hoock, Holger (2017), *Scars of Independence: America's Violent Birth*, New York: Crown.
Hopkins, A. G. (1997), *Future of the Imperial Past*, Cambridge: Cambridge University Press.
Hopkins, A. G. (1999), "Back to the Future: From National History to Imperial History," *Past and Present*, 164: 198–243.
Hopkins, A. G., ed. (2002), *Globalization in World History*, London: Pimlico.
Hopkins, A. G. (2007), "Capitalism, Nationalism and the New American Empire," *Journal of Imperial and Commonwealth History*, 35/1 (March): 95–117.
Hopkins, A. G. (2008), "Rethinking Decolonization," *Past and Present*, 200: 211–48.
House, Jim, and Andrew Thompson (2013), "Decolonisation, Space and Power: Immigration, Welfare and Housing in Britain and France, 1945-1974," in Andrew Thompson (ed.), *Writing Imperial Histories*, 240–67. Manchester: Manchester University Press.
Howe, Stephen (2000), *Ireland and Empire: Colonial Legacies in Irish History and Culture*, Oxford: Oxford University Press.
Howe, Stephen (2006), "When (if ever) did the Empire End? 'Imperial Decolonization' in British Culture since the 1950s," in Martin Lynn (ed.), *The British Empire in the 1950s: Retreat or Revival?* 214–37. Basingstoke: Palgrave Macmillan.
Howe, Stephen (2012), "British Worlds, Settler Worlds, World Systems, and Killing Fields," *The Journal of Imperial and Commonwealth History*, 40/4: 672–91.
Huggan, Graham (2013), "General Introduction," in Graham Huggan (ed.), *The Oxford Handbook of Postcolonial Studies*, 1–26. Oxford: Oxford University Press.
Hughes, Robert (1993), "Envoy to Two Cultures," *Time*, 141/22 (June 21): 60–63.
Hunt, Lynn, ed. (1989), *The New Cultural History*, Berkeley: University of California Press.
Hunt, Nancy Rose, Tessie P. Liu, and Jean Quataert, eds. (1997), *Gendered Colonialisms in African History*, Oxford: Blackwell.
Hunt, Tristram (2014), *Ten Cities That Made an Empire*, London: Allen Lane.
Husain, Aiyaz (2014), *Mapping the End of Empire: American and British Strategic Visions in the Postwar World*, Cambridge, MA: Harvard University Press.
Hyam, Ronald (1993), *Britain's Imperial Century, 1815-1914: A Study of Empire and Expansion*, 2nd ed., London: Palgrave Macmillan.
Hyam, Ronald (2006), *Britain's Declining Empire: The Role to Decolonisation 1918-1968*, Cambridge: Cambridge University Press.
Ignatieff, Michael (2003), "The Burden," *New York Times Magazine* (January 5): 22–54.

Ignatiev, Noel (1995), *How the Irish Became White*, New York: Routledge.
Ingram, Edward (2003), "Hegemony, Global Reach and World Power," in *The British Empire as a World Power*, 16–48. London: Routledge.
Ingram, Edward (2005), "Pairing off Empires: The United States as Great Britain in the Middle East," in T. T. Petersen (ed.), *Controlling the Uncontrollable? The Great Powers in the Middle East*, 1–21. Trondheim, Norway: Tapir.
Irwin, Robert (2006), *Dangerous Knowledge: Orientalism and Its Discontents*, Woodstock: Overlook Press.
Islamoglu, Huricihan, and Peter C. Perdue, eds. (2009), *Shared Histories of Modernity: China, India, and the Ottoman Empire*, London: Routledge.
Jackson, J. R. (1845), *What to Observe; or, the Traveller's Remembrancer*, 2nd ed., London: Madden and Malcolm.
Jacoby, Russell (1995), "Marginal Returns: The Trouble with Post-Colonial Theory," *Linguafranca*, 5/6: 30–37.
James, Lauren (2016), *Colonial Food in Interwar Paris: The Taste of Empire*, London: Bloomsbury.
James, Lawrence (1994), *The Rise and Fall of the British Empire*, New York: St. Martins.
James, Lawrence (2012), "Yes, Mistakes were Made, but we Must Never Stop Being Proud of the Empire," *The Mail Online* (April 18).
Jasanoff, Maya (2005), "What New Empires Inherit From Old Ones," *History News Network* (December 12), accessed online.
Jayawardena, Kumari (1995), *The White Woman's Other Burden: Western Women and South Asia during British Rule*, London: Routledge.
Jeal, Tim (1973), *Livingstone*, New York: Putnam.
Jeal, Tim (2007), *Stanley: The Impossible Life of Africa's Greatest Explorer*, New Haven: Yale University Press.
Jeal, Tim (2011), "Remembering Henry Stanley," *The Telegraph* (March 16), accessed online.
Jeffrey, Keith, ed. (1996), *'An Irish Empire'? Aspects of Ireland and the British Empire*, Manchester: Manchester University Press.
Joffe, Josef (2006), *Überpower: The Imperial Temptation of America*, New York: W. W. Norton.
Johns, Elizabeth, Andrew Sayers, Elizabeth Mankin Kornhauser, and Amy Ellis (1998), *New Worlds from Old: 19th Century Australian and American Landscapes*, Canberra: National Gallery of Australia.
Johnson, Chalmers (2000), *Blowback: The Costs and Consequences of American Empire*, New York: Holt.
Johnson, Chalmers (2004) *The Sorrows of Empire: Militarism, Secrecy, and the End of the Republic*, New York: Holt.
Jones, Aled, and Bill Jones (2003), "The Welsh World and the British Empire c. 1851-1939," in Carl Bridge and Kent Fedorowich (eds.), *The British World*, 57–81. London: Frank Cass.
Judd, Denis (1996), *Empire: The British Imperial Experience from 1765 to the Present*, London: Harper Collins.
Judis, John B. (2004), *The Folly of Empire: What George W. Bush Could Learn From Theodore Roosevelt and Woodrow Wilson*, New York: Oxford University Press.
Kagan, Kimberly, ed. (2010), *The Imperial Moment*, Cambridge, MA: Harvard University Press.

Kahler, Miles (1984), *Decolonization in Britain and France: The Domestic Consequences of International Relations*, Princeton: Princeton University Press.
Kaplan, Robert D. (2002), *Warrior Politics: Why Leadership Demands a Pagan Ethos*, New York: Vintage.
Kaplan, Robert D. (2005), *Imperial Grunts: The American Military on the Ground*, New York: Vintage.
Kaplan, Robert D. (2014), "In Defense of Empire," *The Atlantic* (April), accessed online.
Keighren, Innes M., Charles W. J. Withers, and Bill Bell (2015), *Travels into Print: Exploration, Writing, and Publishing with John Murray, 1773-1859*, Chicago: University of Chicago Press.
Kelley, Patrick A. (2008) *Imperial Secrets: Remapping the Mind of Empire*, Washington, DC: National Defense Intelligence College.
Kennedy, Dane (1996), "Imperial History and Post-Colonial Theory," *Journal of Imperial and Commonwealth History*, 24/3: 345–63.
Kennedy, Dane (2001), "The Boundaries of Oxford's Empire," *The International History Review*, 13/3: 604–22.
Kennedy, Dane (2005), *The Highly Civilized Man: Richard Burton and the Victorian World*, Cambridge, MA: Harvard University Press.
Kennedy, Dane (2007), "On the American Empire from a British Imperial Perspective," *The International History Review*, 29/1: 83–108.
Kennedy, Dane (2013a), *The Last Blank Spaces: Exploring Africa and Australia*, Cambridge, MA: Harvard University Press.
Kennedy, Dane (2013b), "Postcolonialism and History," in Graham Huggins (ed.), *The Oxford Handbook of Postcolonial Studies*, 467–88. Oxford: Oxford University Press.
Kennedy, Dane, ed. (2014), *Reinterpreting Exploration: The West in the World*, New York: Oxford University Press.
Kennedy, Paul (1976), *The Rise and Fall of British Naval Mastery*, New York: Scribner.
Kennedy, Paul (1987) *The Rise and Fall of the Great Powers*, New York: Random House.
Kenny, Michael, and Nick Pearce (2015), "The Rise of the Anglosphere: How the Right Dreamed up a New Conservative World Order," *New Statesman* (February 10), accessed online.
Khalidi, Rashid (2004), *Resurrecting Empire: Western Footprints and America's Perilous Path in the Middle East*, Boston: Beacon.
King, R. D., and Robin W. Kilson, eds. (1999), *The Statecraft of British Imperialism: Essays in Honour of Wm. Roger Louis*, London: Routledge.
King Baudouin Foundation (2007), *Africa in Images, Stanley I Presume?* Brussels: King Baudouin Foundation.
Kitchen, Martin (1996), *The British Empire and Commonwealth: A Short History*, New York: Palgrave.
Kinzer, Stephen (2006), *Overthrow: America's Century of Regime Change from Hawaii to Iraq*, New York: Times Books.
Klare, Michael (2004), *Blood and Oil: The Dangers and Consequences of America's Growing Petroleum Dependency*, New York: Holt.
Klose, Fabian (2013), *Human Rights in the Shadow of Colonial Violence: The Wars of Independence in Kenya and Algeria*, Philadelphia: University of Pennsylvania Press.

Koditschek, Theodore (2011), *Liberalism, Imperialism and the Historical Imagination: Nineteenth Century Visions of a Greater Britain*, Cambridge: Cambridge University Press.

Koivunen, Leila (2009), *Visualizing Africa in Nineteenth-Century British Travel Accounts*, New York: Routledge.

Konishi, Shino, Maria Nugent, and Tiffany Shellam, eds. (2015), *Indigenous Intermediaries: New Perspectives on Exploration Archives*, Canberra: ANU Press.

Kramer, Paul A. (2011), "Power and Connection: Imperial Histories of the United States in the World," *The American Historical Review*, 116/5: 1315–53.

Krauthammer, Charles (2002/2003), "The Unipolar Moment Revisited," *The National Interest*, 70 (Winter): 5–17.

Kuklick, Henrika (1991), *The Savage Within: The Social History of British Anthropology*, Cambridge: Cambridge University Press.

Kumar, Krishan (2012), "Greece and Rome in the British Empire: Contrasting Models," *Journal of British Studies*, 51/1: 76–101.

Kumar, Krishan (2015), "Empire, Nation, and National Identities," in Andrew Thompson (ed.), *Britain's Experience of Empire in the Twentieth Century*, 298–329. Oxford: Oxford University Press.

Kwarteng, Kwasi (2011), *Ghosts of Empire: Britain's Legacies in the Modern World*, New York: Public Affairs.

Lahiri, Shompa (2000), *Indians in Britain: Anglo-Indian Encounters, Race, and Identity*, London: Routledge.

Lamar, Howard, and Leonard Thompson, eds. (1981), *The Frontier in History: North America and Southern Africa Compared*, New Haven: Yale University Press.

Lamb, Jonathan (2001), *Preserving the Self in the South Seas 1680–1840*, Chicago: University of Chicago Press.

Landes, David S. (1998), *The Wealth and Poverty of Nations*, New York: W. W. Norton.

Lake, Marilyn, and Henry Reynolds (2008), *Drawing the Global Colour Line: White Men's Countries and the International Challenge of Racial Equality*, Cambridge: Cambridge University Press.

Lakshmi, Rama (2013), "In India, Cameron Voices Regret for 1919 Massacre," *The Washington Post* (February 21): A10.

Lal, Deepak (2004), *In Praise of Empires: Globalization and Order*, New York: Palgrave Macmillan.

Lambert, David, and Alan Lester, eds. (2006), *Colonial Lives across the Empire: Imperial Careering in the Long Nineteenth Century*, Cambridge: Cambridge University Press.

Lambert, R. D. (1996), "Domains and Issues in International Studies," *International Education Forum*, 16: 1–19.

Landau, Paul (1995), *The Realm of the Word: Language, Gender, and Christianity in a Southern African Kingdom*, London: Heinemann.

Landau, Saul (2003), *The Pre-Emptive Empire: A Guide to Bush's Kingdom*, London: Pluto.

Laycock, Stuart (2012), *All the Countries We've Ever Invaded: And the Few We Never Got Round To*, London: The History Press.

Leask, Nigel (2002), *Curiosity and the Aesthetics of Travel Writing, 1770–1840*, Oxford: Oxford University Press.

Lenin, V. I. (1970 [1916]), *Imperialism, the Highest Stage of Capitalism*, Moscow: International Publishers.
Lester, Alan (2001), *Imperial Networks: Creating Identities in Nineteenth-Century South Africa and Britain*, London: Routledge.
Levine, Philippa (1998), "Battle Colors: Race, Sex, and Colonial Soldiery in World War I," *Journal of Women's History*, 9/4: 104–30.
Levine, Philippa (2003), *Prostitution, Race, and Politics: Policing Venereal Disease in the British Empire*, London: Routledge.
Levine, Philippa, ed. (2004), *Gender and Empire*, Oxford: Oxford University Press.
Lewis, Martin W., and Kären Wigen (1997), *The Myth of Continents: A Critique of Metageography*, Berkeley: University of California Press.
Linenthal, Edward T., and Tom Engelhardt (1996), *The History Wars: The Enola Gay and Other Battles for the American Past*, New York: Henry Holt.
Livingstone, David N. (1993), *The Geographical Tradition: Episodes in the History of a Contested Enterprise*, Oxford: Blackwell.
Lloyd, Trevor (1996), *The British Empire, 1558-1995*, 2nd ed., Oxford: Oxford University Press.
Lloyd, Trevor (2000), "On *The Oxford History of the British Empire* Volume V, *Historiography*," *Comparative Criticism*, 22: 251–56.
Louis, W. R. (1976), *Imperialism: The Robinson and Gallagher Controversy*, New York: New Viewpoints.
Louis, W. R. (1978), *Imperialism at Bay: The United States and the Decolonization of the British Empire, 1941-1945*, New York: Oxford University Press.
Louis, W. R. (1984), *The British Empire in the Middle East 1945-1951: Arab Nationalism, the United States, and Postwar Imperialism*, Oxford: Clarendon Press.
Louis, W. R., editor in chief (1998–99), *The Oxford History of the British Empire*, 5 vols., Oxford: Oxford University Press.
Louis, W. R. (1999), "Introduction," in Robin W. Winks (ed.), *The Oxford History of the British Empire, Vol. V: Historiography*, 1–42. Oxford: Oxford University Press.
Louis, W. R. (2000), "The Ways of Empire: A Conversation with Wm. Roger Louis," *Humanities*, 21: 8–9.
Louis, W. R. (2006), "Suez and Decolonization: Scrambling Out of Africa and Asia," in *Ends of British Imperialism: The Scramble for Empire, Suez, and Decolonization*, 1–33. London: I. B. Tauris.
Louis, W. R., and Ronald Robinson (1994), "The Imperialism of Decolonization," *The Journal of Imperial and Commonwealth History*, 22/3 (July): 462–511.
Lowry, Donal (2003), "The Crown, Empire Loyalism and the Assimilation of Non-British White Subjects in the British World," in Carl Bridge and Kent Fedorowich (eds.), *The British World: Diaspora, Culture and Identity*, 96–120. London: Frank Cass.
Lunt, James (1981), *Imperial Sunset: Frontier Soldiering in the 20th Century*, London: Futura.
Macintyre, Stuart, and Anna Clark (2003), *The History Wars*, Melbourne: University of Melbourne Press.
Mackay, David (1985), *In the Wake of Cook: Exploration, Science and Empire 1780–1801*, New York: St. Martin's Press.
MacKenzie, John (1984), *Propaganda and Empire: The Manipulation of British Public Opinion, 1880-1960*, Manchester: Manchester University Press.

MacKenzie, John, ed. (1986), *Imperialism and Popular Culture*, Manchester: Manchester University Press.
MacKenzie, John (1994), "Edward Said and the Historians," *Nineteenth-Century Contexts*, 18/1: 9–25.
MacKenzie, John (1995), *Orientalism: History, Theory and the Arts*, Manchester: Manchester University Press.
MacKenzie, John (1995b), "The Provincial Geographical Societies in Britain, 1884–1914," in Morag Bell, Robin Butlin, and Michael Heffernan (eds.), *Geography and Imperialism 1820–1940*, 93–124. Manchester: Manchester University Press.
MacKenzie, John, ed. (1996), *David Livingstone and the Victorian Encounter with Africa*, London: National Portrait Gallery.
MacKenzie, John (2007), "The British World and the Complexities of Anglicisation: The Scots of Southern Africa in the Nineteenth Century," in Kate Darian-Smith, et al. (eds.), *Britishness Abroad: Transnational Movements and Imperial Culture*, 109–30. Melbourne: Melbourne University Press.
MacKenzie, John (2009), *Museums and Empire: Natural History, Human Cultures and Colonial Identity*, Manchester: Manchester University Press.
MacKenzie, John (2015), "The British Empire: Ramshackle or Rampaging? A Historiographical Reflection," *Journal of Imperial and Commonwealth History*, 43/1: 99–124.
MacMillan, Margaret (2009), "History Wars," in *Dangerous Games: The Uses and Abuses of History*, 111–38, New York: Modern Library.
Madden, Frederick, and D. K. Fieldhouse, eds. (1986), *Oxford and the Idea of Commonwealth: Essays Presented to Sir Edgar Williams*, London: Croom Helm.
Magee, Gary B., and Andrew S. Thompson (2010), *Empire and Globalisation: Networks of People, Goods and Capital in the British World, c. 1850-1914*, Cambridge: Cambridge University Press.
Maier, Charles S. (2006), *Among Empires: American Ascendancy and Its Predecessors*, Cambridge, Mass: Harvard University Press.
Maitland, Alexander (1971), *Speke*, London: Constable.
Majeed, Javed (1992), *Ungoverned Imaginings: James Mill's "The History of British India" and Orientalism*, Oxford: Oxford University Press.
Mallon, Florencia (1994), "The Promise and Dilemma of Subaltern Studies: Perspectives from Latin American History," *American Historical Review*, 99/5: 1491–1515.
Mamdani, Mahmood (1996), *Citizen and Subject: Contemporary Africa and the Legacy of Late Colonialism*, Princeton: Princeton University Press.
Mani, Lata (1987), "Contentious Traditions: The Debate on Sati in Colonial India," *Cultural Critique*, 7: 119–56; reprinted in Kumkum Sangari and Sudesh Vaid (eds.), *Recasting Women: Essays in Indian Colonial History*, 88–126. New Brunswick: Rutgers University Press.
Mann, Michael (2003), *Incoherent Empire*, London: Verso.
Mansergh, Nicholas, and Penderel Moon, eds. (1970–83), *The Transfer of Power 1942-47*, 12 vols., London: HMSO.
Mantena, Karuna (2010), *Alibis of Empire: Henry Maine and the Ends of Liberal Imperialism*, Princeton: Princeton University Press.
Marcus, George E., and Michael M. J. Fisher (1986), *Anthropology as Cultural Critique: An Experimental Moment in the Human Sciences*, Chicago: University of Chicago Press.

Marshall, Peter, ed. (1996), *The Cambridge Illustrated History of the British Empire*, Cambridge: Cambridge University Press.
Martel, Gordon (1991), "The Meaning of Power: Rethinking the Decline and Fall of the British Empire," *The International History Review*, 13/4 (December): 662–94.
Matera, Marc (2015), *Black London: The Imperial Metropolis and Decolonization in the Twentieth Century*, Berkeley: University of California Press.
McAleer, John J. (2010), *Representing Africa: Landscape, Exploration and Empire in Southern Africa*, Manchester: Manchester University Press.
McClintock, Anne (1994), "The Angel of Progress: Pitfalls of the Term 'Post-colonialism'," in Patrick Williams and Laura Chrisman (eds.), *Colonial Discourse and Post-Colonial Theory: A Reader*, 291–304. New York: Columbia University Press.
McClintock, Anne (1995), *Imperial Leather: Race, Gender and Sexuality in the Colonial Contest*, New York: Routledge.
McCulloch, Jock (2000), *Black Peril, White Virtue: Sexual Crime in Southern Rhodesia, 1902-1935*, Bloomington: Indiana University Press.
McIntyre, W. David (1998), *British Decolonization, 1946-97*, New York: Palgrave.
McMillen, Liz (1993), "Post-Colonial Studies Plumb the Experience of Living Under, and After Imperialism," *The Chronicle of Higher Education* (May): A6–A9.
McNeill, John (2010), *Mosquito Empires: Ecology and War in the Greater Caribbean, 1620-1914*, Cambridge: Cambridge University Press.
Mead, Walter Russell (2008), *God and Gold: Britain, America, and the Making of the Modern World*, New York: Vintage Books.
Mehta, Uday Singh (1999), *Liberalism and Empire: A Study of British Liberal Thought*, Chicago: University of Chicago Press.
Metcalf, Thomas R. (1994), *Ideologies of the Raj: The New Cambridge History of India*, Cambridge: Cambridge University Press.
Metcalf, Thomas R. (2007), *Imperial Connections: India in the Indian Ocean Area, 1860-1920*, Berkeley: University of California Press.
Meyer, Karl (2003), *The Dust of Empire: The Race for Mastery in the Asian Heartland*, New York: Public Affairs.
Midgley, Clare (1992), *Women against Slavery: The British Campaigns, 1780-1870* London: Routledge.
Midgley, Clare, ed. (1999), *Gender and Imperialism*, Manchester: Manchester University Press.
Milbank, Dana, and Charles Babington (2004), "Bush Visits Hill to Reassure Republicans," *Washington Post* (May 21): A4.
Miller, David Philip, and Peter Hanns Reill, eds. (1996), *Visions of Empire: Voyages, Botany, and Representations of Nature*, Cambridge: Cambridge University Press.
Mills, Sara (1991), *Discourses of Difference: An Analysis of Women's Travel Writing and Colonialism*. London: Routledge.
Mishra, Pankaj (2012), *From the Ruins of Empire: The Intellectuals Who Remade Asia*, New York: Farrar, Straus, and Giroux.
Mitchell, Timothy (1988), *Colonizing Egypt*, Berkeley: University of California Press.
Moore-Gilbert, Bart (1997) *Postcolonial Theory: Contexts, Practices, Politics*, London: Verso.

Moorehead, Alan (1960), *The White Nile*, New York: Harper.
Moorehead, Alan (1963), *The Blue Nile*, New York: Harper and Row.
Morgan, Phillip D., and Sean Hawkins, eds. (2007), *Black Experience and the Empire*, Oxford: Oxford University Press.
Moses, A. Dirk, ed. (2004), *Genocide and Settler Society: Frontier Violence and Stolen Indigenous Children in Australian History*, New York: Berghahn Books.
Murgatroyd, Sarah (2002), *The Dig Tree: The Extraordinary Story of the Ill-Fated Burke and Wills 1860 Expedition*, London: Bloomsbury.
Murphy, Philip (2013), *Monarchy and the End of Empire: The House of Windsor, the British Government, and the Post-war Commonwealth*, Oxford: Oxford University Press.
Murphy, Philip (2015), "Acceptable Levels? The Use and Threat of Violence in Central Africa, 1953-64," in Miguel Bandeira Jeronimo and Antonio Costa Pinto (eds.), *The Ends of European Colonial Empires: Cases and Comparisons*, 178–96. Houndmills: Palgrave Macmillan.
Muthu, Sankar (2003), *Enlightenment against Empire*, Princeton: Princeton University Press.
Nairn, Tom (1977), *The Break-Up of Britain: Crisis and Neo-Nationalism*, London: Verso.
Naughtie, James (2004), *The Accidental American: Tony Blair and the Presidency*, New York: Public Affairs.
Nandy, Ashis (1995), *The Intimate Enemy: Loss and Recovery of Self under Colonialism*, Delhi: Oxford University Press.
Newhouse, John (2003), *Imperial America: The Bush Assault on the World Order*, New York: Knopf.
Newman, James L. (2004), *Imperial Footprints: Henry Morton Stanley's African Journeys*, Washington, DC: Potomac.
Newsinger, John (2002), *British Counterinsurgency: From Palestine to Northern Ireland*, Houndmills: Palgrave Macmillan.
Newsinger, John (2006), *The Blood Never Dried: A People's History of the British Empire*, London: Bookmarks.
Nielsen, Jimmi Ostergaard, and Stuart Ward (2015), "'Cramped and Restricted at Home'? Scottish Separatism at Empire's End," *Transactions of the Royal Historical Society*, 25: 159–85.
Norton, Anne (2004), *Leo Strauss and the Politics of American Empire*, New Haven: Yale University Press.
Nye, Joseph (2002), "Lessons in Imperialism," *The Financial Times* (June 16), accessed online.
Obeyesekere, Gananath (1992), *The Apotheosis of Captain Cook: European Myth-Making in the Pacific*, Princeton: Princeton University Press.
O'Brien, Patrick (2002), "The Pax Britannica and American Hegemony," in Patrick, O'Brien and Armand Clesse (eds.), *The Two Hegemonies*, 3–6. Aldershot: Ashgate.
O'Brien, Patrick, and Armand Clesse, eds. (2002), *Two Hegemonies: Britain 1846-1914 and the United States 1941-2001*, Aldershot: Ashgate.
Olson, James, and Robert Shadle, eds. (1996) *Historical Dictionary of the British Empire*, Westport: Greenwood.
Orde, Anne (1996), *The Eclipse of Great Britain: The United States and British Imperial Decline, 1856-1956*, London: Palgrave.

Ortner, Sherry, ed. (1999), *The Fate of 'Culture': Geertz and Beyond*, Berkeley: University of California Press.
Osnos, Evan (2015), "The Opportunist," *The New Yorker* (November 30), accessed online.
Osterhammel, Jurgen (1999), "Britain and China, 1842-1914," in Andrew Porter (ed.), *The Oxford History of the British Empire, Vol. III: The Nineteenth Century*, 146–69. Oxford: Oxford University Press.
Pagden, Anthony (2005), "Imperialism, Liberalism and the Quest for Perpetual Peace," *Daedalus*, 134/2 (Spring): 46–57.
Palat, Ravi A. (1996), "Fragmented Visions: Excavating the Future of Area Studies in a Post-American World," *Review*, 10: 269–315.
Palmer, Alan (1996), *Dictionary of the British Empire and Commonwealth*, London: John Murray.
Pandey, Gyanendra (1990), *The Construction of Communalism in Colonial North India*, Delhi: Oxford University Press
Parry, Benita (1987), "Problems in Current Theories of Colonial Discourse," *The Oxford Literary Review*, 9/1: 27–58.
Parsons, Timothy (1999), *The British Imperial Century, 1815-1914*, Lanham: Rowman and Littlefield.
Parsons, Timothy (2010), *The Rule of Empires: Those Who Built Them, Those Who Endured Them, and Why They Always Fall*, New York: Oxford University Press.
Paul, Kathleen (1997), *Whitewashing Britain: Race and Citizenship in the Postwar Era*, Ithaca: Cornell University Press.
Paxman, Jeremy (2012), "'Our Empire was an Amazing Thing'," *The Telegraph* (February 16), accessed online.
Paxton, Nancy (1992), "Mobilizing Chivalry: Rape in British Novels about the Indian Uprising of 1857," *Victorian Studies*, 36/1: 5–30.
Pearson, Charles Henry (1893), *National Life and Character: A Forecast*, London: Macmillan.
Peers, Douglas M. (1998), "Privates Off Parade: Regimenting Sexuality in the Nineteenth-Century Indian Empire," *International History Review*, 20/4: 823–54.
Pells, Peter, and Oscar Salemink, eds. (1999), *Colonial Subjects: Essays on the Practical History of Anthropology*, Ann Arbor: University of Michigan Press.
Penny, Laurie (2010), "Michael Gove and the Imperialists," *The New Statesman* (June 1), accessed online.
Perry, Adele (2001) *On the Edge of Empire: Gender, Race, and the Making of British Columbia 1849-1871*, Toronto: University of Toronto Press.
Pettitt, Clare (2007), *Dr. Livingstone, I Presume? Missionaries, Journalists, Explorers and Empire*, Cambridge, MA: Harvard University Press.
Pettitt, Clare (2014), "Exploration in Print: From the Miscellany to the Newspaper," in Dane Kennedy (ed.), *Reinterpreting Exploration: The West in the World*, 80–108. New York: Oxford University Press.
Pierson, Ruth Roach, and Nupur Chaudhuri, eds. (1998), *Nation, Empire, Colony: Historicizing Gender and Race*, Bloomington: Indiana University Press.
Pietsch, Tamson (2013), "Rethinking the British World," *Journal of British Studies*, 52/2: 441–63.
Pitts, Jennifer (2005), *A Turn to Empire: The Rise of Imperial Liberalism in Britain and France*, Princeton: Princeton University Press.

Pocock, J. G. A. (1975), "British History: A Plea for a New Subject," *Journal of Modern History*, 47/4: 601–21.

Pocock, J. G. A. (2005), *The Discovery of Islands: Essays in British History*, Cambridge: Cambridge University Press.

Pomeranz, Kenneth (2000), *The Great Divergence: China, Europe, and the Making of the Modern World Economy*, Princeton: Princeton University Press.

Pomeranz, Kenneth (2005), "Empire and 'Civilizing' Missions, Past and Present," *Daedalus*, 134/2 (Spring): 34–45.

Pomeranz, Kenneth (2014), "Histories for a Less National Age," *American Historical Review*, 119/1: 1–22.

Porter, Andrew, ed. (1999), *The Oxford History of the British Empire, Vol. 3: The Nineteenth Century*, Oxford: Oxford University Press.

Porter, Bernard (1996), *The Lion's Share: A Short History of British Imperialism, 1850-1995*, 3rd ed. London: Longman.

Porter, Bernard (2004), *The Absent-Minded Imperialists: Empire, Society and Culture in Britain*, New York: Oxford University Press.

Porter, Bernard (2006), *Empire and Superempire: Britain, America and the World*, New Haven: Yale University Press.

Porter, Dennis (1983), "*Orientalism* and Its Problems," in Francis Barker et al. (eds.), *The Politics of Theory*, 189–93. Colchester: University of Essex Press.

Porter, Dennis (1991), *Haunted Journeys: Desire and Transgression in European Travel Writing*, Princeton: Princeton University Press.

Potter, Simon J. (2007), "Webs, Networks, and Systems: Globalization and the Mass Media in the Nineteenth- and Twentieth-Century British Empire," *Journal of British Studies*, 46/3: 621–46.

Powell, Eve M. Troutt (2003), *A Different Shade of Colonialism: Egypt, Great Britain, and the Mastery of the Sudan*, Berkeley: University of California Press.

Prakash, Gyan (1990), "Writing Post-Orientalist Histories of the Third World: Perspectives from Indian Historiography," *Comparative Studies in Society and History*, 32/2: 383–408.

Prakash, Gyan (1994), "Subaltern Studies as Postcolonial Criticism," *American Historical Review*, 99/5: 1475–90.

Prakash, Gyan (1999), *Another Reason: Science and the Imagination of Modern India*, Princeton: Princeton University Press.

Pratt, Mary Louise (1992), *Imperial Eyes: Travel Writing and Transculturation*, London: Routledge.

Preble, C. (2004), "'Empire'—A Losing Political Issue," *The Hill* (April 20), accessed online.

Prestholdt, Jeremy (2008), *Domesticating the World: African Consumerism and the Genealogies of Globalization*, Berkeley: University of California Press.

Pryce-Jones, David (2002), "The End of the Pax Britannica," *The Wall Street Journal* (September 23): A16.

Reed, Charles V. (2016), *Royal Tourists, Colonial Subjects and the Making of the British World, 1860-1911*, Manchester: Manchester University Press.

Remnick, David (2003), "War Without End?," *The New Yorker* (April 21 and 28), accessed online.

Reeves, Richard (2010), "That Mau Mau in the White House," *Real Clear Politics* (September 15), accessed online.

Reis, Bruno Cardoso (2015), "Myths of Decolonization: Britain, France, and Portugal Compared," in Miguel Bandeira Jeronimo and Antonio Costa Pinto (eds.), *The Ends of European Empires: Cases and Comparisons*, 126–47. Houndmills: Palgrave Macmillan.

Rhodes, Edward (2005), "Onward, Liberal Soldiers?: The Crusading Logic of Bush's Grand Strategy and What is Wrong with It," in Lloyd C. Gardner and Marilyn Young (eds.), *The New American Empire*, 227–52. New York: New Press.

Richardson, Brian W. (2005), *Longitude and Empire: How Captain Cook's Voyages Changed the World*, Vancouver: University of British Columbia Press.

Ricks, Thomas E. (2001), "Empire or Not? A Quiet Debate over US Role," *The Washington Post* (August 21): A1, A13.

Ricks, Thomas E. (2004), "Shift From Traditional War Seen at Pentagon," *Washington Post* (September 3): A1, A5.

Ricks, Thomas E. (2006), *Fiasco: The American Military Adventure in Iraq*, New York: Penguin.

Rieff, David (1999), "A New Age of Liberal Imperialism?" *World Policy Journal*, 16/2 (Summer): 1–10.

Ritchie, G. S. (1967), *The Admiralty Chart: British Naval Hydrography in the Nineteenth Century*, London: Sydney, Hollis and Carter.

Ritvo, Harriet (1989), *The Animal Estate: The English and Other Creatures in the Victorian Age*, Cambridge, MA: Harvard University Press.

Roberts, Andrew (2016), "CANZUK: After Brexit, Canada, Australia, New Zealand and Britain Can Unite as a Pillar of Western Civilization," *The Telegraph* (September 13), accessed online.

Robin, Corey (2004), "Grand Designs: How 9/11 Unified Conservatives in Pursuit of Empire," *The Washington Post* (May 2): B1.

Robinson, Michael F. (2016), *The Lost White Tribe: Explorers, Scientists, and the Theory that Changed a Continent*, New York: Oxford University Press.

Robinson, Ronald (1972), "Non-European Foundations of European Imperialism: Sketch for a Theory of Collaboration," in Roger Owen and Bob Sutcliffe (eds.), *Studies in the Theory of Imperialism*, 117–42. London: Longman.

Robinson, Ronald (1982), "Oxford in Imperial Historiography," in Frederick Madden and D. K. Fieldhouse (eds.), *Oxford and the Idea of Commonwealth*, 30–48. London: Routledge, Kegan Paul.

Robinson, Ronald (1999), "Wm. Roger Louis and the Official Mind of Decolonization," *Journal of Imperial and Commonwealth History*, 27/2: 1–12.

Robinson, Ronald, and John Gallagher with Alice Denny (1981), *Africa and the Victorians: The Official Mind of Imperialism*, 2nd ed. London: Palgrave MacMillan.

Rockel, Stephen J. (2006), *Carriers of Culture: Labor on the Road in Nineteenth-Century East Africa*, Portsmouth, NH: Heinemann.

Roque, Ricardo, and Kim Wagner, eds. (2012), *Engaging Colonial Knowledge: Reading European Archives in World History*, Houndmills: Palgrave Macmillan.

Rosaldo, Renato (1989), "Imperial Nostalgia," *Representations*, 26: 107–22.

Ross, Andrew C. (2002), *David Livingstone: Mission and Empire*, London: Hambledon.

Rotberg, Robert I., ed. (1970), *Africa and Its Explorers: Motives, Methods and Impact*, Cambridge, Mass: Harvard University Press.

Rutherford, Jonathan (1997), *Forever England: Reflections on Masculinity and Empire*, London: Lawrence and Wishart.
Ryan, James R. (1997), *Picturing Empire: Photography and the Visualization of the British Empire*, Chicago, IL: University of Chicago Press.
Ryan, Simon (1996), *The Cartographic Eye: How Explorers Saw Australia*, Cambridge: Cambridge University Press.
Said, Edward W. (1978), *Orientalism*, New York: Pantheon.
Said, Edward W. (1993), *Culture and Imperialism*, New York: Knopf.
Sahlins, Marshall (1995), *How Natives Think, About Captain Cook, For Example*, Chicago: University of Chicago Press.
Salmond, Anne (2004), *The Trial of the Cannibal Dog: Captain Cook in the South Seas*, London: Penguin.
Samuel, Raphael (1989), *Patriotism: The Making and Unmaking of British National Identity*, 3 vols., London: Routledge.
Sangari, Kumkum, and Sudesh Vaid, eds. (1990), *Recasting Women: Essays in Indian Colonial History*, New Brunswick: Rutgers University Press.
Sarkar, Sumit (1994), "Orientalism Revisited: Saidian Frameworks in the Writing of Modern History," *The Oxford Literary Review*, 16/1–2: 205–24.
Satia, Priya (2008), *Spies in Arabia: The Great War and the Cultural Foundations of Britain's Covert Empire in the Middle East*, New York: Oxford University Press.
Schell, Jonathan (2006), "Too Late for Empire," *The Nation*, 283/5 (August 14/21): 13–24.
Scheuer, Michael [Anonymous] (2004), *Imperial Hubris: Why the West is Losing the War on Terror*, Dulles: Potomac Books.
Schneer, Jonathan (1999), *London 1900: The Imperial Metropolis*, New Haven: Yale University Press.
Schwarz, Bill (1996), *The Expansion of England: Race, Ethnicity, and Cultural History*, London: Routledge.
Schwarz, Bill (2007), "'Shivering in the Noonday Sun': The British World and the Dynamics of Nativisation," in Kate Darian-Smith, et al. (eds.), *Britishness Abroad*, 19–44. Melbourne: Melbourne University Press.
Schwarz, Bill (2011), *Memories of Empire, Vol. 1: The White Man's World*, Oxford: Oxford University Press.
Schwarz, Bill (2015), "An Unsentimental Education: John Darwin's Empire," *Journal of Imperial and Commonwealth History*, 43/1: 125–44.
Scott, David (1999), *Refashioning Futures: Criticism after Postcoloniality*, Princeton: Princeton University Press.
Scott, Joan Wallach (1986), "Gender: A Useful Category of Historical Analysis," *American Historical Review*, 91/5: 1053–75.
Scott, L. V. (1993), *Conscription and the Attlee Government: The Politics and Policy of National Service, 1945-1951*, New York: Oxford University Press.
Sharpe, Jenny (1993), *Allegories of Empire: The Figure of Woman in the Colonial Text*, Minneapolis: University of Minnesota Press.
Sheets-Pyenson, Susan (1987), "Civilizing by Nature's Example: The Development of Colonial Museums of Natural History, 1850–1900," in Nathan Reingold and Marc Rothenberg (eds.), *Scientific Colonialism: A Cross-Cultural Comparison*, 351–77. Washington, DC: Smithsonian Institution Press.
Shepard, Todd (2006), *The Invention of Decolonization: The Algerian War and the Remaking of France*, Ithaca: Cornell University Press.

Shoefield, Camilla (2013), *Enoch Powell and the Making of Postcolonial Britain*, Cambridge: Cambridge University Press.
Showalter, Elaine (1994), "The Rise of Theory—a Symposium," *Times Literary Supplement*, 4763 (July 15): 12.
Siegel, Jennifer (2002), *Endgame: Britain, Russia and the Final Struggle for Central Asia*, London: I. B. Tauris.
Simpson, Donald (1976), *Dark Companions: The African Contribution to European Exploration of East Africa*, New York: Barnes and Noble.
Sinclair, Georgina (2006), *At the End of the Line: Colonial Policing and the Imperial Endgame, 1945-80*, Manchester: Manchester University Press.
Sinha, Mrinalini (1995), *Colonial Masculinity: The "Manly Englishman" and the "Effeminate Bengali" in the Late Nineteenth Century*, Manchester: Manchester University Press.
Sinha, Mrinalini (2006), *Specters of Mother India: The Global Restructuring of an Empire*, Durham: Duke University Press.
Smith, Bernard (1985), *European Vision and the South Pacific*, 2nd ed., New Haven: Yale University Press.
Smith, Evan, and Steven Gray (2016), "Brexit, imperial nostalgia and the 'white man's world'," *History and Policy* (June 20), accessed online.
Smith, Simon C. (1998), *British Imperialism, 1750-1970*, Cambridge: Cambridge University Press.
Smith, Tony (1981), *The Patterns of Imperialism: The United States, Great Britain, and the Late-Industrializing World Since 1815*, Cambridge: Cambridge University Press.
Spector, Ronald (2007), *In the Ruins of Empire: The Japanese Surrender and the Battle for Post-war Asia*, New York: Random House.
Spivak, Gayatri Chakravorty (1985), "Subaltern Studies: Deconstructing Historiography," in Ranajit Guha (ed.), *Subaltern Studies IV*, 330–63. Delhi: Oxford University Press.
Spivak, Gayatri Chakravorty (1988), "Can the Subaltern Speak?" in Gary Nelson and Lawrence Grossberg (eds.), *Marxism and the Interpretation of Culture*, 271–313. Urbana: University of Chicago Press.
Spivak, Gayatri Chakravorty (1990), *The Post-Colonial Critic*, edited by Sarah Harasym, New York: Routledge.
Sprinker, Michael, ed. (1992), *Edward Said: A Critical Reader*, Oxford: Wiley-Blackwell.
Spurr, David (1993), *The Rhetoric of Empire: Colonial Discourse in Journalism, Travel Writing, and Imperial Administration*, Durham: Duke University Press.
Stafford, Robert A. (1989), *Scientist of Empire: Sir Roderick Murchison, Scientific Exploration and Victorian Imperialism*, Cambridge: Cambridge University Press.
Stafford, Robert A. (1999a), "Scientific Exploration and Empire," in Andrew Porter (ed.), *The Oxford History of the British Empire, Vol. 3, The Nineteenth Century*, 294–319. Oxford: Oxford University Press.
Stafford, Robert A. (1999b), "Exploration and Empire," in Robin W. Winks (ed.), *The Oxford History of the British Empire, Vol. V: Historiography*, 290–302. Oxford: Oxford University Press.
Steinmetz, George (2006), "Imperialism or Colonialism? From Windhoek to Washington, by Way of Basra," in Craig Calhoun, et al. (eds.), *Lessons of Empire: Imperial Histories and American Power*, 135–56. New York: New Press.

Stepan, Nancy L. (2001), *Picturing Tropical Nature*, Ithaca: Cornell University Press.
Stern, Philip J. (2004), "'Rescuing the Age from the Charge of Ignorance': Gentility, Knowledge, and the Exploration of Africa in the late Eighteenth Century," in Kathleen Wilson (ed.), *A New Imperial History: Culture, Identity and Modernity in Britain and the Empire, 1660–1840*, 115–35. Cambridge: Cambridge University Press.
Stern, Philip J. (2011), *The Company-State: Corporate Sovereignty and the Early Modern Foundations of the British Empire in India*, New York: Oxford University Press.
Stocking, George W. Jr. (1987), *Victorian Anthropology*, New York: Free Press.
Stocking, George W. Jr. (1991), *Colonial Situations: Essays on the Contextualization of Ethnographic Knowledge*, Madison: University of Wisconsin Press.
Stoddard, D. R. (1980), "The RGS and the 'New Geography': Changing Aims and Changing Roles in Nineteenth-Century Science," *The Geographical Journal*, 146/2: 190–202.
Stoler, Ann Laura (1989), "Making Empire Respectable: The Politics of Race and Sexual Morality in 20th-century Colonial Culture," *American Ethnologist*, 16/4: 634–59.
Stoler, Ann Laura (1995), *Race and the Education of Desire: Foucault's History of Sexuality and the Colonial Order of Things*, Durham: Duke University Press.
Stoler, Ann Laura (2002), *Carnal Knowledge and Imperial Power: Race and the Intimate in Colonial Rule*, Berkeley: University of California Press.
Stoler, Ann Laura, and Frederick Cooper (1997), "Between Metropole and Colony: Rethinking a Research Agenda," in Ann Laura Stoler and Frederick Cooper (eds.), *Tensions of Empire: Colonial Cultures in a Bourgeois World*, 1–58. Berkeley: University of California Press.
Suleri, Sara (1992), *The Rhetoric of English India*, Chicago: University of Chicago Press.
Suskind, Ron (2004), "Without a Doubt," *The New York Times Sunday Magazine* (October 17), accessed online.
Tabili, Laura (1994), *We Ask for British Justice: Workers and Racial Difference in Late Imperial Britain*, Ithaca: Cornell University Press.
Thiong'o, Ngugi wa (1986), *Decolonizing the Mind: The Politics of Language in African Literature*, London: Heinemann.
Thomas, Martin (2008), *Empires of Intelligence: Security Services and Colonial Disorder After 1914*, Berkeley: University of California Press.
Thomas, Martin (2014), *Fight or Flight: Britain, France, and their Roads from Empire*, Oxford: Oxford University Press.
Thomas, Martin, ed. (2015), *Expedition into Empire: Exploratory Journeys and the Making of the Modern World*, New York: Routledge.
Thomas, Nicholas (1994), *Colonialism's Culture: Anthropology, Travel and Government*, Princeton: Princeton University Press.
Thomas, Nicholas (2003), *Cook: The Extraordinary Voyages of Captain James Cook*, New York: Walker.
Thompson, Andrew (2005), *The Empire Strikes Back? The Impact of Imperialism on Britain from the Mid-Nineteenth Century*, Harlow: Pearson Longman.

Thompson, Andrew, ed. (2012), *Britain's Experience of Empire in the Twentieth Century*, Oxford: Oxford University Press.
Thompson, Andrew, ed. (2013), *Writing Imperial Histories*, Manchester: Manchester University Press.
Thompson, Andrew, and Gary Magee (2011), *Empire and Globalisation: Networks of Peoples, Goods and Capital in the World c.1850–1914*, Cambridge: Cambridge University Press.
Thompson, Willie (1999), *Global Expansion: Britain and Its Empire, 1870-1914*, London: Pluto Press.
Thompson, William R. (2001), "Martian and Venusian Perspectives on International Relations: Britain as System Leader in the Nineteenth and Twentieth Centuries," in Colin Elman and Miriam Fendius Elman (eds.), *Bridges and Boundaries: Historians, Political Scientists, and the Study of International Relations*, 253–92. Cambridge, MA: MIT Press.
Travers, Robert (2007), *Ideology and Empire in Eighteenth-Century India: The British in Bengal*, Cambridge: Cambridge University Press.
Tsin, Michael (1999), *Nation, Governance, and Modernity in China*, Stanford: Stanford University Press.
Tyrrell, Ian (1999), *True Gardens of the Gods: Californian-Australian Environmental Reform, 1860-1930*, Berkeley: University of California Press.
Tyson, Ann Scott (2005). "A Brain Pentagon Wants to Pick," *The Washington Post* (October 19): A19.
Tyson, Ann Scott (2005b), "Marine General is Told to Speak 'More Carefully'," *Washington Post* (February 4): A5.
Vail, Leroy, ed. (1991), *The Creation of Tribalism in Southern Africa*, Berkeley: University of California Press.
Vasagar, Jeevan (2010), "Niall Ferguson aims to shape up history curriculum with TV and war games," *The Guardian* (July 9), accessed online.
Vaughan, Megan (1991), *Curing Their Ills: Colonial Power and African Illness*, Stanford: Stanford University Press.
Veracini, Lorenzo (2010), *Settler Colonialism: A Theoretical Overview*, Houndmills: Palgrave Macmillan.
Veracini, Lorenzo (2015), *The Settler Colonial Present*, Houndmills: Palgrave Macmillan.
Visram, Rozina (1986), *Ayahs, Lascars, and Princes: Britain, 1700-1947*, London: Routledge.
Viswanathan, Gauri (1989), *Masks of Conquest: Literary Study and British Rule in India*, New York: Columbia University Press.
Viswanathan, Gauri (1998), *Outside the Fold: Conversion, Modernity, and Belief*, Princeton: Princeton University Press.
Waller, Derek (1990), *The Pundits: British Exploration of Tibet and Central Asia*, Louisville: University of Kentucky Press.
Wallerstein, Immanuel (1976, 1980, 1989), *The Modern World System*, 3 vols., New York: Academic Press.
Wallerstein, Immanuel (2003), *The Decline of American Power: The U.S. in a Chaotic World*, New York: New Press.
Wallerstein, Immanuel (2005), *World-Systems Analysis: An Introduction*, Durham: Duke University Press.

Ward, Stuart, ed. (2001), *British Culture and the End of Empire*, Manchester: Manchester University Press.
Ward, Stuart (2005), "Worlds Apart: Three 'British' Prime Ministers at Empire's End," in Philip Buckner and R. Douglas Francis (eds.), *Rediscovering the British World*, 399–419. Calgary: Calgary University Press.
Ward, Stuart (2007), "The 'New Nationalism' in Australia, Canada and New Zealand: Civic Culture in the Wake of the British World," in Kate Darian-Smith, et al. (eds.), *Britishness Abroad*, 231–63. Melbourne: Melbourne University Press.
Ward, Stuart (2008), "Imperial Identities Abroad," in Sarah Stockwell (ed.), *The British Empire*, 219–43. Oxford: Blackwell.
Warren, Jane (2012), "Why should we apologise for the Empire?" *The Express. Co.UK* (May 12), accessed online.
Walker, Adrian (1993), *Six Campaigns: National Servicemen on Active Service 1948-1960*, London: Leo Cooper.
Walker, Michael (2002), "What Kind of Empire?" *The Wilson Quarterly*, 26/3: 36–49.
Walsh, Joan (2011), "Mike Huckabee's Mau Mau Fantasies," *Salon* (March 2), accessed online.
Walton, Calder (2013), *Empire of Secrets: British Intelligence, the Cold War and the Twilight of Empire*, New York: Overlook.
Weaver, John C. (2003), *The Great Land Rush and the Making of the Modern World, 1650-1900*, Montreal: McGill-Queen's University Press.
Webster, Wendy (2005), *Englishness and Empire 1939-1965*, Oxford: Oxford University Press.
Webster, Wendy (2012), "The Empire Comes Home: Commonwealth Migration to Britain," in Andrew Thompson (ed.), *Britain's Experience of Empire in the Twentieth Century*, 122–60. Oxford: Oxford University Press.
West, Shearer, ed. (1996), *The Victorians and Race*, Aldershot: Ashgate.
White, Luise (1995), "'They Could Make Their Victims Dull': Genders and Genres, Fantasies and Cures in Colonial Southern Uganda," *American Historical Review*, 100/5: 1379–1402.
White, Nicholas J. (1999), *Decolonization: The British Experience since 1945*, London: Longman.
Whiting, Richard (2012), "The Empire and British Politics," in A. Thompson (ed.), *Britain's Experience of Empire in the Twentieth Century*, 161–210. Oxford: Oxford University Press.
Wiener, Martin J. (1982), *English Culture and the Decline of the Industrial Spirit, 1850-1980*, Cambridge: Cambridge University Press.
Wiener, Martin J. (2013), "The Idea of 'Colonial Legacy' and the Historiography of Empire," *The Journal of the Historical Society*, 13/1: 1–32.
Williams, Patrick, and Laura Chrisman, eds. (1994), *Colonial Discourse and Post-Colonial Theory: A Reader*, New York: Columbia University Press.
Williams, William Appleman (1969), *The Roots of the Modern American Empire*, New York: Random House.
Wilson, Jon (2016), *The Chaos of Empire: The British Raj and the Conquest of India*, New York: Public Affairs.
Wilson, Kathleen (2003), *The Island Race: Englishness, Empire and Gender in the Eighteenth Century*, London: Routledge.

Wilson, Kathleen (2004), "Introduction: Histories, Empires, Modernities," in Kathleen Wilson (ed.), *A New Imperial History: Culture, Identity, and Modernity in Britain and the Empire, 1660-1840*, 1–26. Cambridge: Cambridge University Press.

Winder, Simon (2006), *The Man Who Saved Britain: A Personal Journey into the Disturbing World of James Bond*, New York: Picador.

Winks, Robin W. (1984), "Problem Child of British History: The British Empire-Commonwealth," in Richard Schlatter (ed.), *Recent Views on British History*, 451–92. New Brunswick: Rutgers University Press.

Winks, Robin W., ed. (1999), *The Oxford History of the British Empire, Vol. 5: Historiography*, Oxford: Oxford University Press.

Withers, Charles W. J. (2010), *Geography and Science in Britain, 1831-1939: A Study of the British Association for the Advancement of Science*, Manchester: Manchester University Press.

Winstone, H. V. F. (1978), *Gertrude Bell*, London: Constable.

Wolf, Eric (1982), *Europe and the People without History*, Berkeley: University of California Press.

Wolfe, Patrick (1997), "History and Imperialism: A Century of Theory, from Marx to Postcolonialism," *American Historical Review*, 102/2: 388–420.

Wolfe, Patrick (1999), *Settler Colonialism and the Transformation of Anthropology: The Politics and Poetics of an Ethnographic Event*, London: Cassell.

Wolfe, Patrick (2001), "Land, Labor, and Difference: Elementary Structures of Race," *American Historical Review*, 106/3: 866–905.

Wolfe, Patrick (2006), "Settler Colonialism and the Elimination of the Native," *Journal of Genocide Research*, 8/4: 387–409.

Wolfe, Patrick(2016), *Traces of History: Elementary Structures of Race*, London: Verso.

Woodcock, George (1974), *Who Killed the British Empire? An Inquest*, New York: Quadrangle.

Wulf, Andrea (2015), *The Invention of Nature: Alexander Von Humbold's New World* (New York: Knopf).

Young, Marilyn B. (2005), "Imperial Language," in Lloyd C. Gardner and Marilyn Young (eds.), *The New American Empire*, 32–49. New York: New Press.

Young, Robert J. C. (1990), *White Mythologies: Writing History and the West*, London: Routledge.

Young, Robert J. C. (1995), *Colonial Desire: Hybridity in Theory, Culture and Race*, London: Routledge.

Youngs, Tim (1994), *Travellers in Africa: British Travelogues, 1850-1900*, Manchester: Manchester University Press.

Zastoupil, Lynn (1994), *John Stuart Mill and India*, Stanford: Stanford University Press.

Zimmerman, Andrew (2013), "Africa in Imperial and Transnational History: Multi-Sited Historiography and the Necessity of Theory," *Journal of African History*, 54/3: 331–40.

INDEX

Abulafia, David 175 n.5
Abyssinian war 127
Achebe 17
Aden 145
Afghanistan 3, 5, 50, 55, 99, 101, 103, 105, 106, 108, 112–14, 117, 120, 123, 124, 138–40, 142, 146, 174 n.36
Africa and Its Explorers (Rotberg) 59
Africa and the Victorians (Robinson and Gallagher) 30
African Association 64
Ahmad, Aijaz 10
Albright, Madeleine 116, 138, 168 n.5
Algeria 81, 93, 94, 97
Althusser 10
American Academy of Arts and Sciences 107
Among Empires (Maier) 107
Anderson, David 91, 92, 99, 145
Anderson, Warwick 44
anglobalization 139
Angola 81
Antarctica 71
anthropology 4, 8, 18, 19, 33, 35, 41, 43, 58, 59, 61–2, 80, 134, 160 n.44
Anti-Oedipus (Deleuze and Guattari) 11
Argentina 165 n.14
armchair geographers 66
Armitage, David 51
Arnn, Larry 153–4
Arnold, David 44, 48, 68
Arnold, Matthew 20
Asad, Talal 41, 59
Attenborough, David 142, 174 n.52
Auerbach, Erich 10

Auerbach, Jeffrey 32
Austen, Jane 20, 34
Australia 5, 33, 45, 64, 65, 68, 74–6, 78, 80–2, 84, 96, 97, 110, 150

Bacevich, Andrew 105
Bailkin, Jordanna 97
Bakhtin, Mikhael 10
Ballantyne, Tony 49
Banivanua-Mar, Tracey 48
Banks, Joseph 64
Bannon, Steven 153
Barnett, Correlli 88
Barnett, Thomas P. M. 104, 115
Barthes, Roland 10
Bayly, C. A. 32, 92, 134
Bayly, Susan 27
Belgium 97
Belich, James 27, 74, 75, 78–80, 84
Bell, Gertrude 67
Belmessous, Sahila 85
Beloff, Lord 24
Benjamin, Walter 10
Bennett, Huw 93, 145
Bentham, Jeremy 53
Bhabha, Homi K. 8, 11, 12, 16, 134
Bickford-Smith, Vivian 76
biopower 43
Black Atlantic, The (Gilroy) 49
Blair, Tony 141–3, 168 n.9
Blood Never Dried, The (Newsinger) 143
Boehner, John 153
Boot, Max 104, 111
Botswana 81
Boucher, Ellen 97
Bourdieu, Pierre 10
Boyce, D. George 91
Brantlinger, Patrick 15

INDEX

Brazil 45, 82
Bremer, Paul 112
Brexit 3, 6, 73, 96, 100, 149–52
Bridge, Carl 74–6
Britain's Declining Empire (Hyam) 91
Britain's Empire (Gott) 143
British Association for the Advancement of Science, The 65
British Decolonization, 1946-1997 (McIntyre) 91
British Documents at the End of Empire series 89, 90
British East India Company 64
British Imperialism (Cain and Hopkins) 8, 134
British Museum 65, 67
British Natural History Museum 65
Britishness 44, 75–9, 84, 96, 174 n.46
British Shintoism 95
British World 5, 45, 48, 74–81, 83–5, 137
Britons (Colley) 44, 78
Bronte, Charlotte 17
Brown, Gordon 142, 143, 174 n.46
Brown, Judith 30
Bruce, James 70
Buchanan, Patrick 103, 139
Buckner, Phillip 26, 74, 76, 133, 158 n.10, 159 n.32
Buettner, Elizabeth 96
Burbank, Jane 107
Bureau of Labor Statistics 128
Burke, Edmund 51
Burke, Timothy 44
Burma 144
Burnett, Graham 69
Burton, Antoinette 3, 20, 34, 44, 46, 48, 52–3, 134, 173 n.16
Burton, Richard 47, 66, 70, 71
Bush, George W. 103, 104, 109, 115, 117–21, 123, 152, 168 n.9, 152
Butler, Judith 41

Cain, P. J. 8, 27, 29, 30, 116, 134, 157 n.75
Caldwell, C. E. 114

Cambridge History of the British Empire 23, 25, 26
Cameron, David 142, 143
Cameron, Verney Lovett 70
Canada 5, 25, 28, 36, 64, 68, 74–6, 80, 81, 84, 96, 97, 110, 134, 150
Cannadine, David 46, 130
Canny, Nicholas 24
CANZUK 150
Carey, Jane 81
Carroll, Siobhan 71
Carter, Paul 59, 60, 68
cartography 48, 59, 69
caste 19, 34, 42, 46, 157 n.51, 160 n.40
Castes of Mind (Dirks) 42
Cell, John 27
Ceylon 165 n.14
Chakrabarty, Dipesh 52–5
Chamberlain, Joseph 27, 117, 129, 130
Chatterjee, Partha 48
Chavez, Hugo 169 n.22
Cheney, Dick 117
China 26, 29, 75, 111, 116, 130, 138, 165 n.14
Chomsky, Noam 105, 139
Chronicle of Higher Education, The 8
Churchill, Caryl 98
Churchill, Winston 6, 95, 96, 130, 141, 152–4, 166 n.1, 175 n.7
Churchill's Trial (Arnn) 153
Civilizing Subjects (Hall) 46
Clapperton, Hugh 69
class 15, 17, 20, 34, 42, 44–6, 112, 113, 119, 133, 136, 175 n.68
Clayton, Anthony 26
Clifford, James 10
Cloud 9 (Churchill) 98
Cohen, David William 43
Cohen, Eliot 104
Cohn, Bernard 19, 41, 42, 134
Cole, Juan 108, 118
Colley, Linda 44, 46, 75, 78, 108, 172 n.1
Collingham, Elizabeth 44
Collini, Stefan 10

colonialism 1, 25–35, 59, 62, 64, 69, 76–8, 80, 125–7, 134, 135, 137, 138, 141, 142, 144–6, 156 nn.17, 45, 157 n.51, 158 n.7, 160 n.34, 165 n.17
   British imperial perspective of 104, 110–12, 114–15, 117–19
   exceptionalism and 89–99
   imperial history and postcolonial theory and 8, 9, 11–13, 15–20, 40–4, 46, 48–50, 52–4
   settler 3, 5, 26, 36, 68, 74–6, 78–85, 92, 95, 137, 166 nn.28–9
Colonial Lives Across the British Empire (Lambert and Lester) 47
Colonial Masculinity (Sinha) 43
Colonizing Egypt (Mitchell) 48
Colossus: The Price of America's Empire (Ferguson) 139
Comaroff, Jean 41, 62
Comaroff, John 41, 62
communalism 19, 42, 160 n.4
Companion Series to the Oxford History 137
Condorcet, Marquis de 53
Conrad 17
constructive imperialism 27
Continental Drift (Grob-Fitzgibbon) 96
Cook, Captain 48, 58, 62–3
Coombes, Annie 81
Cooper, Frederick 33, 46, 53, 107, 135
Cooper, Robert 141
Council of Foreign Relations 104
counterinsurgency operations 26, 90, 92–3
Creation of Tribalism in Southern Africa, The (Vail) 43
"Critics of Empire in Britain" (Owen) 34
Crocker III, W. H. 140
Crosby, Alfred 36, 85
Cuba 110, 111
cultural identity 77–8
Curthoys, Ann 50
Curtin, Philip 58
Cyprus 145

Daedalus journal 107
Dalrymple, William 108
Darwin, Charles 65
Darwin, John 2, 74, 88–90, 175 n.69
Davies, Norman 146
decentralized despotism 52
Decline, Revival, and Fall of the British Empire, The (Gallagher) 129
Decline and Fall of the Roman Empire (Gibbon) 129
Decolonisation: The British Experience Since 1945 (White) 91
Decolonisation and the British Empire, 1775-1997 (Boyce) 91
decolonization 7, 19, 28, 29, 48, 83–4, 89–91, 93–9, 126, 133, 135, 167 nn.24, 42
Decolonization in Britain and France (Kahler) 95
Decolonizing Feminisms (Donaldson) 13
de Gaulle, Charles 95
Denham, Dixon 69
Deleuze, Gilles 11
de Man, Paul 10
Denny, Alice 30
Denoon, Donald 78
Derrida, Jacques 10, 11, 40
de Saussure, Ferdinand 40
D'Sousa, Dinesh 140–1
"Development and the Utopian Ideal" (Hopkins) 32
Diderot, Denis 53
Dilke, Charles 73, 77, 83
Dirks, Nicholas 42, 51
dirty wars 92
Dominican Republic 111
Donaldson, Laura E. 13
Donnelly, Thomas 103
Drawing the Global Colour Line (Lake and Reynold) 78
Drayton, Richard 32, 34, 36, 64
Driver, Felix 68
Dycorp 115
Dyer, Reginald 140

Ecological Imperialism (Crosby) 85
ecstasis 71

Eden, Anthony 95
Edgerton, David 92
Edmonds, Penelope 81
Edney, Matthew 64
Egypt 49, 111, 112, 118, 165 n.14
Eisenhower, Dwight 117
Elementary Aspects of Peasant Insurgency in Colonial India (Guha) 40
Elkins, Caroline 85, 91, 92, 99, 108, 145
Empire (Hardt and Negri) 55
Empire: The Rise and Demise of the British World Order and the Lessons for Global Power (Ferguson) 139
Empire and Globalization (Magee and Thompson) 78
empires and hegemons, distinction between 125
Empire Writes Back: Theory and Practice in Post-Colonial Literatures 13
Enlightenment 53, 61
Epstein, James 172 n.1
Etherington, Norman 35
European Vision and the South Pacific (Smith) 61
Euroscepticism 96
Evans, Richard J. 149
exceptionalism 57, 72, 87–100, 102, 106, 124–6, 139, 168 n.4
Expansion of England (Seeley)
exploration 57–72
Eyre, Edward 46

Fabian, Johannes 59, 71
Falwell, Jerry Jr. 153
Fanon, Frantz 10, 17
Farage, Nigel 149, 150, 152
Fedorowich, Kent 75, 76
Fein, Sinn 150
Feisal, King 113
Feith, Douglas 108
Ferguson, Moira 20
Ferguson, Niall 104, 106, 108, 116, 121, 125, 139, 140, 142, 144, 174 nn.50, 59

Fernández-Armesto, Felipe 57
Fieldhouse, D. K. 19, 30, 132–3
Fight or Flight (Thomas) 93
"First British Empire, The" (Marshall) 32
Fitzpatrick, David 26
Forgotten Wars (Bayly and Harper) 92
Forster, E. M. 17
Foucault, Michel 9, 10, 40, 43, 54
Fox, Liam 150
France 93, 94, 97, 110, 138
Francis, Douglas 76
Franklin, John 63
French, David 93
Friedman, Thomas 138, 169 n.14
Frykenberg, Robert 27
"Future of Imperial History, The" (Winks) 32

Gallagher, John 7, 25, 28–33, 41, 89, 112, 126, 129, 133, 134, 137
Galton, Francis 66
gender 15, 16, 19, 20, 34–5, 41–5, 81, 134, 137, 160 n.40
Genocide and Settler Society (Moses) 81
Germany 114, 116
Ghosh, Durba 54
Ghosts of Empire (Kwarteng) 143
Gibbon, Edward 25, 129
Gilroy, Paul 49
Gingrich, Newt 141
globalization 32, 36, 49, 55, 72, 79, 104, 116, 125, 136, 151
Go, Julian 5, 108–9, 124–9, 140
Gott, Richard 143
Gove, Michael 142, 149
Gramsci, Antonio 10, 40
Greater Britain 73, 77, 83, 97, 165 n.8
Greater Britain (Dilke) 73
Great Land Rush and the Making of the Modern World, The (Weaver) 84, 85
Great Trigonometrical Survey 64, 69
Green, E. H. H. 27
Grenada 111, 128–9
Grob-Fitzgibbon, Benjamin 92, 96

Guam   110, 111, 126
Guantanamo   110, 114, 145
Guardian newspaper   144, 145
Guattari, Felix   11
Guha, Ranajit   40, 41, 53

Hague, William   142
Haiti   111
Hall, Catherine   44, 46, 134, 172 n.1
Halliburton   117
Hardt, Michael   55
Harkness, David   26
Harland-Jacobs, Jessica   49
Harley, J. B.   41
Harootunian, Harry   118
Harper, Tim   92
Harvey, David   41, 105, 117
Hastings, Max   142
Heidegger, Marin   10
Herder, Johann   53
Her Majesty's Stationary Office   89
Heuman, Gad   27
Hillary, Edmund   71
"Hints for Travellers" (Galton)   66
historical consciousness   13
Histories of the Hanged (Anderson)   145
Hobsbawm, Eric   173 n.11
Hobson, J. A.   8, 116, 117
Holland, Robert   74, 89
Honduras   111
Hong Kong   43
Hooker, Joseph   65
Hooker, William   65
Hopkins, A. G.   8, 29, 32, 36–7, 108, 116, 134, 157 n.75
How Empire Shaped Us (Kennedy and Burton)   3
How the Irish Became White (Ignatiev)   83
Huckabee, Mike   141
Huggan, Graham   41
humanitarianism   20, 35, 88, 104, 169 n.14
Hunt, Tristram   143
Huxley, Thomas   65
Hyam, Ronald   27, 29, 30, 35, 91
hyperpower   109, 113, 129, 138

Ideologies of the Raj (Metcalf)   51
Ignatieff, Michael   104, 138, 139
Ignatiev, Noel   83
Image of Africa, The (Curtin)   58
imaginative geographies   47, 49, 59
imperial bodies   44
Imperial Eyes (Pratt)   14, 59
Imperialism: A Study (Hobson)   117
Imperialism. *See also individual entries*
    criticism of recent studies of   36–7
    liberal   51, 53, 137, 141
    transcolonial-cum-transnational aspects of British   48–9
imperial nostalgia   158 n.7
Imperial Reckoning (Elkins)   145
Imperial Secrets (Kelley)   54
India   25, 27, 40, 43, 48, 49, 52, 64, 65, 68, 75, 119, 126, 143, 150, 157 n.51, 164 n.57, 165 n.14
informal empire   134
Institute of Historical Research   24
internal colonialism   110
Intimate Enemy, The (Nandy)   13
Iran   103, 112
Iraq   3, 5, 55, 99, 101, 103, 105, 106, 108, 112–15, 117, 118, 123, 124, 138, 139, 142, 144, 146
Ireland   26, 76
Israel   81–3

Jackson, J. R.   66
Jamaica   45
James, Lawrence   142, 144
Japan   130
Jasanoff, Maya   107
Jeal, Tim   142–3
Johnson, Boris   1, 149, 150, 153
Johnson, Chalmers   105
Jones, Sir William   15
Journal of Imperial and Commonwealth History, The   8

Kagan, Kimberly   140, 174 n.36
Kahler, Miles   95
Kant, Immanuel   53
Kaplan, Robert   104

Karzai, Hamid 112
Kelley, Patrick 54
Kennedy, Dane 3, 175 n.6
Kennedy, Paul 130
Kenya 76, 81, 91–2, 94, 145–6, 165 n.14
Kew Gardens 64, 65, 67
Khalidi, Rashid 108
Kingsley, Mary 67
Kipling, Rudyard 17, 118
Klose, Fabian 94
Knight, Alan 29
Korea 81, 85
Kowalsky, Meaghan 168 n.47
Kramer, Paul 124
Kristol, Irving 103, 106
Kristol, William 103, 138
Kushner, Jared 153
Kuwait 111
Kwarteng, Kwasi 143–4

Lacan, Jacques 10, 11
Lake, Marilyn 45, 78
Lal, Deepak 104, 116
Lambert, David 47
Latin America 26, 29
Lawrence, T. E. 138
Lenin, Vladimir 116
Leopold, King 142
Lester, Alan 47, 49
Leviathan full-time 104
Levine, Philippa 43, 172 n.1
Lewis, Martin 59
liberalism 51, 53, 77, 91–4, 104, 117–19, 138, 139, 141, 144
Liberalism and Empire (Mehta) 51
Lieven, Dominic 106
Linguafranca (journal) 8
Livingstone, David N.59, 67, 70
Lloyd, Trevor 28
Locke, John 119
London Zoo 65, 67
Lonsdale, John 27
Louis, Roger 23–6, 28, 30, 32, 89, 90, 136–7, 146
Lynn, Martin 30
Lyotard, Jean-Francois 10

MacKenzie, John 12, 18, 21, 34, 44, 46, 76, 134, 135
Macmillan, Harold 95
Magee, Gary 78, 79
Maier, Charles 107, 113, 116, 140
Majeed, Javed 15, 20
Malaya 145, 165 n.14
Mallaby, Sebastian 169 n.14
Mamdani, Mahmood 52, 53
Manchester, William 175 n.7
Mani, Lata 43
Mann, Michael 109, 118
Mansfield Park (Austen) 20
Marshall, Peter J. 24, 32
Martin, Ged 36
Marx, Karl 10
Mason, Philip 168 n.45
Mattis, James 120
Mau Mau rebellion 91–2, 141, 144
May, Theresa 150, 153
McClintock, Anne 52
McIntyre, W. David 26, 91
McMahon, Deirdre 26
Mead, Walter Russell 125
Mehta, Uday 51
Memories of Empire (Schwarz) 78, 95
Metcalf, Thomas 32, 49, 51, 119
Mexico 110
Meyer, Karl 108
military-industrial complex 117–18
Mill, James 15, 51, 53
Mill, John Stuart 20, 34, 51, 53
Miller, Rory 29
Mishra, Pankaj 174 n.59
Mitchell, Timothy 48
modernity 27, 35, 37, 51–3, 118
Mongolia 115
Moore, Robin 27
Moore, Thomas 15
moral authority 44, 64
morality 24, 44, 48, 64, 67, 91, 99, 102, 105, 118, 120, 127, 129, 132, 139, 140, 143, 145, 146, 154
moral judgments 24, 44, 91

Moses, Dirk 81
Mugabe, Robert 158 n.7
multiculturalism 98, 136
Murchison, Roderick 65, 67
Murphy, Philip 95

Naipaul 17
Nairn, Tom 96
Nandy, Ashis 13
Nasson, Bill 74
National War College (Washington, D.C.) 104
Negri, Antonio 55
neoconservatism 103, 121, 123, 139, 141, 168 n.5, 173 n.24
neo-Europes 85
the Netherlands 97
New Caledonia 81
new liberal imperialism 141
Newsinger, John 143
New York Times 145
New Zealand 5, 25, 27, 33, 74–6, 81, 84, 96, 110, 150
Nicaragua 111
Nichols, Peter 98
Nigeria 144
Norgay, Tenzing 71

Obama, Barack 1, 105, 119, 140–1, 152, 153
Odhiambo, Atieno 43
official mind 29, 89, 90, 133
O'Hanlon, Rosalind 34
Orientalism 9–10, 17
Orientalism (Said) 9, 10, 15, 41, 43, 59, 135
Osterhammel, Jurgen 29
Owen, Nicholas 34
Owram, Douglas 28
Oxford Companion to the British Empire series 94
Oxford History of the British Empire, The 2, 4, 23–37, 75, 136, 137, 146
  The Eighteenth Century 24
  The Origins of Empire 24

Pakistan 50
paleoconservatives 139

Panama 111
Park, Mungo 64
Parkyns, Mansfield 70
Parry, William 63
Parsons, Timothy 107, 134, 140
Patterns of Empire (Go) 5, 124, 127
Paxman, Jeremy 142, 143
Pearson, Charles Henry 74
Pedersen, Susan 85
Perham, Margery 24
Petraeus, David 138, 140
Philippines 110, 126
Pocock, J. G. A. 44, 75
Poland 85
Politically Incorrect Guide to the British Empire, The (Crocker III) 140
Porter, Bernard 45, 94, 108–9, 112, 119–20, 140
  The Absent-Minded Imperialists 109
Porter, Dennis 10, 35
Portugal 94, 97
postcolonial theory 4, 32, 33, 36, 59–62, 75, 90, 97, 99, 133–5, 137, 138, 146, 156 nn.17, 32, 45, 157 n.75, 159 nn.27, 31
  future directions of 54–5
  imperial history and 7–21
  and studies 39–55
    epistemologies 50–4
    geographies 47–50
    identities 42–7
postimperialism 6, 89, 95–8, 142, 146, 150
poststructuralism 8–11, 18, 32, 33, 40, 59, 134, 155 n.1
Powell, Colin 168 n.5
Powell, Enoch 95
Powell, Eve Troutt 49
Prakash, Gyan 16
Pratt, Mary Louise 14, 59–61, 68, 70
Price, Richard 172 n.1, 173 n.11
Privates on Parade (Nichols) 98
Project for the New American Century 103

Propaganda and Empire: The Manipulation of British Public Opinion, 1880-1960 135
Puerto Rico 110, 111, 126

Qatar 111

racism 9, 13, 15, 16, 19, 20, 34, 35, 41–3, 45–6, 77–8, 82–3, 95, 97, 98, 119, 134, 136, 137, 141, 150, 152, 154, 156 n.17, 160 n.40, 165 n.5
Rao, Santha Rama 46
Reagan, Ronald 105
"Rebuilding America's Defenses" (Donnelly) 103
recolonization 79
religious identity 19, 27, 34–6, 42, 45, 46, 70, 76, 77, 83, 120, 137, 160 n.40
Replenishing the Earth (Belich) 78
A Republic, Not an Empire (Buchanan) 139
Reynolds, Henry 45, 78
Rhetoric of Empire, The (Spurr) 8, 13
Rhetoric of English India, The (Suleri) 17
Rhodes, Edward 118
Rhodesia *see* Zimbabwe
Rise and Fall of the Great Powers, The (Kennedy) 130
Road to Botany Bay, The (Carter) 59
Roberts, Andrew 142, 150
Robinson, Ronald 7, 25, 28–33, 41, 89, 112, 126, 133, 134, 137
Rockel, Stephen 70
Roots of Obama's Rage, The (D'Sousa) 140
Roque, Ricardo 54
Ross, James Clark 63
Ross, John 63
Rotberg, Robert 58
Royal College of Mines 65
Royal College of Surgeons 65
Royal Geographical Society (RGS) 64–7
Rubio, Marco 153, 175 n.7
Rule of Empires, The (Parsons) 140
Rumsfeld, Donald 115

Rushdie, Salman 17
Russia 110, 114
Ryan, Paul 153
Ryan, Simon 69

Said, Edward W. 4, 8–10, 12, 15, 17–20, 24, 41, 43, 47, 54, 59, 60, 74, 134, 135
Samoa 126
Sarkar, Sumit 15
Satia, Priya 52, 53
Savage, Michael 153
Schomburgh, Robert 69
Schumpeter, Joseph 8
Schwarz, Bill 77, 78, 95
"Science, Medicine, and the British Empire" (Drayton) 34
Scott, Joan Wallach 41
Scott, Robert 71
Scottish Nationalist Party 96
Seeley, John 8, 24, 25, 28
Selected Subaltern Studies (Spivak and Guha) 41
settler colonialism 3, 5, 26, 36, 68, 74–6, 78–85, 92, 95, 137, 166 nn.28–9
Settler Colonialism and the Transformation of Anthropology (Wolfe) 80
Settler Colonialism in the Twentieth Century (Elkins and Pedersen) 85
Settler Colonial Studies journal 80, 81
Sex and the Family in Colonial India (Ghosh) 54
sexuality 19, 34, 41, 43, 81, 137, 160 n.40
Shackleton, Ernest 71
"Shaping of Imperial History, The" (Thornton) 32
Sharpe, Jenny 15, 16
Showalter, Elaine 11
Sinha, Mrinalini 43
Sked, Alan 149
Small Wars (Caldwell) 114
Smith, Adam 53
Smith, Bernard 61
Social Science Research Council 106–7

soft power   116
Somalia   50
South Africa   5, 25, 74–6, 81, 84
Soviet Union   105, 112, 115, 129, 130, 138, 154
Spain   110
Speke, John Hanning   66, 70
Spivak, Gayatri Chakravorty   8, 11, 12, 16, 41, 54
Spurr, David   13, 14
Stanley, Henry Morton   67, 68, 70, 142, 164 n.43
Stanley and African Exhibition (1890)   68
Stansky, Peter   136
Stocking, George Jr.   59
Stockwell, A. J.   30
Stoddard, Lothrop   174 n.59
Stoler, Ann Laura   33, 43, 134, 135
Strafford, Robert   27, 36
Subaltern Studies   12, 13, 34, 40, 48
Sudan   144
Suleri, Sara   17
superempire *see* hyperpower
Syria   103

Taiwan   81
Taylor, A. J. P.   24
Telegraph   146
Ten Cities That Made an Empire (Hunt)   143
Thatcher, Margaret   130
Thiong'o, Ngugi wa   11
Thompson, Andrew   78, 79, 168 n.47
Thompson, E. P.   31, 40, 133
Thornton, A. P.   32
Time magazine   8
Tomlinson, B. R.   27, 30, 36
Traces of History: Elementary Structures of Race (Wolfe)   82
traditionalism   18, 24–8, 31–5, 37, 47, 53–5, 61, 85, 98, 103–5, 107, 120, 127, 133, 139, 152, 157 n.75, 173 n.11, 174 n.46
transculturation   60, 70

trigonometric survey   69
Trudeau, Justin   1
Trump, Donald   5, 6, 117, 119, 149, 152–4
2016: Obama's America (film)   140, 141

überpower *see* hyperpower
Ukraine   146
Ungoverned Imaginings (Majeed)   15
United Arab Emirates   111
United Kingdom Independence Party (UKIP)   149, 150
United States   5, 45, 51, 74, 78–84, 96, 138, 140, 142, 145, 146, 152
   British imperial perspective of   101–21
   role in world   123–30

Vail, Leroy   43
Vaughan, Megan   44
Veracini, Lorenzo   80–1, 84
Vietnam   93, 105
Virgin Islands   126
Viswanathan, Gauri   14, 19
von Humboldt, Alexander   63, 69

Wagner, Kim   54
Ward, Stuart   98
Warfare State (Edgerton)   92
Washbrook, D. A.   27, 32
Washington Post   143
Washington Times   140
Weaver, John   84–5
Weekly Standard, The (magazine)   103
What to Observe; or, the Traveller's Remembrancer (Jackson)   66
Wheeler, Heather   1
White, Nicholas   91
"White Man's Burden, The" (Kipling)   118
whiteness   45, 77–8
Who Killed the British Empire? (Woodcock)   88
Wiener, Martin   172 n.1, 175 n.68
Wigen, Kären   59
Williams, William Appleman   124, 168 n.1

Wilson, Kathleen 45
Winks, Robin W. 25, 28, 32, 133, 158 n.5
Wolfe, Patrick 28, 45, 80, 82–3, 119, 166 n.32
Wolfowitz, Paul 138
Wollstonecraft, Mary 20
Woodcock, George 88
Wylie, Diana 32, 35

Yeats, W. B. 17
YouGov opinion survey (2014) 6
Young, Marilyn 171 n.111
Young, Robert 11, 13, 17, 20
Youngs, Tim 15

Zastoupil, Lynn 20
Zimbabwe 3, 44, 165 n.14